URBAN BEIN(

ANATOMY &
IDENTITY
OF THE CITY

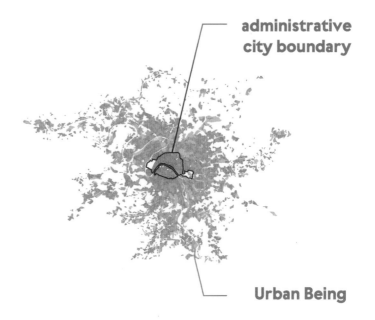

administrative
city boundary

Urban Being

The city lives.

It's man who
brings it alive.

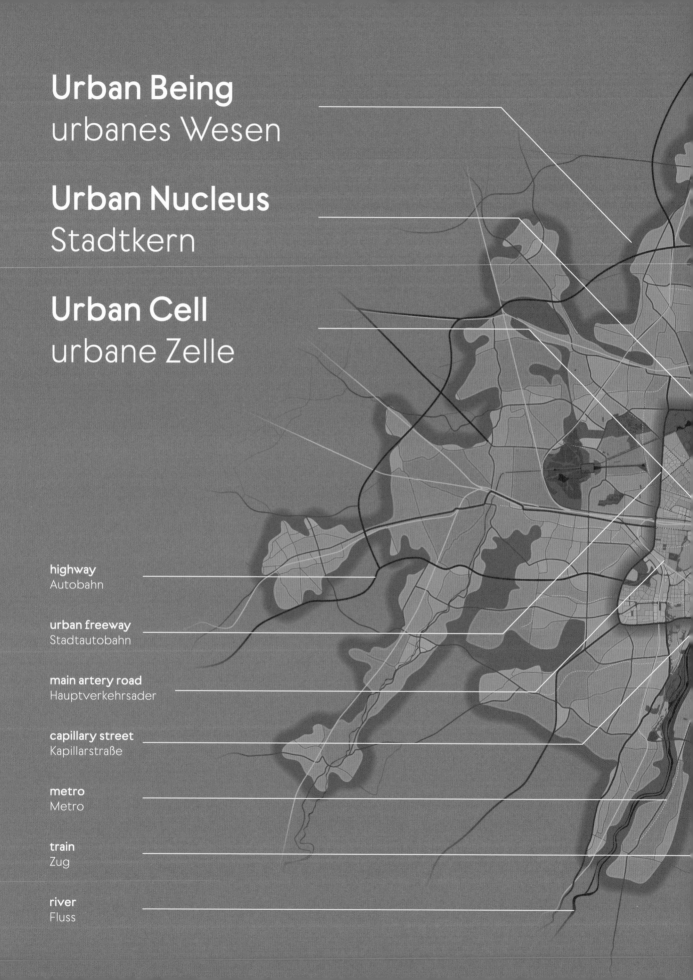

Urban Being
urbanes Wesen

Urban Nucleus
Stadtkern

Urban Cell
urbane Zelle

highway
Autobahn

urban freeway
Stadtautobahn

main artery road
Hauptverkehrsader

capillary street
Kapillarstraße

metro
Metro

train
Zug

river
Fluss

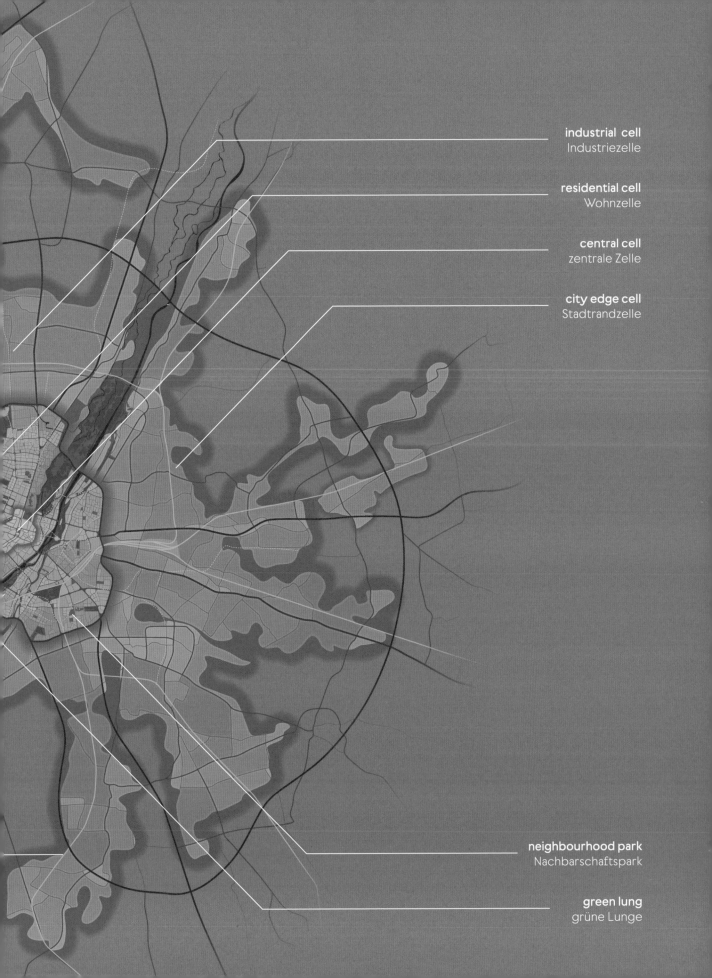

industrial cell
Industriezelle

residential cell
Wohnzelle

central cell
zentrale Zelle

city edge cell
Stadtrandzelle

neighbourhood park
Nachbarschaftspark

green lung
grüne Lunge

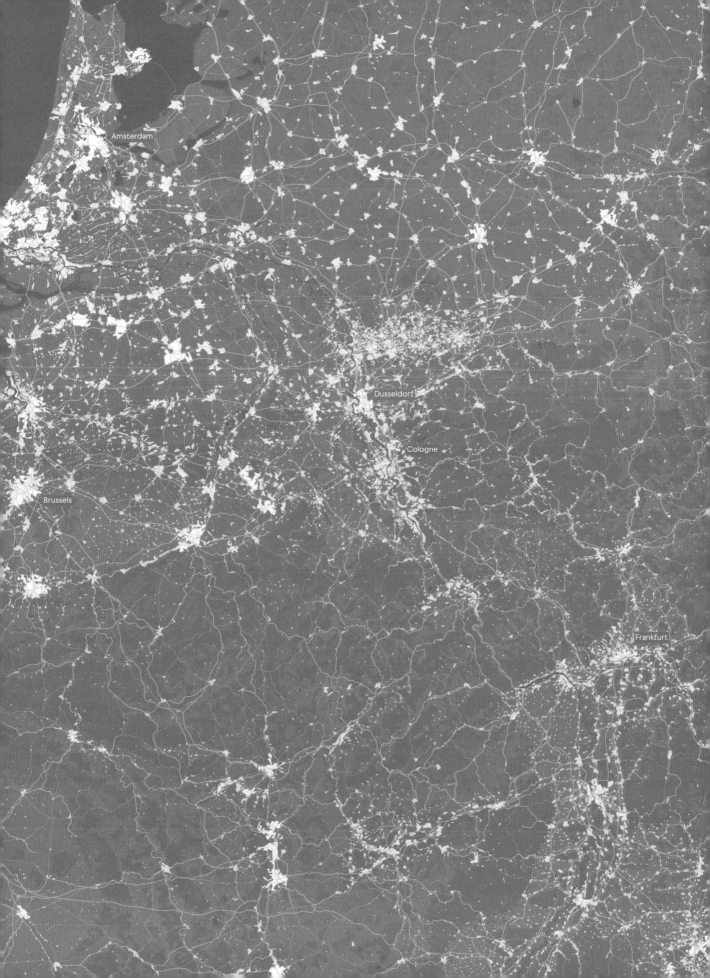

Definition of
Terms

Macroregion
Makroregion

Surrounding
Umgebung

Urban Being
urbanes Wesen

Urban Nucleus
Stadtkern

Urban Cell
urbane Zelle

Content

12   Foreword

16 MACROREGION

18   Definition

20   Descriptive Essay

28   Density and Dimensions
30   Eurasia
32   America

34   Vegetation and City Growth
36   Africa
38   South America

40   The Big Three
42   Europe
44 .   Northeast America
46   Central Asia

48 SURROUNDING

50   Definition
52   Europe
54   Northeast America
56   Central Asia

58   Descriptive Essay

64   Typologies
72   City Cluster - Sudogwon
74   City Densification - Upper Rhine Valley
76   Individual City - Central Velley Chile

78   Urban Nutrition Arteries
80   Yangtze River Delta

81   Northeast-American Axis
82   Central Valley Chile
83   Upper Rhine Valley
84   European Core

86   Topography and City Growth
88   Mexico
90   SP & RJ
92   Sudogwon
93   Central Valley Chile

94   City Cluster
96   Yangtze River Delta
98   Northeast-American Axis
100   European Core
104   North-Italian Lowlands

106 URBAN BEING

108   Definition
109   Paris
110   Berlin

112   Descriptive Essay

120   Typologies

130   Urban Nutrition Arteries
132   Munich
134   Stuttgart
136   Paris
137   London
138   New Delhi
139   Moscow
140   Melbourne
141   Los Angeles
142   Rio de Janeiro
143   Dubai

144 Tokyo
145 Berlin

146 Cellular Structure
148 Rio de Janeiro
150 Los Angeles
152 Paris

154 Industrial Organs
156 Los Angeles
158 London
159 Edmonton

160 Green Systems
162 Munich
164 Edmonton
166 Yaoundé

168 Megacities
170 Los Angeles
172 Shanghai
174 Mexico City
176 London
178 Tokyo

180 URBAN NUCLEUS

182 Definition

186 Descriptive Essay

192 Typologies

202 Freeways
204 Shanghai
206 Munich
208 Stuttgart

210 Green Lungs
212 Central Park, Manhattan
214 English Garden, Munich
216 Victoria Park, Adelaide
218 Schlossgarten, Stuttgart
220 Parque Forestal, Santiago de Chile
222 Shanghai
223 Rio de Janeiro

224 Cellular Structure
226 Cell Sizes and Functions
228 Rio de Janeiro
230 Munich
232 Los Angeles
234 Amsterdam

236 URBAN CELL

238 Definition

240 Descriptive Essay

250 Typologies

260 Urban Nutrition Arteries
262 Main Artery (Boundary of the Cell)
264 Capillary Street (Slow Traffic)
266 Hipódromo, Mexico City
270 Providencia, Santiago de Chile
274 Former French Concession, Shanghai

278 Neighbourhood Parks
280 Hipódromo, Mexico City
282 City Centre, Stuttgart
284 Former French Concession, Shanghai
286 Southeast Edmonton, Edmonton
288 Greenery

290 Commercial Network
292 Copacabana, Rio de Janeiro
294 Central Cell, Stuttgart
296 Dong Qu, Taipeh
298 Epping, Outskirts of London
300 Hipódromo, Mexico City

302 Gastronomy
304 Central Cell, Stuttgart
306 Former French Concession, Shanghai
308 Providencia, Santiago de Chile

310 Commercial Network & Gastronomy
312 Old Town, Munich
314 Manly, Sydney

318 Imprint

Foreword

The city as a habitat of humans is gaining in importance. More than half of humanity already lives in urban areas and the trend is growing. By 2050, an estimated 70 % of the world population will live in megacities, exceeding a population of 10 million people. Targeted urban planning can counteract some of their problems. In order to prevail in international competition, the city must not only grow in size, but also develop its qualities. The first step to improve the quality of a city is to understand its structure. So, how can the structure of a city be described?

There are huge similarities between a city and an organism. Therefore, it makes sense to describe its structure as an anatomy of the city. People and their goods function like urban nutrients flowing through the cities' arteries. The geography, i.e. the form of the landscape, as well as trade routes, airports or fertile surroundings, influence these cycles and play a role in the anatomy. The way a city grows is thus largely determined by external factors. At the same time, a city is always an artificially created habitat of humans and is brought to life by their behaviour. Certain city structures are used very similarly by people, regardless of culture or climate. This means, in reverse, that the anatomy of the city influences its identity. If anatomical structures are applied adequately, specific qualities can be achieved.

Die Stadt als Lebensraum des Menschen gewinnt stetig an Bedeutung. Über die Hälfte der Menschheit lebt bereits in urbanen Gebieten, Tendenz steigend. Bis 2050 werden geschätzte 70 % der Weltbevölkerung in Megastädten mit über 10 Millionen Einwohnern leben. Eine gezielte Stadtplanung kann einigen Problemen dieser Megastädte entgegenwirken. Um im internationalen Wettbewerb bestehen zu können, muss die Stadt nicht nur wachsen, sondern sich auch qualitativ entwickeln. Der erste Schritt zu einer qualitätvollen Stadt ist das Verständnis ihrer Struktur. Wie lässt sich also die Struktur einer Stadt beschreiben?

Die Stadt ähnelt in ihrem Aufbau einem Organismus. Daher ist es sinnvoll, ihre Struktur in einer Anatomie der Stadt zu erörtern. Menschen und ihre Güter funktionieren wie urbane Nährstoffe, die durch die Verkehrsadern der Städte fließen. Die Geografie, also die Form der Landschaft, genauso wie Handelswege, Flughäfen oder fruchtbares Umland beeinflussen diese Kreisläufe und spielen somit eine Rolle in der Anatomie der Stadt. Die Art, wie eine Stadt wächst, wird somit stark von äußeren Faktoren bestimmt. Gleichzeitig ist eine Stadt immer ein künstlich geschaffenes Habitat der Menschen und wird durch deren Verhaltensweisen belebt oder eben nicht. Unabhängig von Kultur und Klima werden gewisse Stadtstrukturen sehr ähnlich durch den Menschen genutzt. Das bedeutet im Umkehrschluss, dass die Anatomie der Stadt ihre Identität beeinflusst. Setzt man anatomische Strukturen adäquat ein, lassen sich gezielte Qualitäten erzeugen.

The Necessity for a new Terminology

In order to understand the range of anatomical characteristics it is necessary to compare cities. This requires a uniform basis. Existing terms like city, metropolitan region or neighbourhood are defined or understood very differently. The metropolitan area of London ends with the urbanised areas. The metropolitan area of Munich includes about 100 kilometers of rural areas around the city. Both metropolitan areas are defined politically and can be adapted purposely. Due to the generous definition of the metropolitan area of Munich, the city appears bigger and more attractive. By comparing cities on this basis, the reality is greatly distorted. A terminology with a uniform definition is therefore absolutely necessary. The terminology in this book refers to five scale levels. They relate exclusively to the physically existing city. Political boundaries and media perceptions are irrelevant to this view. The five described scales are the following:

The Macroregion consists of several hundred cities, which lie at a distance of less than 200 kilometer from each other. These agglomerations of cities form the largest scale level. Shanghai, for example, is located within the Asian Macroregion. The development of Shanghai is also linked to the development of the Asian Macroregion. These Macroregions can be seen in maps such as international flight and trade routes, global population distribution or economic strength by cities.

The Surrounding describes neighbouring cities within a distance of several hundred kilometers. The Surrounding is partly comparable to a megalopolis. There are three basic typologies. The city cluster consists of several cities that have grown together. The city densification is made up of cities within a distance of one to five hours by car. An individual city has no larger neighbouring cities in its Surrounding. These typologies have a great influence on the cities themselves.

Die Notwendigkeit einer neuen Terminologie

Um die Bandbreite anatomischer Merkmale zu verstehen, ist es notwendig, Städte miteinander zu vergleichen. Dazu ist eine einheitliche Grundlage nötig. Existierende Begriffe wie Stadt, Metropolregion oder Nachbarschaft werden sehr unterschiedlich definiert bzw. verstanden, die Metropolregion London endet mit den urbanisierten Bereichen. Die Metropolregion München beinhaltet circa 100 Kilometer ländliche Bereiche um die Stadt. Beide Begriffe wurden politisch definiert und lassen sich zweckmäßig anpassen. Durch die großzügig definierte Metropolregion München erscheint die Stadt größer und attraktiver. Vergleicht man Städte auf dieser Grundlage, wird die Realität stark verzerrt. Eine Terminologie mit einheitlicher Definition ist daher unbedingt notwendig. Die Terminologie in diesem Buch bezieht sich auf fünf Maßstabsebenen. Sie beziehen sich ausschließlich auf die physisch existierende Stadt. Politisch definierte Grenzen und mediale Wahrnehmungen sind für diese Betrachtung irrelevant. Die fünf beschriebenen Maßstäbe sind folgende:

Die Makroregion setzt sich aus mehreren Hundert Städten zusammen, die in einem Abstand von weniger als 200 Kilometer zueinander liegen. Diese Verdichtungen von Städten bilden die größte Maßstabsebene. So liegt Shanghai zum Beispiel in der asiatischen Makroregion. Die Entwicklung Shanghais ist auch mit der Entwicklung der asiatischen Makroregion verknüpft. Makroregionen werden in Grafiken zu internationalen Flug- und Handelsrouten, globalen Bevölkerungsverteilung oder zur wirtschaftlichen Stärke der Städte sichtbar.

Die Umgebung beschreibt die benachbarten Städte in einer Distanz von mehreren Hundert Kilometern. Sie ist teilweise mit Megalopolen vergleichbar. Grundsätzlich gibt es drei Typologien: In Stadtverbänden sind mehrere Städte zusammengewachsen. In Stadtverdichtungen liegen die Städte in einer Distanz von ein bis fünf Autostunden. Individualstädte haben keine größeren Nachbarstädte in ihrer Umgebung. Diese Typologien haben Einfluss auf die Städte selbst.

The Urban Being is an accumulation of urbanised areas in space, possesing an essential peculiarity. It is comparable to a city or metropolitan area, but it describes the physically existing city. Each city has its own character, or its own essence. However, it is not a living being, but is brought to life by humans. Hence the term Urban Being. In terms of urban planning, the term is relevant, as the use of public transport, the amount of traffic or economic strength always refer to the scale of the urban being.

The Urban Nucleus is the core of the Urban Being, limited by physical boundaries. It is comparable to the torso of the Urban Being, including the most important functions. Generally, it is located in the physical centre of the city and is defined by urban freeways, a river or topography.

The Urban Cell is the area between main artery roads within the city. It is the smallest unit in which a resident can survive independently and is comparable to a neighbourhood. It is where the city of cars and the city of humans meet. The cells come in different typologies. Central cells, residential cells or linear cells differ structurally and generate specific urban qualities.

Anatomy and Identity

The anatomy and identity of the city combine analysis with experience. The anatomy analyses the physically existing city. It is important to understand that the only real pictures of cities are satellite images. They show the visible. In contrast, maps are always simplified to emphasise certain parameters. They show structures. The structural maps in this book deal with parameters relating to the anatomy. Similar to tourist maps showing points of interest, these maps show Urban Cells or urban nutrition arteries. They are based on satellite images and other map material. They reflect certain parameters as accurately as possible. The presentation alone highlights unusual aspects and creates a differentiated view on the city.

Das urbane Wesen ist eine Anhäufung städtischer Gebiete im Raum, die eine wesentliche Eigenart besitzen. Es ist mit einer Stadt oder Metropolregion vergleichbar, beschreibt jedoch die physisch existierende Stadt. Jede Stadt hat ihren eigenen Charakter oder ihr eigenes Wesen. Sie ist jedoch kein Lebewesen, sondern wird durch den Menschen zum Leben erweckt. Daher der Begriff urbanes Wesen. Stadtplanerisch ist der Begriff relevant, da sich die Nutzung des öffentlichen Personennahverkehrs, das Verkehrsaufkommen oder die Wirtschaftskraft immer auf das urbane Wesen beziehen.

Der Stadtkern bildet den Kern des urbanen Wesens, der durch physische Grenzen definiert wird. Er ist vergleichbar mit dem Torso des urbanen Wesens, in dem sich die wichtigsten städtischen Funktionen befinden. In der Regel liegt er im physischen Zentrum der Stadt und wird durch einen Stadtautobahnring, einen Fluss oder die Topografie definiert.

Die urbane Zelle ist der Bereich zwischen Hauptverkehrsadern innerhalb der Stadt. Sie ist die kleinste Einheit, in der ein Bewohner selbstständig überleben kann, und mit einer Nachbarschaft vergleichbar. Als Schnittpunkt zwischen der Stadt der Autos und der Stadt der Menschen existiert sie in verschiedenen Typologien. Zentrale Zellen, Wohnzellen oder lineare Zellen unterscheiden sich strukturell und erzeugen spezifische städtische Qualitäten.

Anatomie und Identität

Die Anatomie und Identität der Stadt verbinden die Analyse mit der Erfahrung. Die Anatomie analysiert die physisch existierende Stadt. Hier ist es wichtig zu verstehen, dass die einzigen realen Abbildungen von Städten Satellitenbilder sind. Sie zeigen das Sichtbare. Im Gegensatz dazu sind Karten immer vereinfacht, um gewisse Parameter, hervorzuheben. Sie zeigen Strukturen. Die hier gezeigten strukturellen Karten behandeln Parameter die sich auf die Anatomie der Stadt beziehen. Ähnlich wie touristische Karten Sehenswürdigkeiten hervorheben, zeigen diese

The interpretation of the anatomical drawings is connected to the experience. It can also be described as the identity of the city. With big data, an accurate statement could be made about which road carries the heaviest traffic or which park is used the most. Therefore the interpretation can be scientifically substantiated in the future. To understand the identity, however, a city must be lived in. The years spend abroad by the author provided him with a multi-faceted expertise for this book. He lived in six cities and experienced them each for one or two years. Mexico City, Santiago de Chile, Rio de Janeiro, Shanghai, Munich and Stuttgart. They feature all scales and form the basis for conclusions about the anatomy.

Urban theories are often developed on a theoretical basis. Despite of sharp theoretical considerations, the theory often differs from reality. As a consequence, new districts have to grow and develop their own character in the beginning. This process is an adaptation of theory to reality. The goal of the anatomy of the city is to minimise this adjustment process. Here, grown urban structures are analysed and interpreted through everyday life. In other words, the impact of the anatomy on the identity of the city is described. The combination of experience and analysis makes it possible to say why a certain neighbourhood park is popular, which street edge has the biggest potential for commerce or why an Urban Cell has more residential qualities than another. These conclutions can be applied to both new planning and existing structures.

Karten urbane Zellen oder Nährstoffadern. Diese Karten basieren auf Satellitenbildern und anderem Kartenmaterial und geben den untersuchten Parameter so exakt wie möglich wieder. Allein die Darstellungsweise hebt ungewohnte Aspekte hervor und erzeugt ein differenziertes Bild auf die Stadt.

Die Interpretation der anatomischen Zeichnungen ist mit der Erfahrung verbunden. Sie kann auch als Identität der Stadt beschrieben werden. Über Big Data ließe sich eine genaue Aussage treffen, wie stark welche Straße befahren oder welcher Park am meisten genutzt wird. Daher kann die Interpretation in Zukunft wissenschaftlich untermauert werden. Um ihre Identität zu verstehen, muss eine Stadt jedoch erlebt werden. Die jahrelangen Auslandsaufenthalte des Autors bilden eine vielschichtige Expertise für diese Interpretation. Zwischen ein und zwei Jahren wurden sechs Städte kennengelernt und erlebt. Mexiko-Stadt, Santiago de Chile, Rio de Janeiro, Shanghai, München und Stuttgart. Sie ziehen sich durch alle Maßstäbe und bilden die Grundlage für Rückschlüsse über die Anatomie.

Städtebauliche Theorien werden oft auf theoretischer Basis entwickelt. Trotz scharfsinniger Überlegungen ist die Theorie von der gelebten Realität meist weit entfernt. In Konsequenz müssen neue Stadtteile erst wachsen und ihren eigenen Charakter entwickeln. Dieser Prozess ist die Anpassung der Theorie an die Realität. Das Ziel der Anatomie der Stadt ist es, diesen Anpassungsprozess zu minimieren. Hier werden gewachsene städtische Strukturen analysiert und durch den gelebten Alltag interpretiert. Anders gesagt, es wird die Auswirkung der Anatomie auf die Identität der Stadt beschrieben. Die Kombination aus Erfahrung und Analyse ermöglicht es, Aussagen darüber zu treffen, warum gerade dieser Nachbarschaftspark funktioniert, warum sich der Kommerz genau an dieser Stelle niederlässt oder warum eine urbane Zelle mehr Wohnqualitäten besitzt als eine andere. Diese Erkenntnisse lassen sich sowohl auf neue Planungen, als auch auf gewachsene Stadtstrukturen anwenden.

Macroregion

Macroregion

Definition

The Macroregion consists of several hundreds of cities, which lie at a distance of less than 200 kilometers from each other.

Die Makroregion besteht aus mehreren Hundert Städten, die eine Entfernung von weniger als 200 Kilometer zueinander haben.

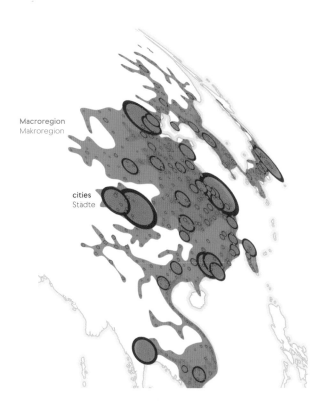

Macroregion
Makroregion

cities
Städte

Macroregion

Descriptive Essay

The term Macroregion has different interpretations, but always describes a vast area in relation to a specific defining aspect. In this book is a clear definition of the term Macroregion, however, other uses of the term are more vague.

Existing Use of the Term

The Macroregions as described by the United Nations have the most extensive scale. Their designation was introduced for use in statistical surveys and includes whole continents or smaller sub regions. South America is viewed as one single Macroregion, while Africa is divided into five. Both, South America and Africa, have strong geographic diversity within their borders, so clearly it is not only the geography of an area that lends to its definition as a Macroregion. However, other relevant aspects are not mentioned.

The term Macroregion also appears in geographical scales. In his paper *On the term and the concept of "region" from the perspective of geography*, Prof. Dr. Werner Bätzing states that 'the whole of Europe can be divided into about 10 Macroregions'. His use of the term describes a certain scale, but lacks any further defining aspect.

Der Begriff Makroregion hat verschiedene Auslegungen, beschreibt aber immer ein großflächiges Gebiet hinsichtlich eines bestimmten Aspektes. Während die Makroregion in diesem Buch eindeutig definiert ist, ist der Begriff in seiner bisherigen Verwendung oft vage.

Bisherige Verwendung des Begriffes

Am großflächigsten sind die geografischen Makroregionen der Vereinten Nationen. Sie wurden für statistische Erhebungen eingeführt und umfassen ganze Kontinente oder kleinere Subregionen. So wird Südamerika von den Vereinten Nationen als eine Makroregion zusammengefasst, während Afrika in fünf Makroregionen unterteilt ist. Da sowohl Südamerika wie auch Afrika eine starke geografische Vielfalt besitzen, zeigt sich, dass die im Namen enthaltene Geografie nicht der einzige Aspekt der Definition ist. Weitere relevante Aspekte werden jedoch nicht genannt.

Der Begriff Makroregion taucht auch in den Maßstabsebenen der Geografie auf. Prof. Dr. Werner Bätzing definiert in seinem Papier *Zum Begriff und zur Konzeption von „Region" aus Sicht der Geografie* die Makroregionen als „große Teilräume in Europa, sodass ganz

The term Macroregion is also used in China, Brazil and Europe. It describes geographically connected regions. In these cases, actual geographical circumstances define the Macroregions. The mountain range of the *Alps* or the *Danube* River Basin constitute geographical Macroregions defined by the European Union. Background is a reinforced political cooperation of the relevant states.

The American anthropologist G. William Skinner proposed several Macroregions in China in his paper A *note Regarding the Physiographic and Socioeconomic Macro Regions of China*. Later he described them in his book *The City in Late Imperial China* as 'nine areas according to the drainage basins of the major rivers and other travel-constraining geomorphological features. They are distinct in terms of environment, economic resources, culture and more or less interdependent histories with often unsynchronised developmental macrocycles'. Here we see a geomorphological aspect and its impact on the social economy emerging as the defining aspect of these Macroregions.

In contrast to the UN, which views South America as one Macroregion, the government of Brazil divides the country into five Macroregions. Each consist of three or more states and are based on geographical, social and economic aspects. How these aspects define the Brazilian Macroregions is not described in detail.

The existing use of the term is very different. These Macroregions differ in their size, their aspects and the quality of their definition. They do, however, describe relevant aspects. In this book, the Macroregion is defined through the density of cities. Therefore, geography, culture and economy are included indirectly in the definition. It is a further development of the term.

Europa etwa in zehn Makroregionen gegliedert werden kann". Damit wird der Begriff zwar in eine Maßstabsebene gebracht, der relevante Aspekt, durch welche sich die Region definiert, bleibt jedoch unklar. Große Staaten wie China, Brasilien, aber auch Europa, benutzen den Begriff, um geografisch zusammenhängende Regionen zu definieren. Gleiche geografische Gegebenheiten definieren hier die Makroregion. So bildet der Gebirgszug der **Alpen** oder das *Donaueinzugsgebiet* eine geografische Makroregion in Europa. Hintergrund ist eine verstärkte politische Zusammenarbeit der entsprechenden Staaten. In China wurden die Makroregionen vom amerikanischen Anthropologen G. William Skinner in seinem Papier A *note regarding the Physiographic and Socioeconomic Macroregions of China* vorgeschlagen. Später beschreibt er sie in seinem Buch *The City in Late Imperial China* als „neun Regionen, die sich auf die Entwässerungsbecken der größten Flüsse beziehen. Andere geomorphologische Gegebenheiten, die das Reisen erschweren, werden ebenfalls miteinbezogen. Die Regionen zeichnen sich durch einzigartige Umwelt, wirtschaftliche Ressourcen, Kultur und mehr oder weniger ähnliche Geschichte aus". Der geomorphologische Aspekt und seine Auswirkungen auf die Sozialökonomie sind hier als definierendes Element der Makroregion eindeutig beschrieben. In Brasilien sind die insgesamt fünf Makroregionen weniger eindeutig definiert. Sie bestehen aus drei oder mehreren Staaten und orientieren sich an geografischen, sozialen und wirtschaftlichen Aspekten. Wie diese Aspekte die brasilianischen Makroregionen definieren, wird nicht näher beschrieben.

Die bisherige Verwendung des Begriffes ist sehr unterschiedlich. Diese Makroregionen unterscheiden sich in ihrer Größe, ihren Aspekten und der Qualität ihrer Definition. Sie beschreiben jedoch relevante Aspekte. In diesem Buch wird die Makroregion durch die Verdichtung von Städten definiert. Geografie, Kultur und Wirtschaft werden so indirekt in die Definition miteinbezogen. Dadurch erfährt der Begriff eine Weiterentwicklung.

What is a Macroregion?

Was ist eine Makroregion?

Cities do not spread evenly across earth. Some regions have a high density of cities, while others are less populated. The Macroregions described in this book are the densely populated areas. Their defining element is the density of cities. Macroregions consist of several hundreds of cities, which lie within 200 kilometer of one another. Depending on the number of cities, they can have different dimensions. A number of key conditions directly affect the growth of cities, three of which, vegetation, connectivity and geography, are explored in more detail below.

Städte verteilen sich nicht gleichmäßig auf der Erde. Es gibt Regionen, in denen sich viele Städte befinden, während andere weniger besiedelt sind. Die dicht besiedelten Regionen werden in diesem Buch als Makroregionen beschrieben. Ihr Hauptaspekt ist die Verdichtung der Städte. Makroregionen umfassen mehrere Hundert Städte, die in einer Entfernung von weniger als 200 Kilometer zueinander liegen. Je nach Anzahl der Städte können sie ganz unterschiedliche Dimensionen haben. Mehrere wichtige Voraussetzungen beeinflussen das Wachstum von Städten. Drei davon - Vegetation, Konnektivität und Geografie - werden im Folgenden beschrieben.

Vegetation

Humans create their own habitats, the cities. Every city is therefore decisively determined by the needs of its inhabitants. Food is an important basic requirement of humans. As a result, people have increasingly settled in fertile areas, resulting in a higher number of cities. These fertile regions, which can be seen as bright green areas on satellite images, have produced the largest Macroregions in the world. Through technology, humans are able to transform barren land into fertile land. This creates a potential for new Macroregions.

The largest bright green zones of the earth are steppe and meadows. They differ from the dark green zones, the rainforests, as well as the desert and mountain landscapes. Macroregions are located only in the bright green zones of the earth. The three biggest fertile zones are located in northeastern America, Europe and Central Asia. These zones also have the biggest Macroregions. Other large zones lie in India, the Gulf of Guinea, the northern Andean region, California and parts of Brazil. These large bright green zones are congruent with their Macroregions as well. While urban growth has taken place in suitable regions in the past, the environment is now being adapted to create the ideal conditions. However, the

Vegetation

Menschen schaffen ihr eigenes Habitat, die Städte. Jede Stadt wird daher maßgeblich durch die Bedürfnisse ihrer Bewohner bestimmt. Ein wichtiges Grundbedürfnis des Menschen ist Nahrung. Daher haben sich Menschen verstärkt in fruchtbaren Gebieten niedergelassen, wodurch eine höhere Anzahl an Städten in fruchtbaren Regionen entstanden ist. Diese fruchtbaren Regionen, die als hellgrüne Bereiche auf Satellitenbildern zu sehen sind, haben die größten Makroregionen hervorgebracht. Durch die Technologisierung ist der Mensch im Stande, unfruchtbares Land in fruchtbares zu verwandeln. Dadurch entsteht ein Potenzial für neue Makroregionen.

Die größten hellgrünen Zonen der Erde sind Steppen- und Wiesenlandschaften. Sie unterscheiden sich von den dunkelgrünen Zonen, den Regenwäldern sowie den Wüsten- und Gebirgslandschaften. Makroregionen befinden sich ausschließlich in den hellgrünen Zonen der Erde. Die drei größten fruchtbaren Zonen liegen im Nordosten Amerikas, Europa und Zentralasien. Diese Zonen besitzen auch die größten Makroregionen. Größere Zonen bilden Indien, der Golf von Guinea, die

relationship between Macroregions and veg-etation remains. Barren regions are becoming increasingly more accessible for city settlement and farming through improved supply routes and opportunities. Huge green circles in the des-ert can be seen on satellite images of Saudi Ara-bia. These are plantations, situated next to the city of Buraida. Here, artificial irrigation turns the desert into fertile soil. Similar phenomena can be observed in Israel. The fertile environment is becoming less important, while the identity of the city, its economic and innovative strength is gaining more importance.

Connectivity

Humans and goods act like urban nutrients that keep cities alive. An increased amount of urban nutrition stimu-lates the development of a Macroregion. Good accessibility increases the flow of these urban nutrients and is a precondition for strong urban growth. In turn, an increased number of cities leads to increased connectivity. This leads to a direct correlation between connectivity and increased urban growth.

In the past, trade routes acted as the main supply of these 'urban nutri-ents'. Today the traffic of goods and people is widely separated. The sea is of great interest for the movement of goods, since a majority of the merchandise is shipped in containers. The nodes of this trade network are the ports and it is no coincidence that the largest of these are located in the nuclei of the Macroregions. The high number of people results in a high import traffic. Shanghai, in the middle of Central Asia, has the port with the largest turnover world-wide. Rotterdam, the largest port in Europe, is located directly in the core of the Macroregion. In the U.S.A., goods are distributed to several ports. New York, New Jersey, Philadelphia, Balti-more and Paulsboro are all on the American Axis, which forms the core of the region. Inland, the rivers functions as veins of the trade traffic. Fol-lowing this, the ports of Rotterdam at the *Rhine*

nördliche Andenregion, Kalifornien und Teile Bra-siliens. Auch in diesen Fällen sind die hellgrünen Zonen deckungsgleich mit den Makroregionen. Während Stadtwachstum in der Vergangenheit in dafür geeigneten Regionen stattgefunden hat, wird die Umwelt heutzutage an die idealen Bedingungen angepasst. Die Beziehung zwischen den Makroregionen und der Vegetation bleibt jedoch bestehen. Durch verbesserte Versor-gungswege und -möglichkeiten sind auch karge Regionen zunehmend interessanter für Stadt-besiedelung und Ackerbau. In Saudi-Arabien erkennt man auf Satellitenbildern riesige grüne Kreise in der Wüste. Sie liegen neben der Stadt Buraida und sind Plantagen, die durch künstliche Bewässerung die Wüste in fruchtbaren Boden umwandeln. In Israel sind ähnliche Phänomene zu beobachten. Die fruchtbare Umgebung wird weniger wichtig, während die Identität der Stadt, ihre Wirtschaft und Innovationskraft an Bedeu-tung gewinnen.

Konnektivität

Menschen und Güter wirken wie urbane Nährstoffe, die Städte am Leben erhalten. Eine erhöhte Anzahl an urbanen Nährstoffen fördert die Entstehung einer Makro-region. Eine gute Erreichbarkeit erhöht den Fluss dieser urbanen Nährstoffe und ist Voraussetzung für ein üppiges Stadtwachstum. Gleichzeitig führt eine erhöhte Anzahl an Städten zu einer ver-stärkten Konnektivität. Konnektivität und Stadt-wachstum haben daher eine Wechselwirkung.

Während in der Ver-gangenheit vor allem Handelswege diese urba-nen Nährstoffe brachten, ist der Personen- und Warenverkehr heute weitgehend getrennt. Der Seeweg ist vor allem für den Warenverkehr von großem Interesse, da ein Großteil aller Waren in Containern verschifft wird. Die Knotenpunkte dieses Netzwerkes bilden die Häfen. Und so ist es kein Zufall, dass in den Kernen der Makroregionen die größten Häfen der Welt liegen. Die vielen Men-schen haben einen hohen Import von Gütern zur Folge. Shanghai, in der Mitte Zentralasiens, besitzt

international flight routes

estuary and Shanghai in the *Yantze Delta* gain further importance for trading due to their proximity to the rivermouths. The port of South Louisiana, the largest in the United States, is located at the mouth of the *Mississippi*. The relationship between a navigable river and city growth is visible along the *Nile* and the *Upper Rhine Valley* in Europe. Coal, petroleum or other raw materials are important factors for urban growth as well. Major cities such as Dubai or Singapore have emerged at their place of extraction and transport routes. At the scale of the Macroregion, airports have become the main gateway to the world for passenger traffic. In order for people to travel between two Macroregions, for example from Europe to Asia, the aircraft is used almost exclusively. But even within the Macroregion, the aircraft is gaining importance and consequentially the number of flight connections of the nearest airport. The biggest Macroregions can clearly be seen in graphs of international air traffic. The number of flight routes increases in tandem with the density of cities.

den Hafen mit dem weltweit größten Umschlag. Rotterdam als größter Hafen Europas liegt ebenfalls Mitten im Kern der Makroregion. In den USA wird der Warenverkehr auf mehrere Häfen aufgeteilt. New York, New Jersey, Philadelphia und Baltimore liegen alle in der nordöstlichen Achse. Ins Landesinnere sind es die Flüsse, die als Adern für den Warenverkehr agieren. Rotterdam an der *Rheinmündung* und Shanghai im *Yangtze-Delta* bekommen daher eine Doppelfunktion. Der *Port of South Louisiana*, der größte der USA, liegt an der Mündung des *Mississippi*. Am *Oberrheintal* und dem *Nil* lässt sich der Zusammenhang zwischen einem schiffbaren Fluss und Stadtwachstum ablesen. Die Faktoren für starkes Stadtwachstum sind auch Kohle, Erdöl oder andere Rohstoffe. An ihren Abbauorten und Transportwegen liegen wichtige Städte wie Dubai oder Singapur. Im Maßstab der Makroregion sind Flughäfen die wichtigsten Tore zur Welt für den Personenverkehr geworden. Um zwischen zwei Makroregionen zu reisen, zum Beispiel von Europa nach Asien, wird fast ausschließlich das Flugzeug benutzt. Aber auch innerhalb

The development of a Macroregion is strongly based on connections to other Macroregions, as well as internal connections. Large ports are the main hubs for goods and typically located in the core of the Macroregion, at the mouth of a navigable canal.

Geography

The form of the landscape has an influence on the distribution of cities. The ideal landscape for urban growth is relatively flat ground. There are few cities on the top of a mountain. Cities in valleys are more common, but the most common location is on flat ground. Because of this, large mountain ranges create natural boundaries to Macroregions.

The boundary effect of mountain ranges is recognisable on many continents. In North America, the Rocky Mountains lie between California and the East Coast. Also in South America, a mountain range limits two Macroregions. In the north, the Andes mark the end of the Caribbean Macroregion, in the south they form a strong border for Chile. Through their influence on the weather, mountain ranges also affect the vegetation. The highest mountain range in the world, the Himalayas, creates a clear separation between India and Central Asia. The east-west orientation of these mountains leads to heavy rainfall. The monsoon favours the Indian Macroregion. A small mountain range with a similar effect is the Alps. This mountain range is merely a linguistic boundary within the Euro-Arab Macroregion, but it also stimulates urban growth in Northern Italy. The shape of the landscape also determines the course of rivers and thus the connectivity.

der Makroregion gewinnt das Flugzeug an Bedeutung und in Konsequenz die Anzahl der Flugverbindungen des nächstgrößeren Flughafens. In Grafiken, die den internationalen Flugverkehr zeigen, lassen sich deshalb die großen Makroregionen deutlich ablesen. Die Anzahl der Flugrouten nimmt mit der Verdichtung der Städte zu.

Die Entwicklung einer Makroregion basiert stark auf den Verbindungen zu anderen Makroregionen sowie internen Verbindungen. Große Häfen sind die Hauptumschlagplätze für Waren und liegen idealerweise im Kern der Makroregion und an den Mündungen schiffbarer Kanäle.

Geografie

Die Form der Landschaft hat einen Einfluss auf die Verteilung der Städte. Die ideale Landschaft für Stadtwachstum ist flach. Es gibt kaum Städte auf Berggipfeln. Städte in Tälern sind häufiger, aber am häufigsten liegen sie auf flachem Untergrund. Daher haben große Gebirgszüge eine Grenzwirkung für Makroregionen.

Die Grenzwirkung von Gebirgen ist auf vielen Kontinenten erkennbar. In Nordamerika liegen die Rocky Mountains zwischen Kalifornien und der Ostküste. Auch in Südamerika begrenzt eine Gebirgskette zwei Makroregionen: Im Norden sind die Anden der Abschluss der karibischen Makroregion, im Süden bilden sie eine starke Grenze für Chile. Durch ihren Einfluss auf das Wetter wirken Gebirgszüge auch auf die Vegetation ein. Das höchste Gebirge der Welt, der Himalaya, schafft eine klare Trennung zwischen Indien und Zentralasien. Durch die Ostwest-Ausrichtung dieses Gebirges kommt es zu starken Regenfällen. Der Monsun begünstigt die indische Makroregion. Eine kleinere Gebirgskette mit ähnlichem Effekt sind die Alpen. Der kleinere Gebirgszug bildet lediglich eine Sprachgrenze innerhalb der europäisch-arabischen Makroregion, fördert zugleich aber das Stadtwachstum in Norditalien. Die Form der Landschaft bestimmt auch den Verlauf von Flüssen und damit die Konnektivität.

Macroregions in Detail

In this book, the term Macroregion treats the density of cities as the main defining aspect. Notwithstanding considerations of scale, the Macroregion is an economic and cultural unit, regardless of political boundaries and ideologies. Thus, these regions differ in part from political, national or media perceptions.

The Euro-Arab Macroregion is characterised by a high geographical diversity. It has a multitude of linguistic and cultural spaces and a small-scale structure of towns and cities. No other Macroregion has a similarly high density of capitals. The reason is the geographical condition, which defines smaller areas within the Macroregion. The zones are mainly defined by mountain ranges and water. The most well-known areas are the British Isles, Scandinavia, the Iberian Peninsula, Italy, the Aegean Sea, Turkey, the *Nile* and the Mediterranean Sea coast in the north of Africa and the Arabian Peninsula. The *Rhine* as main axis of movement into the hinterlands has a different effect. The densest collection of city clusters in the entire Macroregion is located at its mouth. It is where the linguistic and cultural areas overlap. Within 300 by 300 kilometers there are five small city clusters with five different languages. The small scale of the geography has led to many small towns. With more than 7,000 cities, the Euro-Arab Macroregion has much more cities than any other Macroregion on earth. At the same time, the size of the cities is very small in international comparison.

The Central Asian Macroregion is structurally different. It also has a few geographically defined areas. Japan, Korea and Taiwan are defined by the sea. They have created the central metropolitan areas of Tokyo, Seoul and Taipei. China forms a large, cohesive region. The urban development concentrates on four strategic points. The Pearl River Delta with Hong Kong, the *Yangtze Delta* with Shanghai and the North China Plain with Beijing are located on the East China Sea. Chongqing is located in the hinterlands, at the *Yangtze* River. The Macroregion

Makroregionen im Detail

Der Begriff Makroregion setzt sich bewusst die Verdichtung der Städte als Aspekt und zeigt real existierende Strukturen und Stadtgrößen. Neben der Maßstabsebene bildet die Makroregion eine wirtschaftliche und kulturelle Einheit, unabhängig von politischen Grenzen und Ideologien. Dadurch unterscheiden sich diese Regionen teilweise von politischen, nationalen oder medialen Wahrnehmungen.

Die europäisch-arabische Makroregion zeichnet sich durch eine hohe geografische Vielfalt aus. Sie hat eine Vielzahl an Sprach- und Kulturräumen und eine kleinteilige Stadtstruktur. Keine andere Makroregion besitzt eine ähnlich hohe Dichte an Hauptstädten. Grund dafür sind die geografischen Gegebenheiten, die kleinere Zonen innerhalb der Makroregion begrenzen. Die Zonen werden hauptsächlich von Gebirgszügen und Wasser definiert. Die bekanntesten Zonen sind die britischen Inseln, Skandinavien, die iberische Halbinsel, Italien, die Ägäis, die Türkei, der *Nil*, die Mittelmeerküste im Norden Afrikas sowie die arabische Halbinsel. Der *Rhein* als Hauptbewegungsachse ins Landesinnere hat eine gegenteilige Wirkung. An seiner Mündung befindet sich die dichteste Ansammlung von Metropolregionen in der gesamten Makroregion. Hier überlappen sich auch die Sprach- und Kulturräume. Innerhalb von 300 mal 300 Kilometern liegen fünf kleine Stadtverbände mit fünf verschiedenen Sprachen. Die Kleinteiligkeit der Geografie hat zu vielen kleinen Städten geführt. Mit über 7.000 Städten hat die europäisch-arabische Makroregion ein Vielfaches mehr an Städten als alle anderen Makroregionen der Erde. Gleichzeitig ist die Größe der Städte im internationalen Vergleich sehr klein.

Die zentralasiatische Makroregion ist strukturell anders aufgebaut. Auch sie hat ein paar abgegrenzte Bereiche: Japan, Korea und Taiwan werden durch das Meer definiert. Diese kleineren Zonen haben die zentralen Metropolregionen Tokio, Seoul und Taipeh hervorgebracht. China bildet eine große zusammenhängende Region. Hier konzentriert sich das

is distinguished by several large agglomerations, with few cities inbetween. They are located at a great distance of 700 - 1,500 kilometer. Even though they are located in different countries, the Asian cities have a quite similar culture. The economic development is similar, despite different political systems and ideologies. Over a period of several decades, it began with Japan, continued with Taiwan and South Korea and is repeated today in China.

Similar to China, North America has a large expanse of east-facing, green lowland. It is limited by the Rocky Mountains in the West. However, this fertile area has a greater geographic diversity. The Great Lakes in the North favour the growth of cities in the interior. Chicago, Detroit, Toronto and Montreal are just a few examples. Houston, New Orleans and, in part, Dallas, benefit from the Gulf of Mexico. The peninsula of Florida had an effect on the growth of Miami and the location of Atlanta at the southern end of the Appalachian Mountains based on its geographic amenities as well. The *American Axis* from Washington, D.C. to New York City, sometimes even to Boston, has the greatest geographical advantage thanks to the numerous bays, rivers and its proximity to the Atlantic.

Macroregions are important, because a city can never be considered in isolation. It is always in close connection to other cities within its Macroregion. Each Macroregion has economic and cultural characteristics that affect every individual city within. The Macroregion forms an economic and cultural unit, which acts independently of national boundaries. The global perception of a city is strongly connected to its Macroregion.

Stadtwachstum auf vier strategische Punkte: Das *Perlfluss-Delta* mit Hong Kong, das *Yangtze-Delta* mit Shanghai und die *nordchinesische Ebene* mit Peking liegen jeweils am *Ostchinesischen Meer*. Chongqing befindet sich im Landesinneren am *Yangtze*. Die Makroregion zeichnet sich durch mehrere große Ballungsräume aus, zwischen denen relativ kleine Städte liegen. Sie befinden sich in einer großen Entfernung von 700–1.500 Kilometern zueinander. Obwohl die Ballungsräume in verschiedenen Ländern liegen, gleichen sie sich kulturell. Trotz verschiedener politischer Systeme und Ideologien dieser Länder ähnelt sich die wirtschaftliche Entwicklung. Über einen Zeitraum von mehreren Jahrzehnten begann sie mit Japan, setzte sich über Taiwan und Südkorea fort und wiederholt sich heute in China.

Ähnlich wie Zentralasien besitzt auch Nordamerika eine nach Osten gewandte, grüne Tiefebene, die im Westen durch einen Gebirgszug, die Rocky Mountains, begrenzt wird. Diese fruchtbare Fläche hat jedoch eine stärkere geografische Diversität. Die großen Seen im Norden begünstigen das Stadtwachstum. Chicago, Detroit, Toronto und Montreal sind nur ein paar Beispiele. Houston, New Orleans und bedingt auch Dallas profitieren vom *Golf von Mexiko*. Die Halbinsel Floridas hat Miami hervorgebracht und auch die Lage Atlantas am südlichen Ende der *Appalachen* ist geografisch begünstigt. Die nordostamerikanische Achse von Washington, D.C. bis New York City, zu der teilweise auch Boston gezählt wird, hat durch ihre Buchten, Flüsse und die Lage am Atlantik jedoch den größten geografischen Vorteil.

Makroregionen sind von Bedeutung, da eine Stadt niemals isoliert betrachtet werden kann. Sie steht immer im engeren Zusammenhang mit anderen Städten in ihrer Makroregion. Jede Makroregion hat wirtschaftliche und kulturelle Eigenheiten, die auch die einzelnen Städte betreffen. Die Makroregion bildet eine wirtschaftliche und kulturelle Einheit, die unabhängig von politischen Grenzen funktioniert. Daher ist die globale Wahrnehmung einer Stadt stark mit ihrer Makroregion verknüpft.

Macroregion

Density and Dimensions

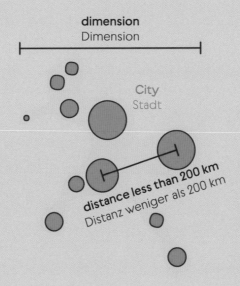

dimension
Dimension

City
Stadt

distance less than 200 km
Distanz weniger als 200 km

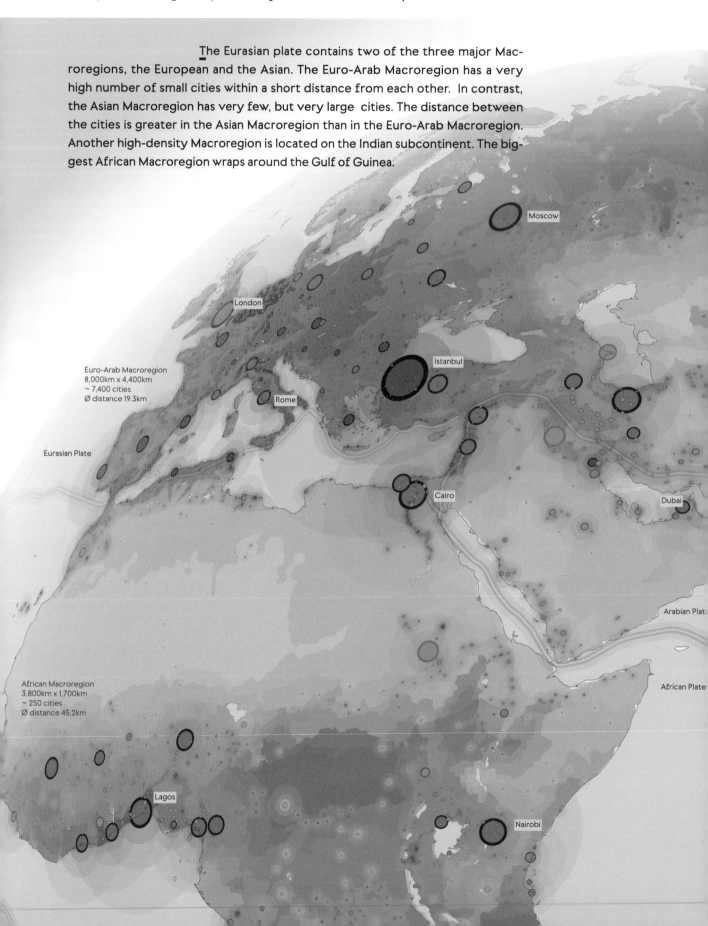

The Eurasian plate contains two of the three major Macroregions, the European and the Asian. The Euro-Arab Macroregion has a very high number of small cities within a short distance from each other. In contrast, the Asian Macroregion has very few, but very large cities. The distance between the cities is greater in the Asian Macroregion than in the Euro-Arab Macroregion. Another high-density Macroregion is located on the Indian subcontinent. The biggest African Macroregion wraps around the Gulf of Guinea.

Moscow

London

Euro-Arab Macroregion
8,000km x 4,400km
~ 7,400 cities
Ø distance 19.3km

Istanbul

Rome

Eurasian Plate

Cairo

Dubai

Arabian Plate

African Macroregion
3,800km x 1,700km
~ 250 cities
Ø distance 45.2km

African Plate

Lagos

Nairobi

Die eurasische Platte umfasst zwei der drei großen Makroregionen, die europäisch-arabische und die asiatische. Die europäisch-arabische besteht aus vielen kleinen Städten mit geringem Abstand. Die asiatische besteht im Gegensatz dazu aus wenigen, aber sehr großen Städten mit großen Abständen. Eine hochverdichtete Makroregion bildet auch der indische Subkontinent. Auf dem afrikanischen Kontinent liegt die höchste Verdichtung am *Golf von Guinea*.

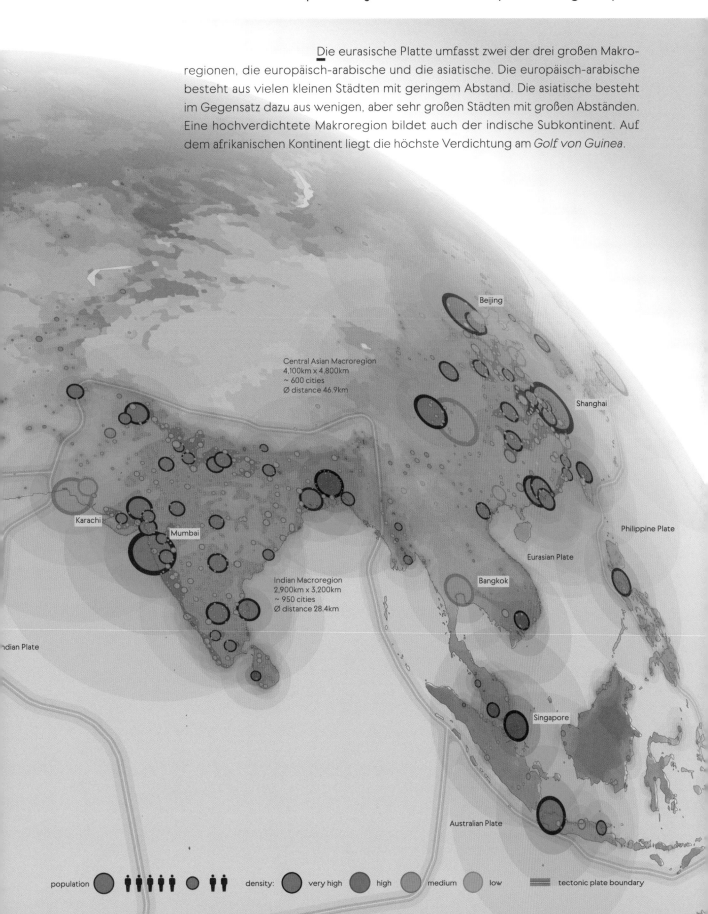

Beijing

Central Asian Macroregion
4,100km x 4,800km
~ 600 cities
Ø distance 46.9km

Shanghai

Karachi

Mumbai

Philippine Plate

Eurasian Plate

Indian Macroregion
2,900km x 3,200km
~ 950 cities
Ø distance 28.4km

Bangkok

Indian Plate

Singapore

Australian Plate

population ⬤ 🚹🚹🚹🚹🚹 ⬤ 🚹🚹   density: ⬤ very high ⬤ high ⬤ medium ⬤ low ▬▬ tectonic plate boundary

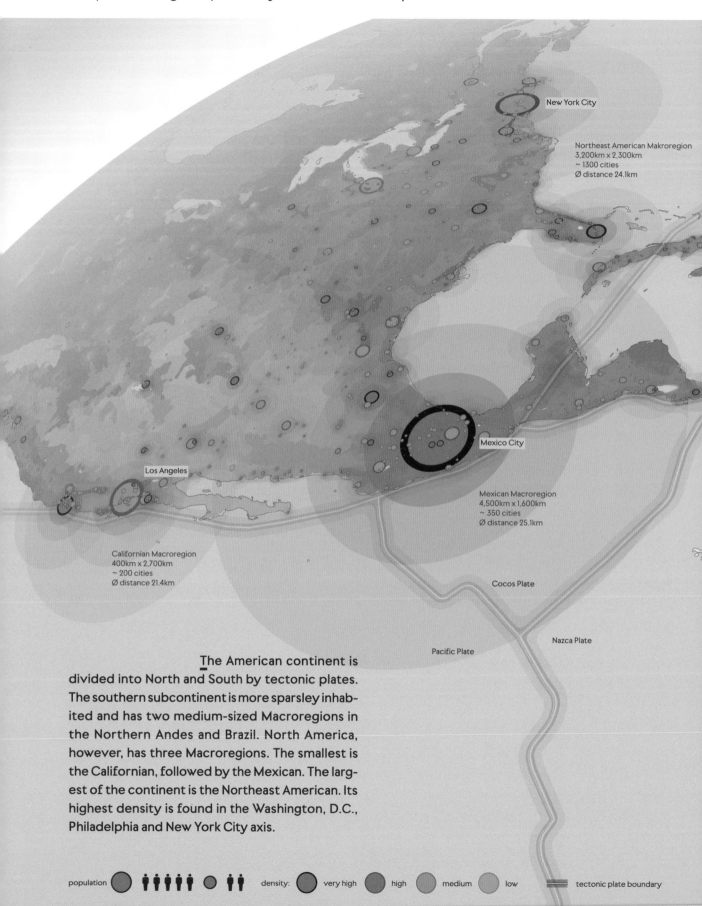

New York City

Northeast American Makroregion
3,200km x 2,300km
~ 1300 cities
Ø distance 24.1km

Mexico City

Mexican Macroregion
4,500km x 1,600km
~ 350 cities
Ø distance 25.1km

Los Angeles

Californian Macroregion
400km x 2,700km
~ 200 cities
Ø distance 21.4km

Cocos Plate

Nazca Plate

Pacific Plate

The American continent is divided into North and South by tectonic plates. The southern subcontinent is more sparsley inhabited and has two medium-sized Macroregions in the Northern Andes and Brazil. North America, however, has three Macroregions. The smallest is the Californian, followed by the Mexican. The largest of the continent is the Northeast American. Its highest density is found in the Washington, D.C., Philadelphia and New York City axis.

population ● ♟♟♟♟♟ ● ♟♟   density: ● very high ● high ● medium ● low   ▬▬ tectonic plate boundary

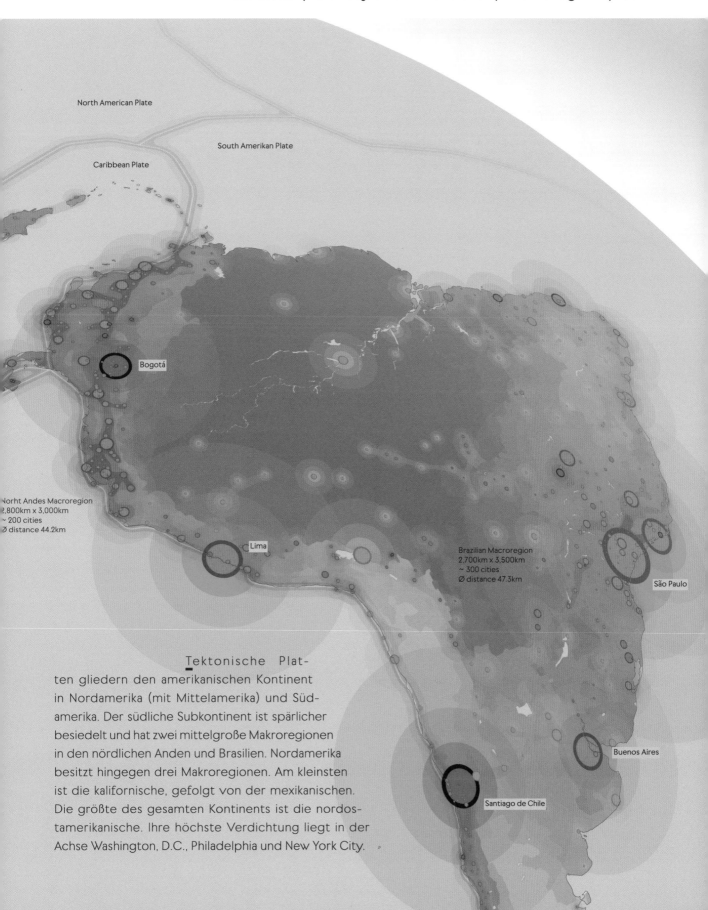

North American Plate

South Amerikan Plate

Caribbean Plate

Bogotá

Norht Andes Macroregion
2,800km x 3,000km
~ 200 cities
Ø distance 44.2km

Lima

Brazilian Macroregion
2,700km x 3,500km
~ 300 cities
Ø distance 47.3km

São Paulo

Buenos Aires

Santiago de Chile

Tektonische Plat-
ten gliedern den amerikanischen Kontinent
in Nordamerika (mit Mittelamerika) und Südamerika. Der südliche Subkontinent ist spärlicher
besiedelt und hat zwei mittelgroße Makroregionen
in den nördlichen Anden und Brasilien. Nordamerika
besitzt hingegen drei Makroregionen. Am kleinsten
ist die kalifornische, gefolgt von der mexikanischen.
Die größte des gesamten Kontinents ist die nordostamerikanische. Ihre höchste Verdichtung liegt in der
Achse Washington, D.C., Philadelphia und New York City.

Macroregion

Vegetation and City Growth

desert, mountains
Wüste, Berge

steppe, grasslands
Steppe, Grasflächen

rainforest
Regenwald

low city growth
niedriges Stadtwachstum

high city growth
hohes Stadtwachstum

low city growth
niedriges Stadtwachstum

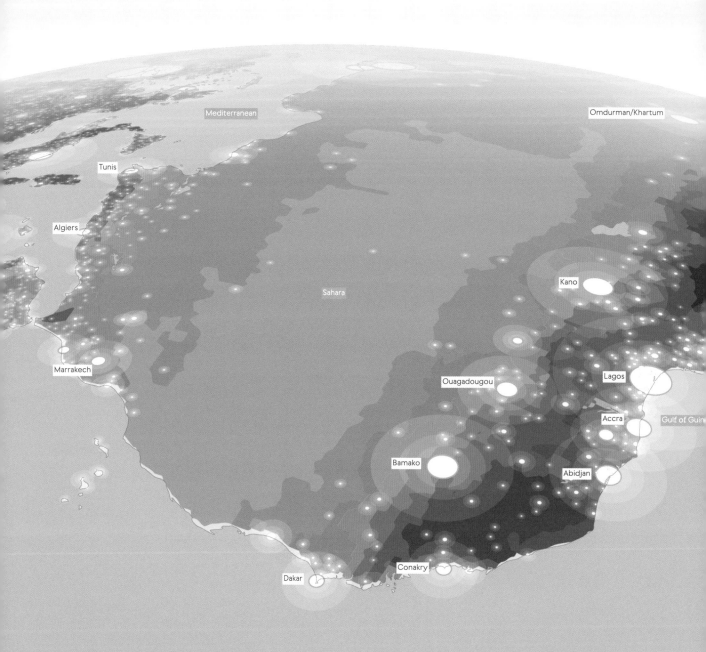

The African continent is marked by three big cities - Kano, Ouagadougou and Bamako. The steppe landscape of is strongly characterised by different climatic zones, which in turn influence the city growth. The highest city densification lies south of the *Sahara* desert, at the *Gulf of Guinea*. Its highest density is located in the region around Lagos and Accra. The transition to the *Sahara* is marked by three big cities - Kano, Ouagadougou and Bamako. The steppe landscape of the southern part of the continent has a uniform scattering of smaller towns and cities. It extends from Luanda, till Nairobi and Cape Town. In the north of the continent, a populated green stripe runs along the Mediterranean *Sea*.

 city   water 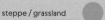 rainforest steppe / grassland desert / mountains

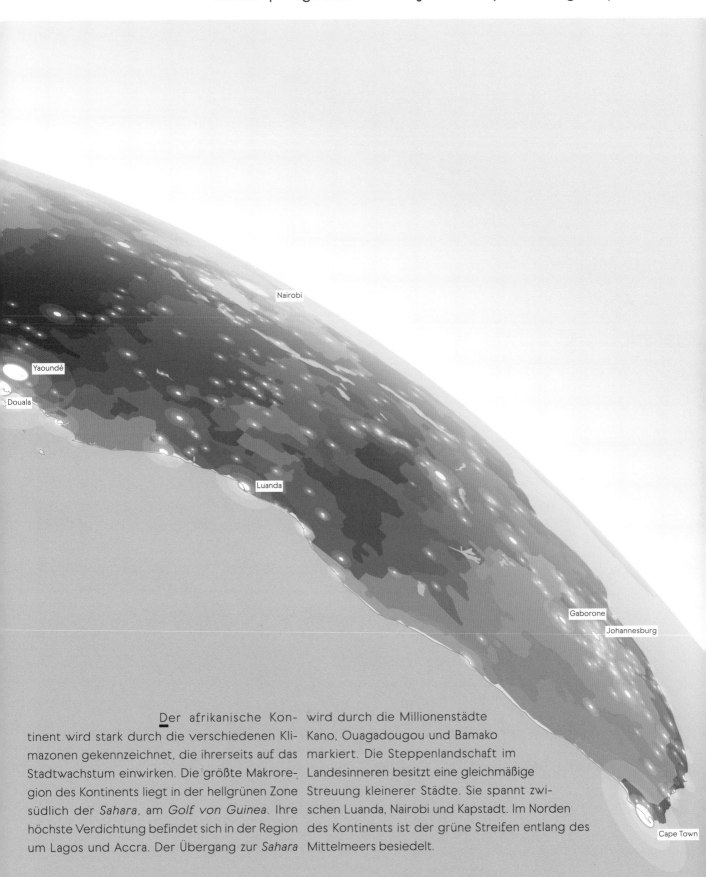

Der afrikanische Kontinent wird stark durch die verschiedenen Klimazonen gekennzeichnet, die ihrerseits auf das Stadtwachstum einwirken. Die größte Makroregion des Kontinents liegt in der hellgrünen Zone südlich der *Sahara*, am *Golf von Guinea*. Ihre höchste Verdichtung befindet sich in der Region um Lagos und Accra. Der Übergang zur *Sahara* wird durch die Millionenstädte Kano, Ouagadougou und Bamako markiert. Die Steppenlandschaft im Landesinneren besitzt eine gleichmäßige Streuung kleinerer Städte. Sie spannt zwischen Luanda, Nairobi und Kapstadt. Im Norden des Kontinents ist der grüne Streifen entlang des Mittelmeers besiedelt.

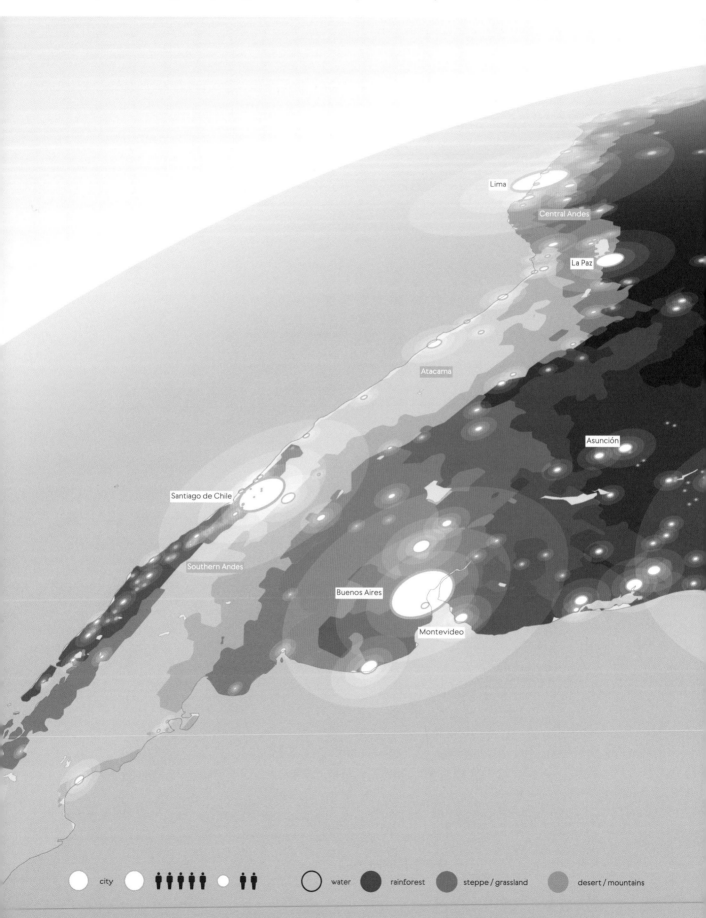

city   water   rainforest   steppe / grassland   desert / mountains

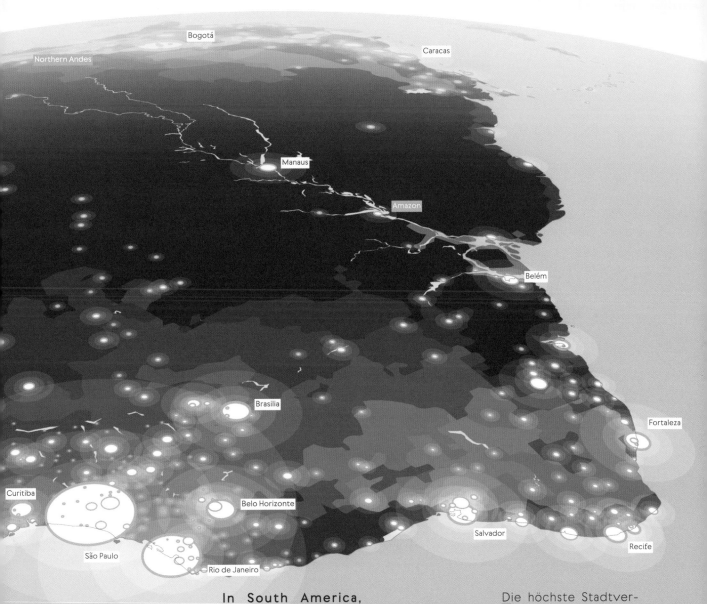

In South America, the highest densification of cities is located around the region of São Paulo, Rio de Janeiro, Belo Horizonte and Brasilia. The northern cities of Salvador, Recife and Fortaleza form a less dense region, while the *Amazon* basin is very sparsely populated. In the northern Andes, the urban growth densifies again in the elongated Macroregion of Lima, via Bogotá to Caracas. The central valley of Chile can easily be recognised in the south of the subcontinent. Cut off by the *Atacama Desert* and the Andes Cordillera, cities start to become denser again in the Argentine plateaus towards Buenos Aires.

Die höchste Stadtverdichtung befindet sich in der Region um São Paulo, Rio de Janeiro, Belo Horizonte und Brasilia. Die nördlich gelegenen Städte Salvador, Recife und Fortaleza bilden eine weniger verdichtete Makroregion, während das *Amazonasbecken* sehr spärlich besiedelt ist. Erst in den nördlichen Anden nimmt das Stadtwachstum in der länglichen Makroregion von Lima über Bogotá bis Caracas wieder zu. Im Süden des Subkontinents lässt sich deutlich das zentrale Tal Chiles ablesen. Abgeschnitten durch die *Atakamawüste* und die Gebirgskette der Anden verdichten sich die Städte erst wieder in den argentinischen Hochebenen Richtung Buenos Aires.

Macroregion

The Big Three

city

streets

water

Satellite Image thanks to:
© NASA Earth Observatory image by Robert Simmon, using Suomi NPP VIIRS data provided courtesy of Chris Elvidge (NOAA National Geophysical Data Center). Suomi NPP is the result of a partnership between NASA, NOAA, and the Department of Defense.

The European Macroregion has its core in London, Paris and the Benelux countries. Another high density area is the north of Italy. The densely populated *Rhine valley* can be observed from Cologne via Frankfurt towards Zurich, which then extends over Lyon to the Mediterranean coast. The sparsely populated Alps form one of the many borders of the continent. In contrast to the mountain range, the coastline works as a catalyst for urban growth due to its connectivity and food supply. The coasts of Spain, Portugal, Morocco, Tunisia and Israel have a high amount of cities. A relatively uniform densification of cities runs from Berlin, via Budapest to Athens. Further east, the cities get sparser until the metropolitan areas of Moscow and Istanbul.

Die europäische Makroregion hat ihren Kern im Bereich der Beneluxländer, Paris und London. Eine weitere hohe Verdichtung liegt im Norden Italiens. Von Köln über Frankfurt in Richtung Zürich ist das dicht besiedelte *Rheintal* ablesbar, dessen Verdichtung über Lyon bis an die Mittelmeerküste reicht. Deutlich erkennt man die spärlich besiedelten Alpen, die eine der vielen Sprachgrenzen des Kontinents darstellen. Wegen der Erreichbarkeit per Schiff sind vor allem die Küstenlinien stark besiedelt. Von Marokko bis Tunesien oder in Portugal und Israel ist dieser Effekt zu sehen. Eine relativ gleichmäßige Stadtverdichtung zieht sich von Berlin über Budapest bis Athen. Weiter östlich nimmt die Dichte der Städte kontinuierlich ab, bis sie auf die großen Ballungsräume von Moskau und Istanbul trifft.

The largest Macroregion of the American continent lies in the northeast. Its core region is formed by the Washington, D.C., Philadelphia and New York City axis. Near the Great Lakes another strong densification is visible. It includes Chicago, Detroit and Toronto. The southernmost cities are Houston, New Orleans and Miami at the Gulf of Mexico. In the west, the densification extends to Minneapolis, Kansas City and Dallas, where it starts to decrease continuously till Denver at the Rocky Mountains. With a few exceptions, such as Salt Lake City, the mountainous region is very sparsely populated. On the Westcoast, the urban growth picks up again. The Californian Macroregion extends from Vancouver and Seattle in the north, to Los Angeles and San Diego in the South. The core of the Mexican Macroregion consists of a group of cities around Mexico City.

San Francisco

Rocky Mountains

Salt Lake City

Los Angeles

Den

Phoenix

Mexico

Dallas

Houston

Guadalajara

New Orleans

Gulf of Mexico

Mexico City

La Habana

Satellite Image thanks to:
© NASA Earth Observatory image by Robert Simmon, using Suomi NPP VIIRS data provided courtesy of Chris Elvidge (NOAA National Geophysical Data Center). Suomi NPP is the result of a partnership between NASA, NOAA, and the Department of Defense.

Die größte Makroregion des amerikanischen Kontinents liegt im Nordosten. Sie hat ihren Kern in der Achse Washington, D.C., Philadelphia und New York City. In der Nähe der großen Seen ist eine weitere starke Verdichtung sichtbar. Zu ihr gehören Chicago, Detroit und Toronto. Die südlichsten Städte der Makroregion sind Houston, New Orleans und Miami am *Golf von Mexiko*. Nach Westen reicht die Makroregion bis Minneapolis, Kansas City und Dallas. Dort nimmt die Stadtverdichtung kontinuierlich ab, bis sie mit Denver an die Rocky Mountains stößt. Mit ein paar Ausnahmen wie Salt Lake City ist die Gebirgsregion sehr spärlich besiedelt. Erst an der Westküste nimmt die Stadtverdichtung in der kalifornischen Makroregion wieder zu. Sie reicht von Vancouver und Seattle im Norden bis Los Angeles und San Diego. Im Süden befindet sich der Kern der mexikanischen Makroregion in der Stadtgruppierung um Mexiko-Stadt.

○ city ◯ streets water

The Central Asian Macroregion has multiple cores with a distance of 700 - 1,500 kilometer between them. Of these, the largest is the *Yangtze Delta* around Shanghai. With around 140 million inhabitants it is the largest urban entity in the world. The city clusters around Hong Kong, Chengdu, Beijing, Seoul and Tokyo form the other cores. The number of smaller cities is comparetively low.

A similar distribution can be found in Southeast Asia. Bangkok, Kuala Lumpur, Singapore and Jakarta are the biggest agglomeratons in this area.

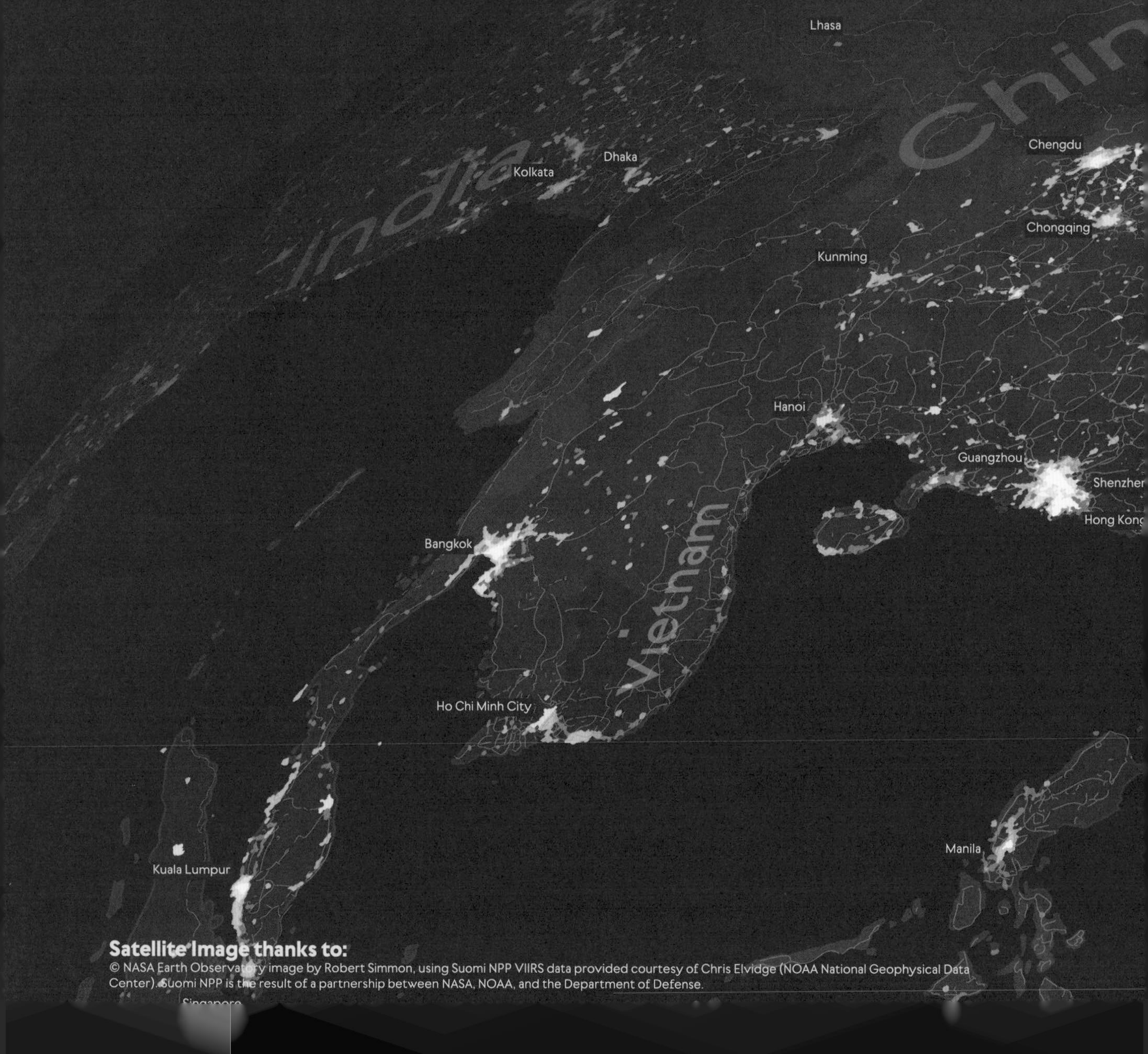

Lhasa

China

India

Chengdu

Chongqing

Kolkata

Dhaka

Kunming

Hanoi

Guangzhou

Shenzhen

Hong Kong

Bangkok

Vietnam

Ho Chi Minh City

Manila

Kuala Lumpur

Singapore

Urumqi

Ulaanbaatar

Xi'an

Beijing

Tianjin

Shenyang

Harbin

Dalian

Qingdao

Pyongyang

Wuhan

Nanjing

Seoul

Hangzhou

Shanghai

Busan

Fuzhou

Taipei

Japan

Osaka

Nagoya

Naha

Tokyo

Die zentralasiatische Mak- Seoul und Tokio bilden die weiteren Kerne. In roregion besitzt mehrere Kerne in einem Abstand Südostasien ist die Verteilung der Städte ähnlich. von 700 - 1.500 Kilometern. Das *Yangtze-Delta* Bangkok, Kuala Lumpur, Singapur und Jakarta bil- um Shanghai ist mit circa 140 Millionen Einwoh- den hier die größten Ballungsräume. nern das größte städtische Gebilde der Welt. Die

Surrounding

Surrounding

Definition

The Surrounding describes neighbouring cities within a distance of several hundred kilometers of each other.

Die Umgebung beschreibt benachbarte Städte in einer Distanz von mehreren Hundert Kilometern zueinander.

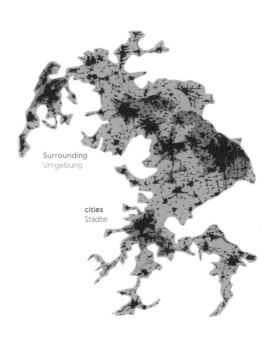

Surrounding
Umgebung

cities
Städte

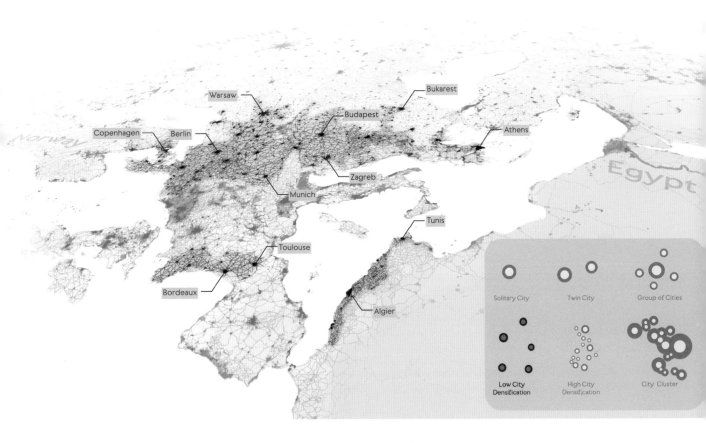

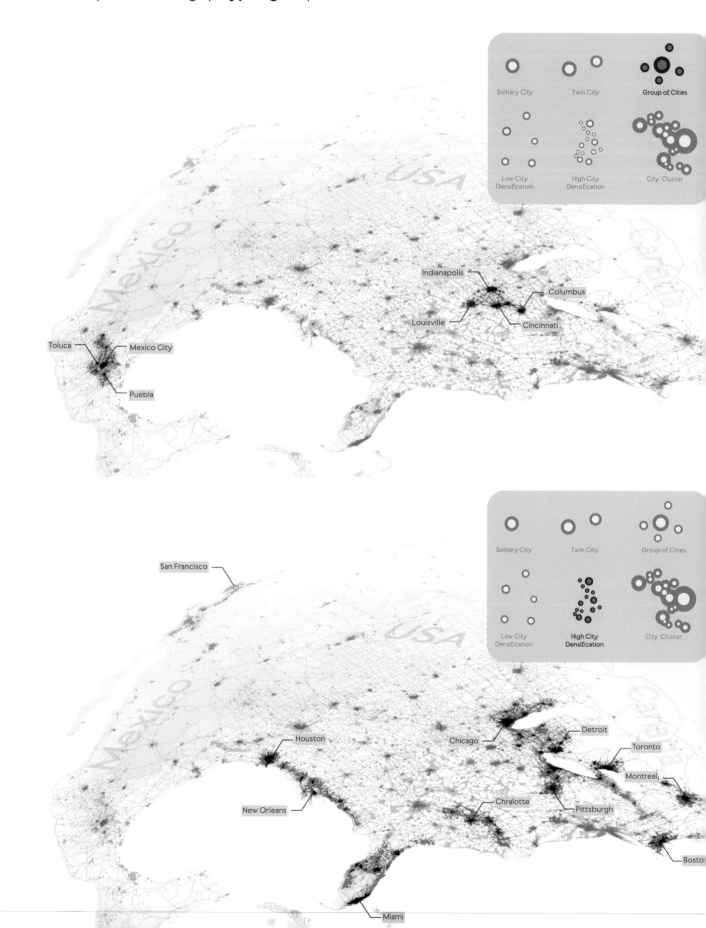

Solitary City   Twin City   Group of Cities

Low City Densification   High City Densification   City Cluster

Indianapolis
Columbus
Louisville
Cincinnati

Toluca — Mexico City
Puebla

San Francisco

Solitary City   Twin City   Group of Cities

Low City Densification   High City Densification   City Cluster

Houston
Chicago
Detroit
Toronto
Montreal
New Orleans
Chralotte
Pittsburgh
Bosto

Miami

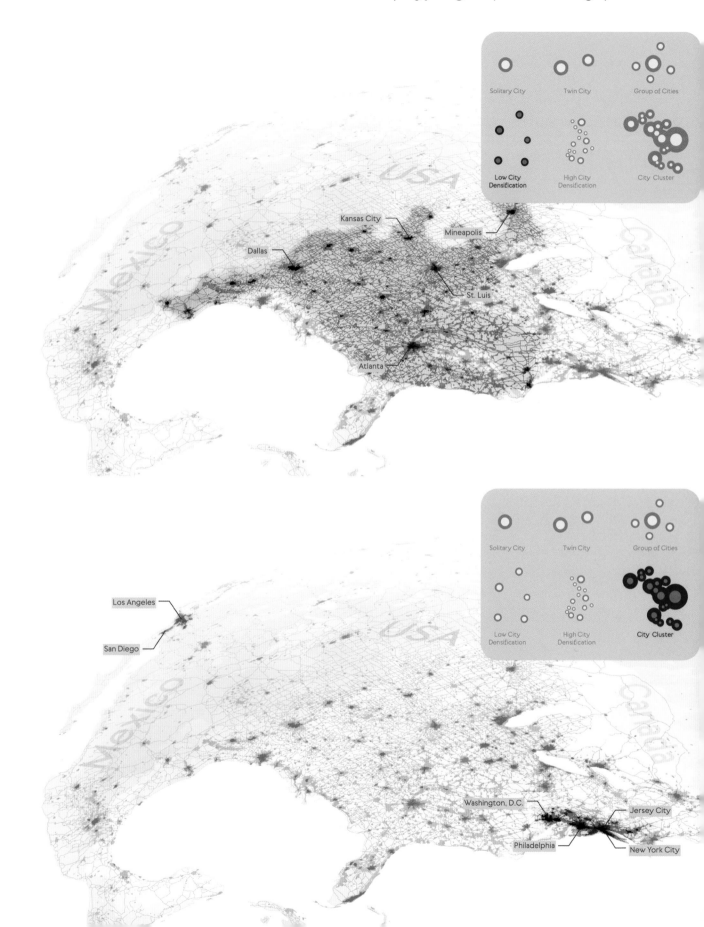

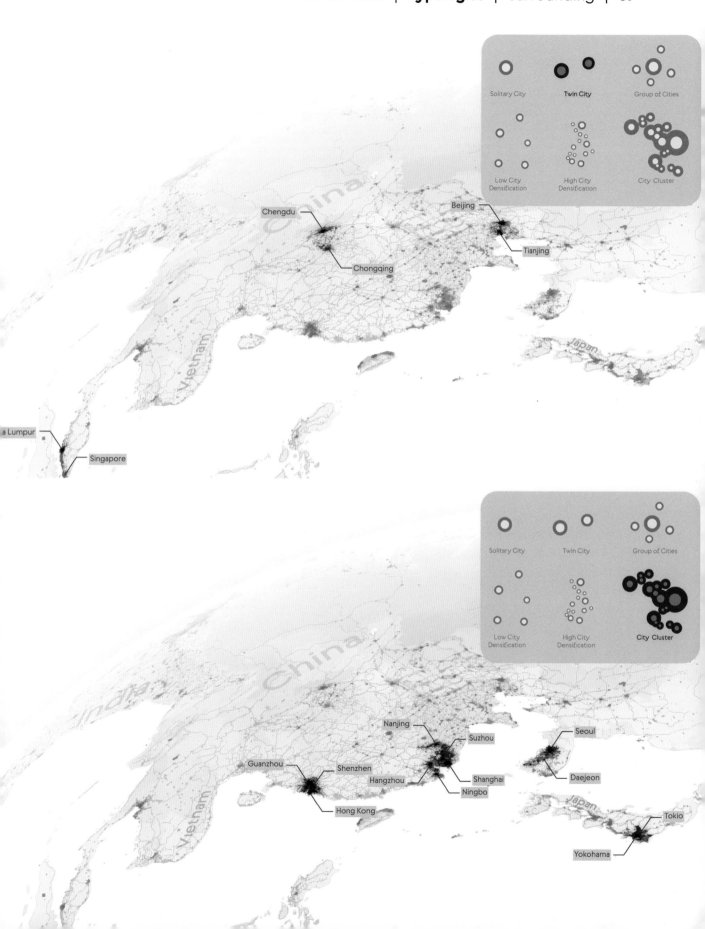

Solitary City
Twin City
Group of Cities
Low City Densification
High City Densification
City Cluster

Chengdu
Chongqing
Beijing
Tianjing
a Lumpur
Singapore

Nanjing
Suzhou
Seoul
Guanzhou
Shenzhen
Hangzhou
Shanghai
Daejeon
Ningbo
Hong Kong
Tokio
Yokohama

Surrounding

Descriptive Essay

The Surrounding shows a city within the context of its neighbouring cities. There are three basic typologies, depending on the density and number of cities. The first typology is the city cluster. It consists of several cities that have grown together. These cities form one connected urban entity. The second typology can be classified as a city densification. The neighbouring cities lie at a distance of 30 to 300 kilometers. The third typology is the individual city. It has no neighbouring cities within a distance of several hundred kilometers. The typology is strongly determined by topography and connectivity. A relatively flat ground and good connections support urban development and form a dense network of cities.

Die Umgebung zeigt den Bezug einer Stadt zu ihren benachbarten Städten. Je nach Dichte und Anzahl der Städte ergeben sich drei grundsätzliche Typologien: Der erste Typ ist der Stadtverband. Er besteht aus mehreren zusammengewachsenen Städten. Der zweite Typ wird als Stadtverdichtung bezeichnet. Die benachbarten Städte liegen in einer Entfernung von 30 bis 300 Kilometern zueinander. Der dritte Typ ist die Individualstadt. Sie hat keine benachbarten Städte in einer Entfernung von mehreren Hundert Kilometern. Die Typologie basiert stark auf der Topografie und Konnektivität. Ein relativ flacher Untergrund und eine gute Anbindung fördern das Stadtwachstum und bilden ein dichtes Netzwerk aus Städten.

Topography and City Growth

Urban growth is strongly linked to topography. The topography determines where we move and forms physical boundaries for cities.

Hard-to-reach valleys in the mountains are usually not very populated. Large valleys with navigable rivers, on the other hand, form important axes of movement. The flat ground between the mountains and the fertile soil are ideal for urban growth. The main axis of movement between São Paulo and Rio de Janeiro

Topografie und Stadtwachstum

Stadtwachstum basiert stark auf Topografie. Die Topografie bestimmt, wo wir uns bewegen, bildet gleichzeitig aber auch physische Grenzen.

Schwer zugängliche Täler in den Bergen sind daher meist wenig besiedelt. Große Täler mit schiffbaren Flüssen bilden hingegen wichtige Bewegungsachsen. Der flache Untergrund und der fruchtbare Boden eignen sich ideal für ein Stadtwachstum. Die Hauptbewegungsachse zwischen São Paulo und Rio de

lies in a valley. It is where several smaller cities started to grow. The central valley in Chile had a similar effect. Several smaller cities grew along this axis of movement. The metropolitan area of Seoul is expanding deep into the valleys of the surrounding mountains. The boundary effect of topography is also visible in Mexico City. The city is limited by volcanoes and mountains. They separate the city from its satellite cities.

Mountain ranges function as boundaries. They stop the urban growth. In contrast, flat ground is highly accessible and stimulates the emergence of cities.

Urban Nutrition Arteries

Urban nutrition arteries function similar to arteries in an organism. They bring the nutrients to the places they are needed. The more populated an area is, the more nutrients it needs. Big flows of nutrients, for example between two cities, always use the easiest way to move.

The urban nutrition arteries depend strongly on the topographical conditions. Highways and navigable canals are located on flat ground and in valleys. The Andes in Chile are notable for their absence of highways. Urban arteries have a strong interaction with urban growth. The increased flow of urban nutrients along rivers favours the growth of cities. At the same time, a large number of cities create a denser road network. Thus, densely populated regions, such as the *Yangtze Delta* in China or the *Upper Rhine Valley* in Europe, have tighter road networks than less densely populated regions, such as Chile. However, the urban arteries do not only function as a link between cities. They concentrate in large cities. Therefore, large cities form a node within the road network. Metropolitan areas are recognisable in the road network. Even structural differences, such as between London, Paris and the *Rhine-Ruhr* area, become clear. Concentrations of small cities, such as those found in Belgium and the Netherlands, can also be seen on the road network.

Janeiro liegt in einem Tal. An ihr sind mehrere kleine Städte gewachsen. Das zentrale Tal in Chile hat einen ähnlichen Effekt. Als Hauptbewegungsachse des Landes sind auch hier viele Städte gewachsen. Die Metropolregion Seoul reicht tief in die Täler der umgebenden Berge. Auch in Mexiko-Stadt ist die Grenzwirkung der Topographie sichtbar. Die Stadt ist von Vulkanen und Bergen umgeben. Diese trennen die Stadt von ihren umgebenden Satellitenstädten ab.

Gebirgszüge bilden starke Grenzen. Sie stoppen das Stadtwachstum. Ein flacher Untergrund ist dagegen einfach zugänglich und stimuliert die Entstehung von Städten.

Urbane Nährstoffadern

Urbane Nährstoffadern funktionieren wie Arterien in einem Organismus. Sie bringen die Nährstoffe an den Ort, an dem sie gebraucht werden. Je dichter ein Gebiet besiedelt ist, desto mehr Nährstoffe benötigt es. Dabei suchen sich Nährstoffe immer den einfachsten Weg.

Die urbanen Nährstoffadern hängen stark mit den topografischen Gegebenheiten zusammen. Autobahnen und schiffbare Kanäle befinden sich auf flachem Untergrund und in Tälern. So machen sich die Anden in Chile durch das Fehlen von Autobahnen bemerkbar. Zudem besteht eine starke Wechselwirkung zwischen urbanen Nährstoffadern und Stadtwachstum. Der erhöhte Fluss von urbanen Nährstoffen entlang von Flüssen begünstigt das Wachstum von Städten. Gleichzeitig erzeugt eine Vielzahl von Städten ein dichteres Straßennetzwerk. So haben dicht besiedelte Regionen wie das *Yangtze-Delta* in China oder das *Oberrheintal* in Europa ein engeres Straßennetzwerk als weniger dicht besiedelte Regionen wie Chile. Die urbanen Nährstoffadern funktionieren jedoch nicht nur als Verbindung zwischen den Städten. Ihre stärkste Verdichtung erfahren sie innerhalb von Großstädten. Große Städte bilden daher einen Knotenpunkt innerhalb des

Urban nutrition arteries, like rivers, highways or train tracks, are partly linked to topography. They avoid topographical obstacles and use the flat ground. But they also reflect the settlement typology. Densifications of cities have a fine mesh of highways, while big metropolitan areas form nodes in the street network.

City Clusters

The largest urban structures are city clusters. They consist of several cities that have physically grown together to become *a single urban unit*. The city cluster is clearly defined by the physical connection. In contrast, the term megalopolis is not clearly defined and used differently in America, China and Europe. Depending on the use, it sometimes coincides with the city cluster.

Comparing American, Chinese and European megalopolises, the different understanding of the term becomes evident. Jean Gottmann used the term megalopolis in 1961 in his landmark study *Megalopolis: The Urbanized Northeastern Seaboard of the United States.* He used it to describe 'the chain of metropolitan areas ... extending from Boston, ... through New York City, Philadelphia, to Washington, D.C.'. This megalopolis is made up of five major cities that are connected. In this case, the megalopolis and the city cluster are the same. Its dimension and structure is similar to the *Yangtze Delta*. This megalopolis around Shanghai consists of six megacities that have grown together. It is a city cluster as well. With a population of over 140 million people, it is the largest cohesive, urban structure in the world. The Tokyo - Yokohama cluster is much smaller. But it is defined as one city, gaining the title as the largest city in the world. The Jingjinji megalopolis around Beijing has two connected megacities, a small city cluster. Yet the politically created region adds a huge surrounding area to the megalopolis as well. This increases the population to 130 million, which makes the capital appear larger than it really is.

Straßennetzwerks. Metropolregionen lassen sich anhand der Autobahnen ablesen. Selbst strukturelle Unterschiede wie zum Beispiel zwischen London, Paris und dem *Rhein-Ruhr-Gebiet* werden deutlich. Auch Verdichtungen von kleinen Großstädten in Belgien und den Niederlanden sind am Straßennetzwerk ablesbar.

Urbane Nährstoffadern wie Flüsse, Autobahnen oder Zuggleise sind teilweise mit der Topografie verknüpft. Sie vermeiden topografische Hindernisse und verlaufen auf flachem Untergrund. Gleichzeitig spiegeln sie die Siedlungsstruktur wider. Stadtverdichtungen haben ein feines Straßennetzwerk, während große Metropolregionen Knotenpunkte bilden.

Stadtverbände

Die größten urbanen Gebilde sind Stadtverbände. Sie bestehen aus mehereren zusammengewachsenen Städten. Der Stadtverband wird durch die physische Verbindung klar definiert. Der Begriff Megalopole ist dagegen nicht klar definiert und wird in Amerika, Europa und China sehr unterschiedlich gebraucht. Je nach Auslegung stimmt er zuweilen mit dem Stadtverband überein.

Vergleicht man die amerikanischen, chinesischen und europäischen Megalopolen miteinander, werden die unterschiedlichen Auffassungen deutlich. Jean Gottmann verwendete den Begriff Megalopole 1961 in seiner Studie *Megalopolis: The Urbanized Northeastern Seaboard of the United States*. Er gebrauchte den Begriff um „die Kette aus Metropolregionen (...) von Boston, (...) New York City, Philadelphia, bis Washington, D.C.' zu beschreiben. Diese Megalopolis besteht aus fünf miteinander verbundenen Großstädten. In diesem Fall sind die Megalopole und der Stadtverband dasselbe. Seine Dimension und Struktur ähneln dem *Yangtze-Delta*. Diese Megalopole um Shanghai besteht aus sechs Megastädten, die zusammengewachsen sind. Sie formen ebenfalls einen Stadtverband. Mit einer Einwohnerzahl von über 140 Millionen Menschen ist der Verband

The city cluster is much smaller than the megalopolis. The European megalopolis *Blue Banana* is much bigger than the American or Chinese megalopolises. It consists of a large city cluster in northern Italy, several smaller clusters in the Benelux Countries, a medium sized cluster in the north of England and several individual cities and city densifications. It is around three times the size of the *American Axis* and ten times the size of the Beijing Cluster. The cluster in northern Italy and the agglomeration of smaller clusters in the Benelux countries both have a similar size to the northeast *American Axis*. Even the quantity of megalopolises varies, due to the unclear definition. The National Development and Reform Commission of China defines 'ten major metropolitan regions forming in China'. The *Economist* magazine comes to a total number of 13 megalopolises.

The definition of the megalopolis can be conveniently adapted. It can be used as a political instrument. Relevant cities appear larger and economic regions more diverse and attractive. The city cluster on the other hand, shows the physically connected cities, their population and density. The most important feature is the cluster or the merging of the cities. The precise definition allows the description of the urban structures more accurately and creates a reality-based perspective.

City Densifications

City densifications are Surroundings where the cities are separated by one to five hours by car. They can be classified as high or low density. A high density of cities increases the potential for a strong economy. The amount of urbanised areas in these densifications can even exceed a large city cluster.

If individual cities are close together, but not connected, they form a city densification. There are different types, depending on the distance between the cities. In Europe, both high and low densifications can be seen. In the east of Europe the cities are

das größte städtische Gebilde der Welt. Der Tokio-Yokohama-Verband ist deutlich kleiner. Aber er wurde als eine Stadt definiert, wodurch er den Titel „größte Stadt der Welt" erlangt hat. Die Jingjinji-Megalopole um Peking hat zwei miteinander verbundene Megastädte, die einen kleineren Stadtverband bilden. Jedoch bezieht die politisch definierte Region einen weiten Teil ihres Umlandes mit ein. Dadurch steigt die Bevölkerung auf 130 Millionen Menschen, wodurch die Hauptstadt wichtiger und größer erscheint. In diesem Fall ist der Stadtverband deutlich kleiner als die Megalopole. Die europäische Megalopole *Blaue Banane* ist deutlich größer als die amerikanischen oder chinesischen Megalopolen. Sie besteht aus einem großen Stadtverband in Norditalien, mehreren kleinen Verbänden in den Beneluxländern, einem mittleren Verband in Nordengland und, mehreren Individualstädten sowie Stadtverdichtungen. Diese Megalopole ist dreimal größer als die amerikanische Achse und zehnmal größer als der Peking-Verband. Der Verband in Norditalien und die kleinen Verbände in den Beneluxländern haben beide ähnliche Dimensionen wie die nordostamerikanische Achse. Auch die Anzahl der Megalopolen unterscheidet sich aufgrund der unterschiedlichen Definitionen. Die *National Development and Reform Commision of China* definiert „zehn größere Metropolregionen, die in China entstehen". Der *Economist* kommt auf insgesamt 13 Megalopolen.

Die Definition der Megalopolis lässt sich zweckmäßig anpassen. Sie kann als ein politisches Instrument benutzt werden. Relevante Städte erscheinen größer und wirtschaftliche Regionen diverser und attraktiver. Der Stadtverband zeigt hingegen die physisch existierenden Städte, ihre Bevölkerung sowie ihre Dichte. Die wichtigste Eigenschaft ist der Verbund, also das Zusammenwachsen der Städte. Die eindeutige Definition erlaubt es, urbane Gebilde akkurater zu beschreiben, und erzeugt eine realitätsbasierte Sichtweise.

separated by two to five hours by car. Berlin, Warsaw, Prague, Munich, Vienna, Budapest and Belgrade lie in a low density Surrounding and have comparatively high distances to each other. A high density Surrounding runs from Frankfurt, Stuttgart, Strasbourg, Basel, Zurich and Geneva to the Mediterranean coast. The cities are at a short distance of one or two hours from one another by road.

Despite their size, city densifications can be more densely populated than city clusters. The region around the Upper *Rhine Valley* has a greater populated area than the North-American Axis. The small cities form a dense network and function as independent nodes. It is easier for smaller cities to specialise and neighbouring cities in the densification benefit from these functions. The economic specialisation in particular is one of the advantages of city densifications. Because of the small size of the cities, rents and production costs tend to be favourable. Individual subsidiaries of large companies can be spread to several cities. Administration and organization are often located in the internationally connected cities, while production takes advantage of the smaller cities in the Surrounding. As a result, city densifications often develop into economically strong regions. This principle works globally. The hinterland of São Paulo has a high density of cities and is at the same time the strongest economic region of the subcontinent. The production facilities of large international companies are located in the satellite cities around Mexico City, a group of cities similar to a high densification. The region around the *Upper Rhine Valley* is one of the strongest economic regions in France, Germany and Switzerland and has a high density as well. Similar urban structures can be found in Northern India. They contribute significantly to the national economy.

City densifications are less obvious than city clusters, but have a huge economic value. They combine a high urban density with rural qualities.

Stadtverdichtungen

Stadtverdichtungen sind Umgebungen, in denen Städte in einer Distanz von ein bis fünf Autostunden zueinander liegen. Sie können durch ihre hohe oder niedere Dichte unterschieden werden. Eine hohe Stadtverdichtung birgt das Potenzial für eine starke Wirtschaft.

Liegen einzelne Städte dicht beieinander, sind jedoch nicht miteinander verbunden, formen sie eine Stadtverdichtung. Sie unterscheiden sich durch die Distanz zwischen den Städten. In Europa erkennt man den Unterschied zwischen hohen und niederen Verdichtungen. In Osteuropas haben die Städte große Distanzen von zwei bis fünf Autostunden zueinander. Berlin, Warschau, Prag, München, Wien, Budapest und Belgrad bilden eine niedere Verdichtung. Eine hohe Verdichtung verläuft von Frankfurt, Stuttgart, Straßburg, Basel, Zürich und Genf bis an die Mittelmeerküste. Hier liegen die Städte in einer geringen Entfernung von ein bis zwei Autostunden zueinander. Stadtverdichtungen sind teilweise dichter besiedelt als Stadtverbände. Die Region um das *Oberrheintal* hat mehr besiedelte Fläche als die *amerikanische Achse*. Die kleinen Städte bilden ein dichtes Netzwerk und funktionieren als eigenständige Knotenpunkte. Sie lassen sich leichter spezialisieren, wovon auch benachbarte Städte profitieren. Die wirtschaftliche Spezialisierung ist ein wichtiger Vorteil von Stadtverdichtungen. Wegen der kleinen Stadtgrößen sind die Mieten und Produktionskosten günstig. Verwaltung und Organisation befinden sich oft in den international vernetzten Großstädten, während die Produktion die Vorteile der kleineren Städte nutzt. Dadurch entwickeln sich Stadtverdichtungen häufig zu wirtschaftlich starken Regionen. Diese Entwicklung ist weltweit erkennbar. Das Hinterland von São Paulo bildet eine hohe Stadtverdichtung und ist zugleich stärkste Wirtschaftsregion des Subkontinents. In den Satellitenstädten um Mexiko-Stadt siedeln sich die Produktionen internationaler Großkonzerne an. Diese Umgebung bildet eine Stadtgruppierung, ähnlich einer hohen Verdichtung. Die Region um das *Oberrheintal* zählt

Individual Cities

When there are no immediately cities in the Surrounding, the individual city incorporates all functions for the surrounding area. A good example is Santiago de Chile. The next major city is a one-day trip away by road, which is why Santiago can be classified as a solitary city. The capital is an economic and cultural centre. Here are the main universities, hospitals, airports and part of the government. Only the port city of Valparaiso, as the seat of the parliament, takes over a few functions. In Europe, Paris, Madrid and Moscow are the most distinct individual cities.

The typologisation of different cities is gradual. This means that not every city can be classified into a distinct category. The transitions are fluid. The *Rhine-Ruhr* area is structurally located between a city cluster and a high city densification. In addition to the structural features, the scale plays an important role as well. A high city densification and a scattered, Urban Being are structurally the same, but differ in size. In the Stuttgart area, the individual villages are only a few minutes' drive away, while the nearest cities are less than two hours away. Thus, Stuttgart is a scattered Urban Being within a high city densification.

zu den wirtschaftlich stärksten Regionen Frankreichs, Deutschlands und der Schweiz. Auch sie zählt zu den hohen Stadtverdichtungen. Ähnliche städtische Strukturen liegen im Norden Indiens. Sie tragen maßgeblich zur nationalen Wirtschaft bei.

Stadtverdichtungen sind weniger bekannt als Stadtverbände, haben jedoch einen großen wirtschaftlichen Wert. Sie kombinieren hohe städtische Dichte mit ländlichen Qualitäten.

Individualstädte

Befinden sich keine anderen Großstädte in der näheren Umgebung, muss die Individualstadt alle Funktionen für das Umland übernehmen. Ein gutes Beispiel dafür ist Santiago de Chile. Die nächste Großstadt ist eine Tagesreise mit dem Auto entfernt. Daher kann Santiago als Solitärstadt eingeordnet werden. Die Hauptstadt ist wirtschaftliches und kulturelles Zentrum. Hier befinden sich die wichtigsten Universitäten, Krankenhäuser, Flughäfen und ein Teil der Regierung. Allein die Hafenstadt Valparaiso übernimmt als Sitz des Parlaments ein paar Funktionen. In Europa sind Paris, Madrid und Moskau die ausgeprägtesten Individualstädte.

Die Typologisierung verschiedener Städte ist graduell. Das bedeutet, das sich nicht jede Stadt in eine eindeutige Kategorie einordnen lässt. Die Übergänge sind fließend. Das *Rhein-Ruhr-Gebiet* befindet sich strukturell zwischen einem Stadtverband und einer hohen Stadtverdichtung. Neben den strukturellen Eigenheiten spielt auch der Maßstab eine wesentliche Rolle. Eine hohe Stadtverdichtung und ein verstreutes urbanes Wesen sind strukturell gleich aufgebaut, unterscheiden sich jedoch in der Größe. Im Großraum Stuttgart liegen die einzelnen Dörfer wenige Autominuten voneinander entfernt, während die nächsten Städte in einer Autostunde erreichbar sind. Stuttgart ist somit ein verstreutes urbanes Wesen innerhalb einer hohen Stadtverdichtung.

Surrounding

Typologies

solitary city
Solitärstadt

twin city
Doppelstadt

group of cities
Stadtgruppierung

low city densification
niedere Stadtverdichtung

high city densification
hohe Stadtverdichtung

star-shaped city cluster
sternförmiger Stadtverband

linear city cluster
linearer Stadtverband

polygonal city cluster
polygonaler Stadtverband

linear city cluster
linearer Stadtverband

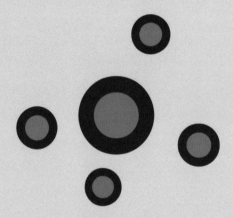

group of cities
Stadtgruppierung

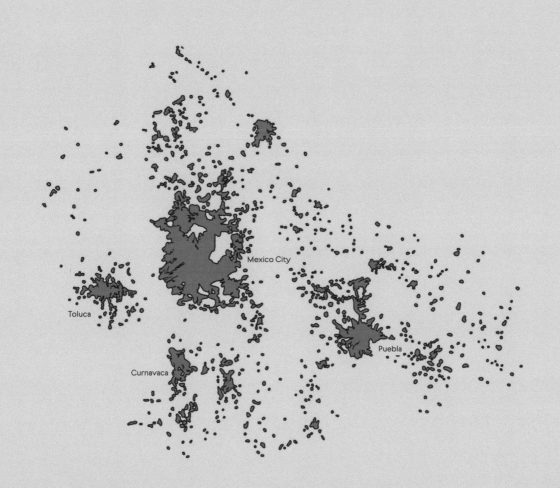

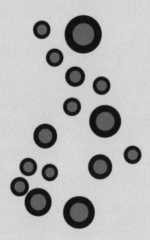

high city densification
hohe Stadtverdichtung

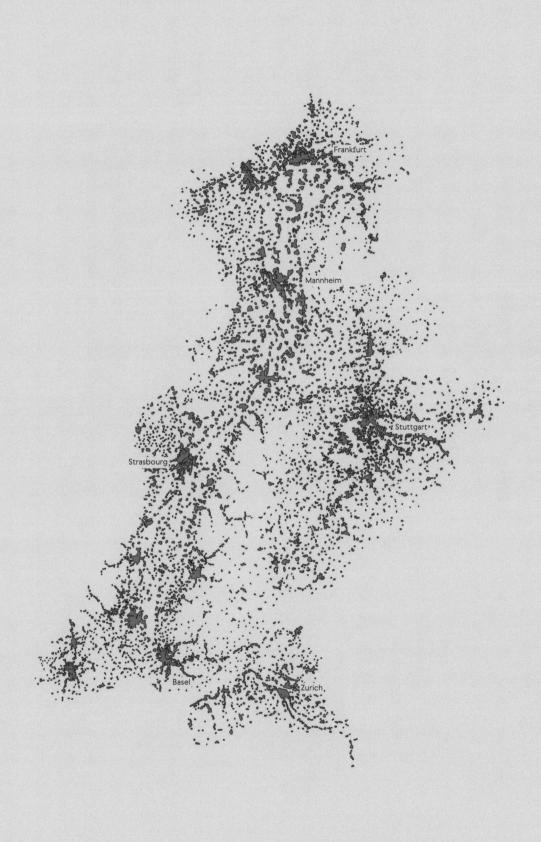

Sudogwon is a city cluster, which consists of a large city, Seoul, and several smaller towns. The city cluster extends to Chuncheon in the east, Cheonan in the south and the *Yellow Sea* in the west. Within its Surrounding it holds an important and central position. The city cluster contains a variety of functions, while the smaller individual cities in the south are mostly industrial.

The mountainous topography of South Korea gives the city cluster a unique structure. While forest covers the mountains, the populated valleys form long urban fingers. These fine extremities of the city reach far inland.

Pyongyang is significantly smaller than Seoul and surrounded by a multitude of small villages. All in all, the north is more village-like and the south more urban. This structural difference can also be seen by the number of highways.

Sudogwon ist ein Stadtverband, der aus einer Großstadt, Seoul, und mehreren kleinen Städten besteht. Der Stadtverband reicht im Osten bis Chuncheon, im Süden bis Cheonan und im Westen bis an das *Gelbe Meer*. Innerhalb seiner Umgebung nimmt der Stadtverband eine sehr zentrale Rolle ein. Er beherbergt eine Vielzahl an Funktionen, während die kleineren Individualstädte im Süden hauptsächlich industriell geprägt sind.

Durch die bergige Topografie Südkoreas hat der Stadtverband eine einzigartige Struktur. Während die Berge naturbelassen sind, bilden die besiedelten Täler lange städtische Finger. Diese feinen Gliedmaßen der Stadt reichen bis weit in das Landesinnere.

Pjöngjang ist deutlich kleiner als Seoul und von einer Vielzahl kleiner Dörfer umgeben. Insgesamt ist der Norden eher dörflich und der Süden eher städtisch geprägt. Dieser strukturelle Unterschied ist auch an den Autobahnen erkennbar.

star-shaped city cluster
sternförmiger Stadtverband

city

highway

water

green-field

forest

The drawing on the right shows several typologies at once. The *Rhine-Ruhr* area, including Cologne, Dusseldorf and Dortmund, forms a small city cluster. It is the largest agglomeration in Germany, but still quite small compared to other city clusters in Asia or the Americas.

The high city densification along the *Upper Rhine Valley* constitutes a rare typology. It stretches from Frankfurt to Basel and continues south via Zurich, Lyon and Marseille to the Mediterranean coast. It consists of small cities that are separated by limited distances of approximately one to two hours by car. The numerous highways and train connections form an extremely densified city network in that area, exceeding the *American Axis*. Typical of Europe, there are many small towns and villages in between. Stuttgart marks the eastern end of the high city densification, which decreases towards Munich.

The lower city densification is the third typology in which cities are separated by two to five hours by car. The lower densification of cities has an enormous size. It ranges from Munich in the east, to Warsaw in the west and from Stockholm in the north, to Athens in the south.

Im rechts dargestellten Ausschnitt werden gleich mehrere Typologien gezeigt. Das *Rhein-Ruhr-Gebiet* im Norden bildet mit Köln, Düsseldorf und Dortmund einen kleinen Stadtverband. Die größte Agglomeration Deutschlands ist im Vergleich zu anderen Stadtverbänden jedoch recht beschaulich.

Eine zweite Typologie ist die hohe Stadtverdichtung entlang des oberen *Rheintals*. Sie zieht sich von Frankfurt bis Basel und verläuft weiter südlich über Zürich, Lyon und Marseille bis an die Mittelmeerküste. Sie besteht aus kleineren Großstädten, die in einem geringen Abstand von ein bis zwei Autostunden zueinander liegen. Die zahlreichen Autobahnen und Zugverbindungen bilden ein extrem verdichtetes Stadtnetzwerk, dass sogar die *amerikanische Achse* übertrifft. Typisch für Europa gibt es viele kleine Städte und Dörfer dazwischen. Nach Osten hin gehört Stuttgart noch zur Stadtverdichtung, während diese Richtung München abnimmt.

Die niedere Stadtverdichtung bildet die dritte Typologie in der Zeichnung. In ihr liegen die Städte in einer Entfernung von zwei bis fünf Autostunden zueinander. Die niedere Verdichtung in Europa hat eine enorme Größe: Sie reicht von München im Osten bis Warschau im Westen, von Stockholm im Norden bis Athen im Süden.

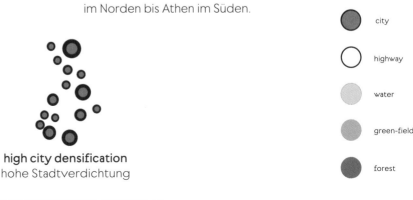

high city densification
hohe Stadtverdichtung

city

highway

water

green-field

forest

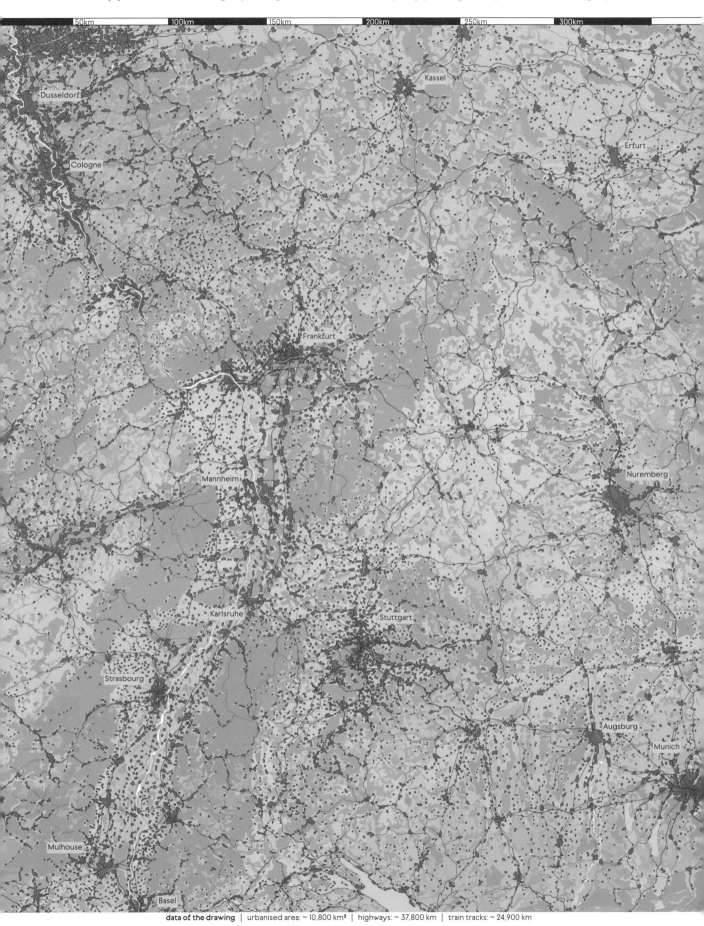

50km 100km 150km 200km 250km 300km

Dusseldorf

Cologne

Kassel

Erfurt

Frankfurt

Mannheim

Nuremberg

Karlsruhe

Stuttgart

Strasbourg

Augsburg

Munich

Mulhouse

Basel

data of the drawing | urbanised area: ~ 10,800 km² | highways: ~ 37,800 km | train tracks: ~ 24,900 km

Its unique location makes Santiago de Chile a solitary city. Natural boundaries, such as the Andes, the *Atacama Desert*, *Patagonia* and the South Pacific, isolate the city. Because of the abundant natural resources and skillful political leadership, the city is the only one in Latin America to achieve a "first world standard".

The large distances to other cities make the solitary city appear relatively introverted. As the only major metropolis in the area, it has to fulfill all the functions of the entire country, except for the political, as its parliament is located in the nearby city of Valparaiso. Santiago de Chile therefore forms the main node of the entire city network in the Surrounding.

A linear arrangement of cities exists only in the central valley to the south. The main axis of movement along the flat valley and fertile soil are the conditions for urban growth. As the only fertile area of the country, the valley forms the backbone of Chilean agriculture.

Die einzigartige Lage macht Santiago de Chile zu einer Solitärstadt. Natürliche Grenzen wie die Anden, die *Atacama-wüste*, *Patagonien* und der Südpazifik isolieren die Stadt stark. Aufgrund der reichlichen Ressourcen dieser Natur und einer geschickten politischen Führung hat die Stadt als einzige Lateinamerikas einen „ersten Welt-Standard" erreicht.

Die große Distanz zu anderen Städten lässt die Solitärstadt vergleichsweise introvertiert erscheinen. Als einzige Großstadt in der Umgebung muss sie die Funktionen des gesamten Landes erfüllen. Lediglich das Parlament befindet sich im nahe gelegenen Valparaiso. Santiago de Chile bildet damit den Hauptknotenpunkt des gesamten Stadtnetzwerkes der Umgebung.

Eine lineare Reihung von Städten gibt es nur im zentralen Tal Richtung Süden. Als einziges fruchtbares Gebiet des Landes bildet das Tal das Rückgrat der chilenischen Landwirtschaft. Die Hauptbewegungsachse durch das flache Tal und der fruchtbare Boden bilden auch hier die Voraussetzungen für ein Stadtwachstum.

solitary city
Solitärstadt

city

highway

water

green-field

forest

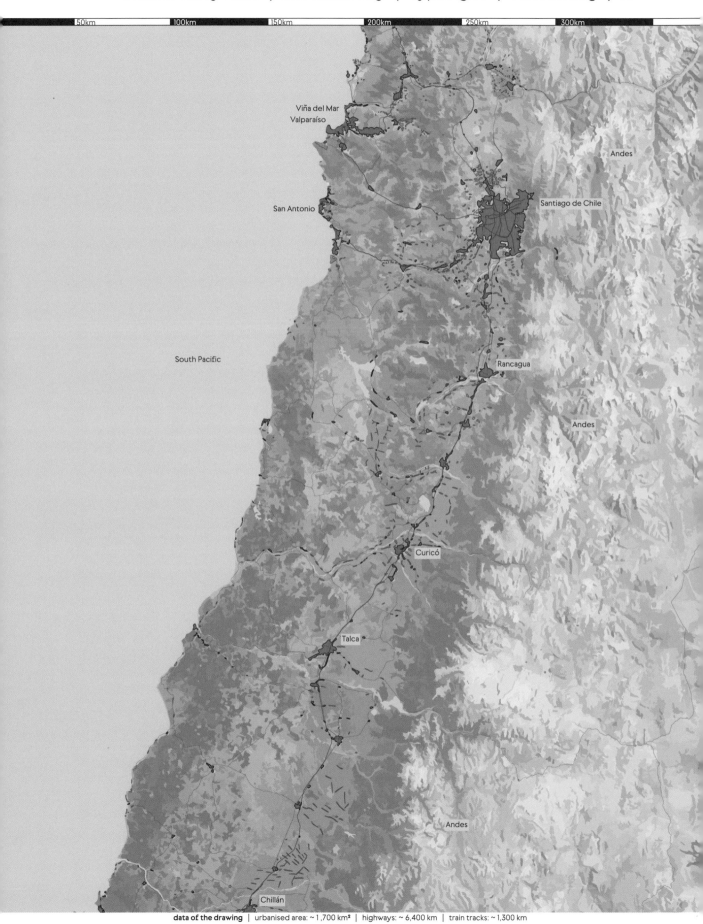

50km 100km 150km 200km 250km 300km

Viña del Mar
Valparaíso

Andes

San Antonio

Santiago de Chile

South Pacific

Rancagua

Andes

Curicó

Talca

Andes

Chillán

data of the drawing | urbanised area: ~ 1,700 km² | highways: ~ 6,400 km | train tracks: ~ 1,300 km

Surrounding

Urban Nutrition Arteries

canals
Kanäle

train tracks
Zuggleise

main artery roads
Hauptverkehrsadern

300km   250km   200km   150km   100km   50km

Pacific

Nanjing

Yangtze River

Suzhou

Shanghai

Hangzhou

Ningbo

data of the drawing | street length: ~26,700 km | train tracks: ~6,200 km

50km 100km 150km 200km 250km 300km

Hudson River

New York City

Philadelphia

Baltimore

Delaware Bay

Washinton, D.C.

Atlantic

Chesapeake Bay

train / metro

highway

water

data of the drawing | street length: ~16,400 kilometer | train tracks: ~9,300 km

300km 250km 200km 150km 100km 50km

Pacific

Santiago de Chile

train / metro

highway

water

data of the drawing | street length: ~6,400 km | train tracks: ~1,400 km

300km   250km   200km   150km   100km   50km

London

Calais

Lille

Lens

○ train / metro

○ highway

○ water

Paris

data of the drawing | street length: ~22,900 km | train tracks: ~12,400 km

50km　　100km　　150km　　200km　　250km　　300km

Amsterdam

Rotterdam

Antwerp

Brussels

Dortmund

Cologne

Frankfurt

Luxembourg

Saarbrucken

Stuttgart

data of the drawing | street length: ~41,100 km | train tracks: ~23,400 km

Surrounding

Topography and City Growth

cities grow on flat ground
Städte wachsen auf flachem Untergrund

300km 250km 200km 150km 100km 50km

Sierra Madre Occidental

León de los Aldama

Santiago de Querétaro

Guadalajara

Morelia

Mexico City is located on a plateau within the *Sierra Madre*. The surrounding mountains to the south, east and west caused the formation of satellite cities. Toluca, Cuernavaca and Puebla are very cut off by the volcanoes *Popocatépetl* and *Iztaccíhuatl*, but are still part of the group of cities around Mexico City.

Mexiko-Stadt liegt in einer Hochebene, inmitten der *Sierra Madre*. Durch die umgebenden Berge im Süden, Osten und Westen haben sich Satellitenstädte gebildet. Toluca, Cuernavaca und Puebla werden zwar stark durch die Vulkane *Popocatépetl* und *Iztaccíhuatl* abgeschnitten, gehören aber dennoch zur Stadtgruppierung.

50km 100km 150km 200km 250km 300km

Gulf of Mexico

Sierra Madre Oriental

Toluca

México City

Iztaccíhuatl

Puebla

Popocatépetl

Cuernavaca

city ◐ street water ◉ topography

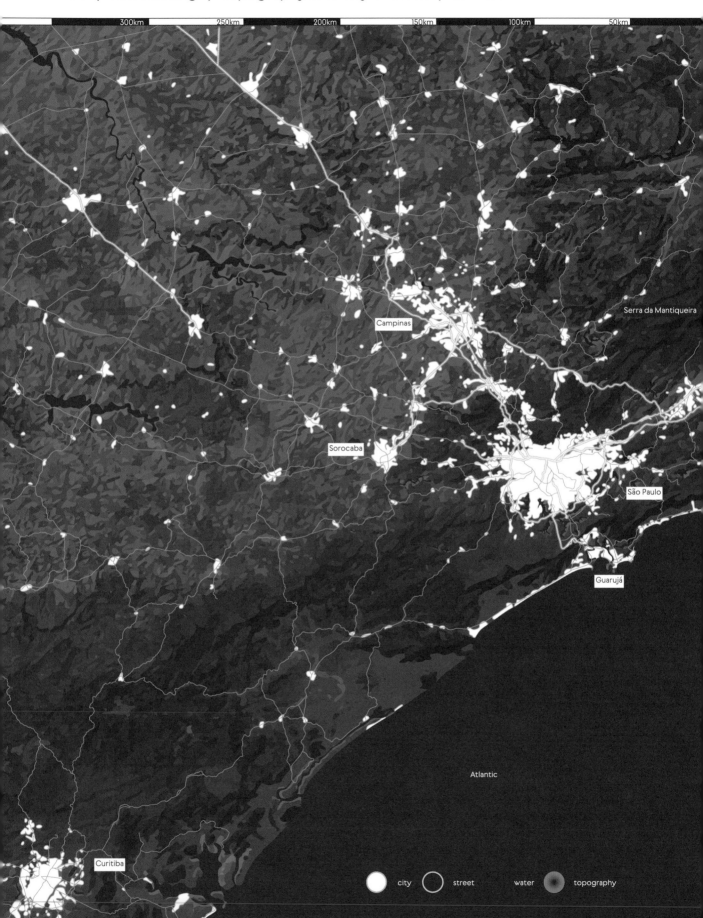

300km 250km 200km 150km 100km 50km

Serra da Mantiqueira

Campinas

Sorocaba

São Paulo

Guarujá

Atlantic

Curitiba

city ◯ street water topography

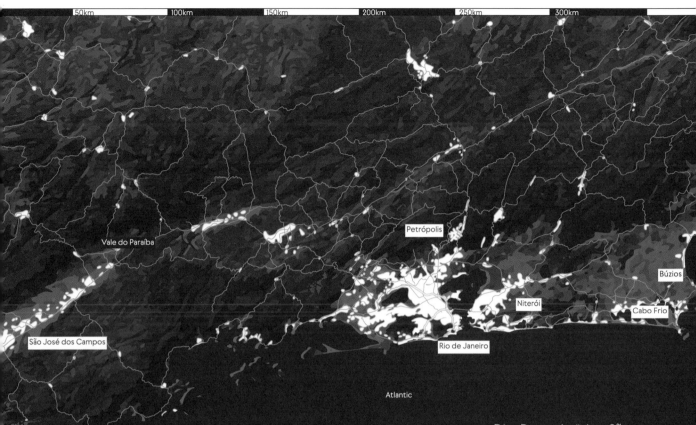

50km　　100km　　150km　　200km　　250km　　300km

Vale do Paraíba

Petrópolis

Búzios

Niterói

Cabo Frio

São José dos Campos

Rio de Janeiro

Atlantic

The twin cities São Paulo (SP) and Rio de Janeiro (RJ) are strongly influenced by the surrounding topography. The main axis of movement between the two cities takes place in a valley that runs parallel to the coast. The bay of *Guanabara* in Rio forms a natural harbour, the most important topographical asset of the city. RJ grows from the mouth of the bay, towards the inland along the valleys created by the surrounding mountain ranges. The combined effect of this topography is the star-shaped growth as seen.

The flat hinterland of SP has led to a relatively high city densification. As in other high densifications, this has enabled the development of a strong economy. This dense city network is located on a plateau and densifies towards the main hub of SP. Due to its location, SP is an ideal hub between the economically strong hinterland and the international trade routes of the nearby Atlantic.

Die Doppelstädte São Paulo (SP) und Rio de Janeiro (RJ) werden stark von der umgebenden Topografie beeinflusst. Die Bucht Guanabara in Rio bildet einen natürlichen Hafen und ist damit der wichtigste topografische Vorteil der Stadt. Die vielen Berge geben die sternförmige Wachstumsrichtung vor. RJ wächst von der Mündung der Bucht in Richtung Landesinnere entlang der Täler.

Die Hauptbewegungsachse zwischen RJ und SP liegt in einem Tal parallel zur Küste. Auch hier beeinflusst die Topografie die Bewegung der Menschen und Güter und damit das Stadtwachstum.

Das flache Hinterland SPs hat zu einer relativ hohen Stadtverdichtung geführt. Ähnlich wie bei anderen Stadtverdichtungen hat diese eine starke Wirtschaft hervorgebracht. Dieses stark verdichtete Stadtnetzwerk liegt in einer Hochebene und läuft in dem Hauptknotenpunkt SP zusammen. SP bildet durch seine Lage den idealen Knotenpunkt zwischen dem wirtschaftlich starken Hinterland und dem internationalen Handel des nahe gelegenen

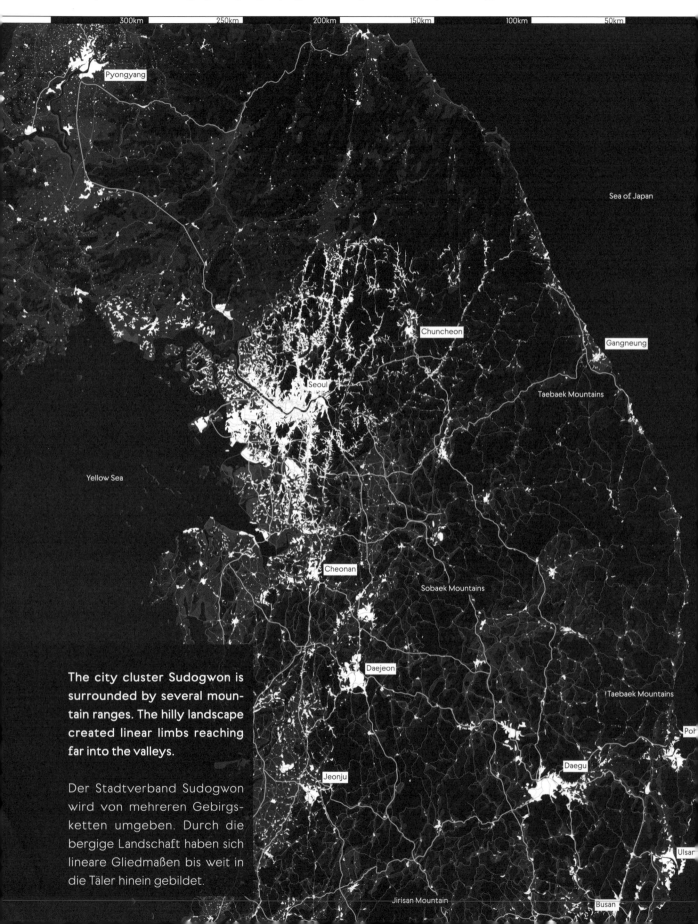

300km 250km 200km 150km 100km 50km

Pyongyang

Sea of Japan

Chuncheon

Gangneung

Seoul

Taebaek Mountains

Yellow Sea

Cheonan

Sobaek Mountains

Daejeon

Taebaek Mountains

Pol

Jeonju

Daegu

Ulsar

Jirisan Mountain

Busan

The city cluster Sudogwon is surrounded by several mountain ranges. The hilly landscape created linear limbs reaching far into the valleys.

Der Stadtverband Sudogwon wird von mehreren Gebirgsketten umgeben. Durch die bergige Landschaft haben sich lineare Gliedmaßen bis weit in die Täler hinein gebildet.

Santiago is located at the northern end of the *Valle Central*, the Central Valley. The valley is formed by the Andes in the east and the coastal mountain range in the west. The city growth mainly occurs in the plain valleys and on the coast near the capital.

Santiago de Chile liegt am nördlichen Ende des *Valle Central*, des zentralen Tals. Das Tal wird im Osten von den Anden und im Westen von der Gebirgskette der Küste geformt. Das Stadtwachstum findet vor allem in den flachen Tälern und an den Küsten in der Nähe der Hauptstadt statt.

city

street

topography

water

Surrounding

City Cluster

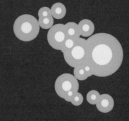

star-shaped city cluster
sternförmiger Stadtverband

linear city cluster
linearer Stadtverband

polygonal city cluster
polygonaler Stadtverband

The *Yangtze Delta* has a population of around 140 million people and is therefore the most densely populated city cluster in the world. With an area of approximately 70,000 sqarekilometer, it is about the size of the Republic of Ireland, with 25 times the population. It is known as the *Golden Triangle*, which extends between the metropolis Shanghai, Nanjing and Hangzhou.

Shanghai harbour has the world's highest turnover. This is in no small part due to its location within the Central Asian Macroregion. The city growth is aided further by the flat ground and the connection via the *Yangtze River* to the Chinese hinterland. The flat ground allows a very high connectivity between major cities. The high speed train takes one hour for the 300 kilometer between Shanghai and Nanjing.

The close proximity between the major cities allows them to benefit economically and culturally from each other. However, the urban concentration results in a severe contamination of air, water, and thus food. As the city cluster increases in size, so does the importance of an environmentally conscious economy, mobility and energy.

Das *Yangtze-Delta* ist mit circa 140 Millionen Menschen der am dichtesten besiedelte Stadtverband der Welt. Mit einer Größe von circa 70.000 Quadratkilometer ist es ungefähr so groß wie die Republik Irland, jedoch 25 Mal dichter bevölkert. Es ist unter dem Namen *Goldenes Dreieck* bekannt, das von den Metropolen Shanghai, Nanjing und Hangzhou aufgespannt wird. Die ideale Lage innerhalb der zentralasiatischen Makroregion und am Meer ist, neben der Wirtschaftslage, Grund für den Containerhafen mit dem weltweit höchsten Umschlag. Ein flacher Untergrund und die Verbindung über den *Yangtze* ins Hinterland haben das Stadtwachstum zudem stark begünstigt. Der flache Untergrund erlaubt eine sehr hohe Konnektivität zwischen den Metropolen. Die 300 Kilometer zwischen Shanghai und Nanjing werden mit dem Schnellzug in einer Stunde zurückgelegt.

Durch ihre Nähe profitieren die Metropolen vor allem wirtschaftlich und kulturell voneinander. Andererseits führt die Konzentration zu extremen Verschmutzungen der Luft, des Wassers und damit der Lebensmittel. Mit der Größe des Stadtverbandes wird eine umweltbewusste Wirtschaft, Mobilität und Energie um ein Vielfaches wichtiger.

polygonal city cluster
polygonaler Stadtverband

 city

 highway / train

 water

50km 100km 150km 200km 250km 300km

Yangzhou

Zhenjiang

Nantong

Nanjing

Changzhou

Wuxi

Suzhou

Shanghai

Jiaxing

Hangzhou

Shaoxing

Ningbo

data of the drawing | urbanised area: ~ 15,900 km² | highways: ~ 26,700 km | train tracks: ~ 5,300 km

The *American Axis* forms the largest city cluster on the American continent. The coastline with numerous bays, canals and rivers is unique. The shoreline creates a curving axis of movement, on which the cities line up like pearls. Each of the cities is connected by a bay to the Atlantic Ocean. The strongest concentration of the axis extends from Washington, D.C. across Baltimore and Philadelphia to New York City / Jersey City. Boston is sometimes included as part of the axis, but is not part of the city cluster.

Another peculiar feature is the structure of American cities. They consist of highly densified centres and ultra-low density suburbs. These low density suburbs are known as urban sprawl. The houses are so far apart, that it can only conditionally be seen as a city. Due to the low density, public facilities such as schools, kindergartens and hospitals, as well as public transport are very uneconomical. The long distances and the strong dependence on cars make the urban sprawl as an unsustainable city model.

Die *amerikanische Achse* formt den größten Stadtverband auf dem amerikanischen Kontinent. Auffällig ist die Küstenlinie mit den unzähligen Buchten, Kanälen und Flüssen. Durch die Küstenlinie entsteht eine geschwungene Bewegungsachse, an der sich die Städte wie Perlen aufreihen. Jede der Großstädte ist durch eine Bucht an den Atlantik angebunden. Die stärkste Verdichtung der Achse reicht von Washington, D.C. über Baltimore und Philadelphia bis New York City / Jersey Stadt. Boston wird teilweise zur Achse hinzugezählt, ist aber nicht mehr Teil des Stadtverbandes.

Auffällig ist auch der Aufbau der amerikanischen Städte. Sie bestehen aus hochverdichteten Zentren und extrem niedrig verdichteten Vororten. Die Vororte sind unter dem Namen *Urban Sprawl*, städtische Wucherung, bekannt. Die Wohnhäuser liegen hier so weit auseinander, dass man nur bedingt von Stadt sprechen kann. Durch die geringe Dichte sind öffentliche Funktionen wie Schulen, Kindergärten und Krankenhäuser sowie öffentlicher Nahverkehr sehr unwirtschaftlich. Die langen Wege und die starke Abhängigkeit vom Auto machen den *Urban Sprawl* zu einem problematischen Stadtmodell.

linear city cluster
linearer Stadtverband

 city

 highway / train

 water

50km 100km 150km 200km 250km 300km

New York City

Jersey City

Philadelphia

Baltimore

Washington D.C.

data of the drawing | urbanised area: ~ 9,700 km² | highways: ~ 16,400 km | train tracks: ~ 9,300 km

The core of the European Macroregion consists of two megacities and a collection of small city clusters. The two megacities London and Paris respectively form the western and southern vertex. In the east, the core extends to the *Rhine-Ruhr* area, in the north it is bordered by the Dutch city cluster. The European capital Brussels is located quite central within the core.

The Dutch city cluster is the second largest in the Surrounding. It comprises Amsterdam, The Hague, Rotterdam and Utrecht, and houses about 7.5 million inhabitants. Several city clusters extend further south as a triangle around the capital Brussels. The triangle begins in the north with the Belgian city cluster consisting of Brussels, Antwerp and Ghent. In the West, the triangle passes through the French cities of Lille and Lens. Through the Meuse valley with Charleroi it connects to the border triangle Maastricht, Liège and Aachen in the east. Further east, the German *Rhine-Ruhr* region forms the largest city cluster. It extends from Dortmund, Essen, Dusseldorf to Cologne. The cluster has a population of about 11.3 million people. The individual cities are highly interconnected via public transport within the cluster. All these city clusters together form the largest part of the European core. This collection of the described clusters has a population of over 30 million people.

Der Kern der europäischen Makroregion besteht aus zwei Megastädten und einer Ansammlung kleiner Stadtverbände. Die beiden Megastädte London und Paris bilden jeweils den westlichen und südlichen Eckpunkt. Im Osten reicht der Kern bis zum *Rhein-Ruhr-Gebiet*, im Norden wird er vom niederländischen Stadtverband begrenzt. Relativ zentral befindet sich die europäische Hauptstadt Brüssel.

Der niederländische Stadtverband ist der zweitgrößte der Umgebung. Er besteht aus den Städten Amsterdam, Den Haag, Rotterdam und Utrecht und hat circa 7,5 Millionen Einwohner. Weiter südlich verlaufen mehrere Stadtverbände als Dreieck um die Hauptstadt Brüssel. Das Dreieck beginnt im Norden mit dem belgischen Stadtverband bestehend aus Brüssel, Antwerpen und Gent. Im Westen verläuft das Dreieck durch den französischen Stadtverband um Lille und Lens. Über das *Maastal* mit Charleroi schließt es im Osten an das Dreiländereck Maastricht, Lüttich und Aachen an. Im Osten bildet das deutsche *Rhein-Ruhr-Gebiet* den größten Stadtverband. Es erstreckt sich von Dortmund über Essen und Düsseldorf bis Köln. Der Verband kommt auf eine Einwohnerzahl von circa 11,3 Millionen Menschen. Die einzelnen Städte sind stark über den öffentlichen Nahverkehr miteinander verbunden. Alle diese Stadtverbände zusammen bilden den größten Teil des europäischen Kerns. Er besitzt eine Einwohnerzahl von über 30 Millionen Menschen.

Paris is the smaller of the two megacities. The Urban Being of Paris has a population of about 10.6 million people and is therefore a megacity. Through centuries of centralised, political structuring of the *Grande Nation*, Paris is the only major city in the immediate Surrounding and can be classified as a solitary city. Cities like Reims, Rouen and Caen are significantly smaller.

The largest Urban Being in the European core is the London metropolitan area. In this instance, the metropolitan area and the Urban Being are congruent, as the metropolitan area is defined by its *practical reachability through public transport*. London, just like Paris, is a solitary city that has no major cities in its immediate Surrounding. The entire Urban Being reaches a population of over 14 million people.

The core of the European Macroregion is strongly influenced by its geographical conditions. The English and French linguistic areas are clearly defined by geography. One could argue, this led to early and strong political structures, the monarchies. They gave rise to their huge capital cities, London and Paris. In contrast to Madrid, Rome or Athens, these two capitals are not located in the centre of their linguistic area. Through their shifted location, they became part of the core. The other part of the core is the collection of city clusters. This collection is a result of connectivity. Ghent, Rotterdam and Amsterdam are known as trade cities. They are located on traditional trade routes, have a proximity to the sea and benefit from the navigable *Rhine*. The flat area around the *Rhine* delta is ideal for urban growth and the long river, running deep into Europe, has a connecting effect. Trough this connection, linguistic and cultural areas started to overlap. In this small collection five languages mix and five city clusters are located in close proximity.

Paris ist die kleinere der beiden Megastädte. Das urbane Wesen kommt auf eine Einwohnerzahl von circa 10,6 Millionen und erreicht damit gerade die notwendige Größe für eine Megastadt. Durch den jahrhundertelangen zentralistischen Aufbau der *Grande Nation* ist Paris die einzige Großstadt in der direkten Umgebung und gehört damit zu den Solitärstädten. Städte wie Reims, Rouen oder Caen sind deutlich kleiner.

Das größte urbane Wesen Westeuropas ist unter dem Namen Metropolregion London bekannt. Diese Metropolregion definiert sich über die *praktische Erreichbarkeit mit dem öffentlichen Nahverkehr*. Durch die intelligente Definition sind die Metropolregion und das urbane Wesen in diesem Fall deckungsgleich. Ähnlich wie Paris ist auch London eine Solitärstadt, die keine größeren Städte in ihrer näheren Umgebung besitzt. Daher macht auch die Definition über den Nahverkehr Sinn. Das gesamte urbane Wesen kommt auf eine Einwohnerzahl von über 14 Millionen.

Der Kern der europäischen Makroregion wird stark durch geografische Gegebenheiten beeinflusst. Die englischen und französischen Sprachräume werden klar durch Geografie definiert. Dies hat unter anderem zu frühen politisch stabilen Strukturen geführt, den Monarchien. Diese haben ihrerseits große Hauptstädte hervorgebracht, in diesem Fall London und Paris. Anders als Madrid, Rom oder Athen liegen diese beiden Hauptstädte nicht im Zentrum ihres Sprachraums. Durch ihre verschobene Lage werden sie Teil des europäischen Kerns. Der andere Teil des Kerns besteht aus der Ansammlung mehrerer Stadtverbände. Diese Ansammlung ist das Resultat hoher Konnektivität. Gent, Rotterdam und Amsterdam sind bekannte Handelsstädte. Sie befinden sich auf traditionellen Handelsrouten, liegen in der Nähe des Meeres und profitieren vom schiffbaren *Rhein*. Der flache Untergrund um das *Rheindelta* ist ideal für Stadtwachstum und der lange Fluss, der bis tief nach Europa hineinreicht, hat einen verbindenden Effekt. Sprach- und Kulturräume überlappen sich durch diese Verbindung. In der kleinen Ansammlung mischen sich fünf Sprachen und fünf Stadtverbände liegen in nächster Nähe.

300km   250km   200km   150km   100km   50km

Leicester

Oxford

London

Dover

Calais

Gh

Tourcoing

Roubaix

Lille

Lens

Amiens

Le Havre

Rouen

Caen

Paris

city

highway / train

water

data of the drawing left side | urbanised area: ~ 10,300 km² | highways: ~ 22,900 km | train tracks: ~ 12,400 km

50km   100km   150km   200km   250km   300km

Amsterdam
Osnabruck
The Haag
Utrecht
Rotterdam
Dortmund
Essen
Antwerp
Dusseldorf
Maastricht
Cologne
Brussels
Aachen
Liège
Charleroi
Frankfurt
Luxembourg
Mannheim
Saarbrucken
Metz
Stuttgart

data of the drawing right side | urbanised area: ~ 14,700 km² | highways: ~ 41,100 km | train tracks: ~ 23,400 km

The *Po Valley* is among the most densely populated regions of Europe. The rivers, coming from the mountains, have favoured a strong urban growth near the Alps. The densest region is the agglomeration around Milan. The city cluster stretches from Brescia and Verona to Venice in the east. In the west it extends to Turin. In the north it reaches far into the valleys of the Alps. At the southern end of the lowlands, the axis of movement through Bologna led to another strong city growth.

Typically for Europe, the city cluster consists of many small settlements. They are mostly just a handful of houses that lie very close together. Despite their small size, the villages have a high density and are very different from the urban sprawl. They form a large city cluster with several centres, making a clear distinction between the Urban Beings impossible.

Die *Po-Ebene* gehört zu den am dichtesten besiedelten Regionen Europas. Die von den Bergen kommenden Flüsse haben am Alpenrand ein starkes Stadtwachstum begünstigt. Am stärksten verdichtet ist der Ballungsraum um Mailand herum. Über Brescia und Verona zieht sich der Stadtverband bis Venedig im Osten. Im Westen erstreckt er sich bis Turin. Durch die Täler zieht er sich im Norden bis weit in die Alpen hinein. Am südlichen Ende der Ebene hat die Bewegungsachse durch Bologna zu einem weiteren verstärkten Stadtwachstum geführt.

Typisch für Europa ist der Stadtverband aus vielen kleinen Siedlungsgebieten. Sie setzen sich teilweise aus einer Hand voll Häusern zusammen und liegen sehr nahe beieinander. Trotz ihrer kleinen Größe besitzen die Dörfer eine hohe Dichte und sind nicht mit dem *Urban Sprawl* vergleichbar. Sie bilden einen großflächigen Stadtverband mit mehreren Zentren und machen eine klare Abgrenzung der urbanen Wesen unmöglich.

polygonal city cluster
polygonaler Stadtverband

 city

highway / train

water

50km 100km 150km 200km 250km 300km

Brescia

Verona

Milan

Venice

Turin

Bologna

Florence

Urban Being

Urban Being

The Urban Being is an accumulation of urbanised areas in space, possessing an essential peculiarity.

Das urbane Wesen ist eine Anhäufung städtischer Gebiete im Raum, die eine wesentliche Eigenart besitzen.

political city boundary
politische Stadtgrenze

Urban Being
urbanes Wesen

Political City

Berlin
3.5 million 👤

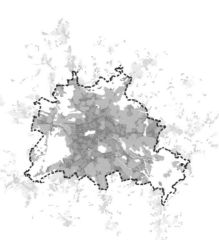

Paris
2.2 million 👤

Urban Being

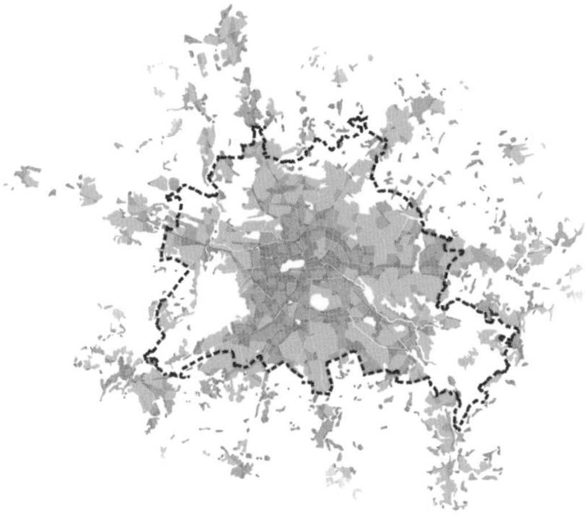

Berlin
4.4 million

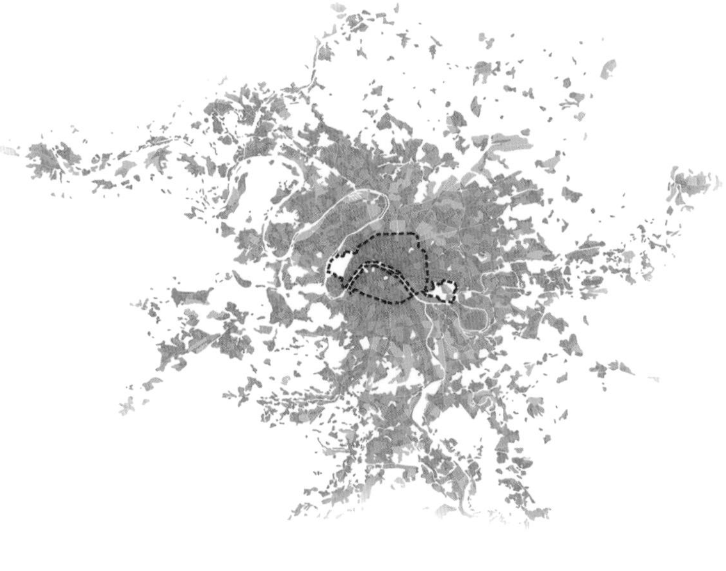

Paris
10.6 million

Urban Being

Descriptive Essay

The city is not a living being, but rather an Urban Being. It does not live by itself, it is humans that bring it to life. The term Urban Being can be interpreted in two ways. On one hand, it refers to the whole urban entity. On the other hand, it describes the people living in the city.

Arbitrarily defined political boundaries of cities distort our perception. In contrast, the Urban Being describes the city in its physical or actual size and thus creates a uniform definition. An Urban Being is an accumulation of urbanised areas in space, possessing an essential peculiarity. The accumulation of urbanised areas is comparable to a metropolitan area or agglomeration. Different cities within the same agglomeration are distinguished by their essential peculiarity. The Urban Being has a high urban planning relevance. Since it describes the actual size of the city, it leads to conclusions about public transport, the amount of traffic and economic strength.

The Physical Size of the City

The relevant size of a city is its physical size. However, existing terms like metropolitan areas or city have very different interpretations and make a uniform definition necessary.

Die Stadt ist kein Lebewesen, sondern vielmehr ein urbanes Wesen. Sie wird durch die Menschen zum Leben erweckt. Der Begriff urbanes Wesen kann daher doppelt gedeutet werden. Zum einen beschreibt er das gesamte städtische Gebilde, zum anderen die Menschen, die in ihm leben.

Willkürlich definierte Stadtgrenzen verzerren unsere Wahrnehmung von Städten. Im Gegensatz dazu beschreibt das urbane Wesen die Stadt in ihrer physischen bzw. realen Größe und schafft dadurch eine einheitliche Definition. Ein urbanes Wesen ist eine Anhäufung städtischer Gebiete im Raum, die eine wesentliche Eigenart besitzen. Die Anhäufung städtischer Gebiete ist mit einem Ballungsraum oder einer Metropolregion vergleichbar. Verschiedene Städte innerhalb desselben Ballungsraums werden durch die wesentliche Eigenart unterschieden. Das urbane Wesen hat eine hohe stadtplanerische Relevanz. Da es die reale Größe der Stadt beschreibt, lässt es Rückschlüsse auf den öffentlichen Personennahverkehr, das Verkehrsaufkommen oder die Wirtschaftskraft zu.

Die physische Größe der Stadt

Die relevante Größe einer Stadt ist ihre physische Größe. Existierende Begriffe wie Metropolregion oder Stadt haben jedoch sehr

The different interpretations become evident in the comparison of several cities. The city of Paris is comparatively small. It has 2.2 million inhabitants. The Urban Being of Paris amounts to 10.6 million inhabitants. The public transport system does not stop at the political city boundaries. It serves the entire Urban Being. The amount of traffic reflects the mega city with over 10 million inhabitants as well. Describing Paris as a metropolis of 2 million inhabitants does not do justice to the actual size of the city. But this distortion exists in the other extreme as well. The term metropolitan region has no clear definition either. The metropolitan area of Munich covers approximately 100 kilometers of rural areas around the agglomeration. Therefore, it becomes more populated and appears larger than it is. As described before, the metropolitan area of London has one of the most articulate definitions. It defines itself through the practical accessibility by public transport. In this case, the metropolitan area and the Urban Being are identical.

A constant factor of every city is the higher density of development compared to rural areas. The first factor in the definition of the Urban Being is this density. Every Urban Being is defined by its higher development density compared to the surrounding. The density is an important factor to understand the size of the city. Not only the accumulation of urban areas, but also the density of urban areas itself plays a role. Los Angeles has a very low density and thus attains enormous dimensions. The city is much bigger than Shanghai, although it has only half as many inhabitants. Area and density together affect the size of the city.

The second part of the definition is about the essential peculiarity. Through this addition, Urban Beings can be distinguished from each other within the same agglomeration. The definition by practical accessibility works for individual cities. The city cluster in the *Rhine-Ruhr* area also has a common public transport network, but consists of several cities. The cities form a common accumulation of urbanised areas in space, but each city

unterschiedliche Auslegungen und machen eine einheitliche Definition notwendig.

Die unterschiedliche Auslegung der Begriffe wird durch den Vergleich mehrerer Städte deutlich. Die Stadt Paris ist vergleichsweise klein. Sie besitzt 2,2 Millionen Einwohner. Das urbane Wesen Paris kommt auf eine Größe von 10,6 Millionen Einwohnern. Betrachtet man den öffentlichen Nahverkehr, zieht sich dieser durch das gesamte urbane Wesen. Auch das Verkehrsaufkommen von Paris ist das einer Megastadt mit über 10 Millionen Einwohnern. Paris als 2-Millionen-Einwohner-Metropole zu beschreiben, wird der eigentlichen Größe der Stadt nicht gerecht. Doch diese Verzerrung existiert auch im anderen Extrem. Der Begriff Metropolregion besitzt ebenfalls keine eindeutige Definition. Die Metropolregion München bezieht circa 100 Kilometer dörfliche Gebiete um den Ballungsraum mit ein. Dadurch bekommt sie mehr Einwohner und erscheint größer, als sie ist. Wie bereits beschrieben, besitzt die Metropolregion London eine der verständlichsten Definitionen. Sie definiert sich über die praktische Erreichbarkeit mit dem öffentlichen Nahverkehr. In ihrem Fall sind die Metropolregion und das urbane Wesen deckungsgleich.

Ein konstanter Faktor jeder Stadt ist die höhere Dichte der Bebauung im Vergleich zum ländlichen Raum. Der erste Faktor in der Definition des urbanen Wesens ist diese Dichte. Jedes urbane Wesen definiert sich durch seine höhere Bebauungsdichte im Vergleich zum Umland. Die Dichte ist ein wichtiger Faktor, um die Größe der Stadt zu verstehen. Nicht nur die Ansammlung städtischer Gebiete, auch die Dichte der städtischen Gebiete selbst spielt eine Rolle. Los Angeles hat eine sehr geringe Dichte und erlangt dadurch enorme Dimensionen. Die Stadt ist flächenmäßig um ein Vielfaches größer als Shanghai, obwohl sie nur halb so viele Einwohner besitzt. Fläche und Dichte beeinflussen zusammen die Größe der Stadt.

Der zweite Teil der Definition besteht aus der wesentlichen Eigenart. Durch diesen Zusatz lassen sich urbane Wesen innerhalb eines Ballungsraums voneinander abgrenzen. Die Definition über die praktische

has its own essential peculiarity. In this way, political, economic or city planning decisions can be made specifically for the Urban Being or the city cluster. The appendix of the definition applies to the other extreme as well. The area of Stuttgart is a scattered Urban Being. It is a metropolitan region of a thousand villages. Economically, the region considers itself one Urban Being. Politically and socially, however, the essential peculiarity of the metropolitan area has not yet matured. This causes constant problems in the area of traffic planning, since every small part of the Urban Being acts independently.

On the one hand, the Urban Being rectifies the perception of the city. Paris is a mega city with over 10 million inhabitants and should be perceived as such. On the other hand, the Urban Being is a relevant factor in urban planning. Traffic volumes, public transport systems, green systems, innovative power and economic strength always relate to the Urban Being.

Typologies

Depending on density and shape, Urban Beings can be divided into different typologies. The majority of cities have a high or low density, while medium densities are less common.

The condensed and highly condensed Urban Beings constitute the largest group. Their boundaries are clearly visible in the analytical drawings. Their high density makes them appear more urban and bigger than they actually are. In this typology, even the small Urban Beings tend to appear large. The densification leads to short distances within the city. These short ways increase the number of urban functions in the immediate vicinity. This means that parks, theaters, hospitals, as well as supermarkets, schools and other functions tend to be more easily accessible. This increases sustainability.

The scattered Urban Beings form the second largest group. They are

Erreichbarkeit funktioniert bei Individualstädten. Der Stadtverband im *Rhein-Ruhr-Gebiet* hat ebenfalls ein gemeinsames öffentliches Personennahverkehrs-Netz, besteht jedoch aus mehreren Städten. Die Städte bilden eine gemeinsame Anhäufung von städtischen Gebieten im Raum, jedoch besitzt jede Stadt ihre wesentliche Eigenart. Dadurch können politische, wirtschaftliche oder stadtplanerische Entscheidungen spezifisch für das urbane Wesen oder den Stadtverband getroffen werden. Auch im anderen Extrem greift der Zusatz der Definition. Der Raum Stuttgart gehört zu den verstreuten urbanen Wesen. Er ist eine Metropolregion, die sich aus vielen einzelnen Dörfern zusammensetzt. Wirtschaftlich versteht sich die Region als ein urbanes Wesen. Politisch und gesellschaftlich ist die wesentliche Eigenart des Ballungsraums jedoch noch nicht im Bewusstsein angelangt. Gerade bei der Verkehrsplanung führt dies immer wieder zu Problemen, da einzelne Bereiche des urbanen Wesens unabhängig voneinander agieren.

Das urbane Wesen entzerrt zum einen die Wahrnehmung der Städte. Paris ist eine Megastadt mit über 10 Millionen Einwohnern und sollte auch als solche wahrgenommen werden. Zum anderen ist das urbane Wesen eine planerisch relevante Größe. Verkehrsaufkommen, öffentlicher Nahverkehr, grüne Systeme, Innovationskraft oder wirtschaftliche Stärke beziehen sich immer auf das urbane Wesen.

Typologien

Je nach Dichte und Form lassen sich urbane Wesen in unterschiedliche Typologien unterscheiden. Dabei hat der Großteil der Städte eine hohe oder niedere Dichte, mittlere Dichten sind weniger verbreitet.

Die verdichteten und hochverdichteten urbanen Wesen stellen den größten Anteil. Ihre Grenzen sind in den analytischen Zeichnungen klar ablesbar. Durch ihre Dichte wirken sie sehr städtisch. Selbst kleine urbane Wesen in dieser Typologie wirken durch ihre Verdichtung meistens größer. Die Komprimierung führt zu geringen Distanzen innerhalb der Stadt. Diese kurzen

made up of a large number of towns and villages. They are very similar to small City Clusters and at a certain scale impossible to distinguish. Due to their fragmented structure, it is difficult to define an exact border. Scattered Urban Beings tend to run gradually into rural areas. They appear much smaller as they really are, since the whole agglomeration is rarely perceived as such. Often, only the central core is referred to as the actual city. This typology combines the advantages of rural life with the economic power of a large metropolis. Structurally it has a high space consumption, but with a small amount of urbanised area. It is the typology with the highest amount of natural areas. This leads to long distances, high amount of traffic and difficult accessibility by public transport.

Medium density typologies include special variations, such as the fried egg type. It occurs only in the North East of the USA and consists of two very different densities. On the one hand the high-density and sustainable centre. On the other hand the low density suburbs, which can only conditionally be described as a city. These suburbs are known as urban sprawl and pose problematic structures of urban growth. As a whole, the fried egg typology reaches medium sustainability. The tentacle type is based on topographical conditions. The tentacles or urban fingers grow into the surrounding valleys. This type tends to have a high-density centre and a high amount of nature. But, in contrast to the scattered Urban Beings, it does not appear that small. The urban fingers seem to be part of the city, with a high access to the nearby nature.

In order to improve the qualities of a city it is necessary to understand its structure and typology. Each type has its own challenges and benefits. By understanding the type, structural problems can be targeted specifically.

Wege erhöhen die Anzahl städtischer Funktionen in unmittelbarer Nähe. Das bedeutet, dass Parks, Theater, Krankenhäuser, aber auch Supermärkte, Schulen und andere Funktionen tendenziell schneller erreichbar sind. Dadurch wird die Nachhaltigkeit erhöht.

Die verstreuten urbanen Wesen bilden die zweitgrößte Gruppe. Sie setzen sich aus einer Vielzahl kleiner Städtchen und Dörfer zusammen und bilden einen nahtlosen Übergang zu den kleinen Stadtverbänden. Durch ihre Kleinteiligkeit ist eine exakte Grenze nur schwer zu definieren, da sie meist graduell in den ländlichen Raum auslaufen. Sie wirken um ein Vielfaches kleiner, da der gesamte Ballungsraum selten als solcher wahrgenommen wird. Oft wird nur der zentrale Kern als eigentliche Stadt bezeichnet. Diese Typologie kombiniert die Vorzüge des ländlichen Lebens mit der Wirtschaftskraft einer großen Metropole. Strukturell hat sie einen hohen Platzverbrauch, jedoch mit einem kleinen Anteil urbanisierter Fläche, wodurch sie zur Typologie mit dem höchsten Anteil natürlicher Flächen wird. Das führt zu großen Distanzen, hohem Verkehrsaufkommen und erschwerter Erreichbarkeit durch den öffentlichen Nahverkehr.

Die Typologien mit mittlerer Dichte beinhalten Sondertypologien wie den Spiegelei-Typ. Er kommt nur im Nordosten der USA vor und setzt sich aus zwei sehr unterschiedlichen Dichten zusammen. Zum einen das hoch verdichtete und nachhaltige Zentrum, zum anderen die Vororte, die durch ihre niedere Dichte nur bedingt als Stadt bezeichnet werden können. Diese Vororte sind unter dem Namen *Urban Sprawl* schon lange als problematisches Stadtwachstum bekannt. Der Tentakel-Typ basiert dagegen auf topografischen Gegebenheiten. Die Tentakel, oder städtischen Finger, wachsen in die umgebenden Täler hinein. Auch dieser Typ hat meist ein hochverdichtetes Zentrum, wirkt weiter außen jedoch sehr natürlich durch seinen hohen Grünanteil.

Um die Qualitäten einer Stadt zu verbessern, ist es notwendig, ihre Struktur und Typologie zu verstehen. Jeder Typ besitzt eigene Herausforderungen und Vorzüge. Durch das Verständnis des Typus lassen sich strukturelle Probleme gezielt beheben.

Urban Nutrition Arteries, Industry & Cell Structure

Urbane Nährstoffadern, Industrie & Zellstruktur

As mentioned before, people and goods are crucial for every Urban Being. They function as nutrients for the organism and move through urban nutrition arteries, such as freeways, main traffic arteries, train tracks, navigable canals and rivers. These arteries form physical and mental barriers for humans. The spaces between them are described as Urban Cells. They influence the functioning and thus the quality of the city.

The road network is the main component of the urban nutrition arteries. The city type and topography create different systems. The most common one is the ring system. The rings form bypass roads for the different car speeds. The speed outside the city is that of the highway. It is about 120 km/h and has no disruptions, such as traffic lights or crosswalks. The outermost ring is ideally a highway around the Urban Being. Long-distance traffic, which does not have to enter the city, is kept outside the Urban Being. Munich and Santiago de Chile are close to mountains. As there is not much traffic from the mountains, their highway rings are open in this direction. If the highway runs through the city, for example in Stuttgart, extreme traffic congestion occurs. If the highway ring runs inside the Urban Being, like in Paris, it cuts the city into pieces. This highway was planned for the political city, not for the Urban Being. Perfect highway rings can be seen in London and Moscow.

The next lower speed of the car is the one of the inner city freeway. It is about 60 km/h and also has no interruptions. In the ring system, the freeway usually defines the Urban Nucleus. It serves as a bypass around the centre for the traffic within the city. The formation of rings can be observed in Urban Beings on a flat ground. The freeways of Urban Beings located on hills pass their freeways through the valleys. The formation of a ring system becomes impossible, the orientation more difficult and the traffic flow slower. A common traffic system is the rectangular grid. It is mostly limited to the

Wie bereits beschrieben, beleben Menschen und Güter jedes urbane Wesen. Sie funktionieren wie Nährstoffe für den Organismus Stadt und bewegen sich auf urbanen Nährstoffadern wie Stadtautobahnen, Hauptverkehrsadern, Zuggleisen, schiffbaren Kanälen und Flüssen. Diese Adern sind physische und mentale Grenzen für den Menschen. Die Bereiche zwischen ihnen werden als urbane Zellen beschrieben. Sie beeinflussen die Funktionsweise und damit die Qualität der Stadt.

Das Straßennetzwerk ist der Hauptbestandteil der urbanen Nährstoffadern. Je nach Stadttyp und Topografie entstehen unterschiedliche Systeme. Am weitesten verbreitet ist das Ringsystem. Die Ringe bilden Umgehungsstraßen für die unterschiedlichen Geschwindigkeiten des Autoverkehrs. Die Geschwindigkeit außerhalb der Stadt ist die der Autobahn. Sie beträgt circa 120 km/h und besitzt keine Unterbrechungen wie Ampeln oder Zebrastreifen. Der äußerste Ring ist idealerweise eine Autobahn, die den Durchgangsverkehr um das urbane Wesen herumleitet und das Verkehrsaufkommen im Inneren minimiert. München und Santiago de Chile liegen in unmittelbarer Nähe zu Bergen. Da aus dieser Richtung wenig Verkehr kommt, sind ihre Autobahnringe dort geöffnet. Verläuft die Autobahn durch die Stadt, wie im Beispiel Stuttgart, entstehen extreme Verkehrsbehinderungen. Verläuft der Ring innerhalb des urbanen Wesens, wie in Paris, zerschneidet er die Stadt. Er wurde für die politische Stadt und nicht für das urbane Wesen geplant. Stark ausgeprägte Autobahnringe sind in London und Moskau zu sehen.

Die nächst langsamere Geschwindigkeit ist die der Stadtautobahn. Sie ist circa 60 km/h schnell und hat ebenfalls keine Unterbrechungen. Im Ringsystem definiert die Stadtautobahn meist den Stadtkern. Sie dient als Umfahrung der inneren Bereiche für den internen Verkehr des urbanen Wesens. Eine Ringbildung ist vor allem bei urbanen Wesen auf flachem Untergrund zu beobachten. Befindet sich

main artery roads and operates independently of the urban freeways. Los Angeles has such a grid. Despite the rectangular structure, the major city freeways run as a ring around the relatively small Urban Nucleus. This densification of urban freeways causes traffic congestion. Large cities are generally burdened by traffic. The basic idea of the ring system is to keep the traffic out of the city and optimise it as much as possible. It meets the requirements of long-distance traffic and the inhabitants. This street structure can improve the traffic situation within the Urban Being and constitute a step towards a more equitable city. However, it requires further measures, such as a cheap, fast and inclusive public transport, selective bans of cars and city planning that encourages short distances, to reduce the dependence on the car. While the first two measures have a political nature, the third measure can be achieved through specific Urban Cell structures.

Urban Cells favour various functions, depending on the shape and design. The linear cells, described in the chapter *Urban Cell,* are strong sub-centres. If they are strategically located in suburbs, they can constitute an alternative to the city centre. Within a close proximity to residential areas, they can be reached by foot. The ride to the centre is redundant and the traffic decreases. The sub-centre will strengthen the quality of the neighbourhood. The most common example is *Copacabana*. The density of shops on main road exceeds European shopping streets. Even living cells change their quality with the size. Large residential cells have long distances to public transport, which mostly runs on main roads. They tend to appear empty and have less commerce and gastronomy. The nature of the road network has a direct impact on the quality of life within the Urban Cell.

The industry is another important part of any Urban Being. The death of an industry, such as in Detroit, brings great harm to the Urban Being. Without work there are no goods or people. The urban nutrients that keep the city alive dwindle. The type of industry that

das urbane Wesen auf einer hügeligen Topografie, verlaufen die Autobahnen durch Täler, wodurch keine Ringbildung entsteht. Die Orientierung wird erschwert und die Verkehrsführung behindert. Eine verbreitete Verkehrsführung im englischsprachigen Raum ist das rechtwinklige Raster. Es beschränkt sich hauptsächlich auf die Hauptverkehrsadern und funktioniert unabhängig von den Stadtautobahnen. Los Angeles besitzt dieses Raster. Trotz der rechtwinkligen Struktur verlaufen die großen Stadtautobahnen um den vergleichsweise kleinen Stadtkern, wodurch sie stark verdichtet werden. Große Städte werden grundsätzlich vom Verkehr belastet. Der Grundgedanke des Ringsystems ist es, den Verkehr so weit wie möglich aus der Stadt draußen zu halten und trotzdem zu optimieren. Das System wird dem Fernverkehr und den Stadtbewohnern gerecht. Das Straßenraster kann die Verkehrssituation innerhalb des urbanen Wesens verbessern und einen Schritt zur gerechten Stadt bedeuten. Es bedarf aber noch weiterer Maßnahmen wie einem günstigen, schnellen und integrativen Nahverkehr, selektiver Fahrverbote und einer Stadtplanung, die kurze Distanzen fördert, um die Abhängigkeit vom Auto zu verringern. Während die ersten beiden Maßnahmen politischer Natur sind, lässt sich die dritte gezielte durch urbane Zellstrukturen verbessern.

Urbane Zellen begünstigen je nach Form und Ausführung verschiedene Funktionen. Die im Kapitel *urbane Zelle* beschriebenen linearen Zellen sind starke Subzentren. Setzt man sie gezielt in Vororten ein, bilden sie eine Alternative zum Zentrum der Stadt. In unmittelbarer Nähe zu Wohngebieten können sie fußläufig erreicht werden. Die Fahrt ins Zentrum wird überflüssig und der Verkehr verringert sich. Gleichzeitig stärkt das Subzentrum die Qualität des Viertels. Ein bekanntes Beispiel ist *Copacabana*. Die Ladendichte der Hauptstraße übersteigt der europäischer Einkaufsstraßen. Auch Wohnzellen verändern ihre Qualität mit der Größe. Große Wohnzellen haben weite Distanzen zum öffentlichen Nahverkehr, der meist auf den Hauptstraßen verläuft. Die Wohngegend wirkt tendenziell leerer und besitzt weniger Kommerz

keeps a city alive depends on many factors. Political decisions, natural resources, specialisation and labour are just a few examples. However, the location of industrial areas follows a certain logic. Manufacturing industries have to move their goods and lie ideally in close proximity to train tracks, highways, rivers, ports and airports. An even distribution of industry within the Urban Being reduces the daily commute for workers. Short distances create quality of life for people, while a direct connection to a strong nutrition artery favours the industry. The goal of a just city should be to meet both of these requirements.

Green Systems

Many Urban Beings do not possess large green systems. They are an option that can provide additional qualities to the city. Depending on the design, they can fullfill a few or many functions. The most basic are forest areas within the city. They generate fresh air and have a cleansing effect. They are often compared with the lungs of a city. Normally they offer few programmes for the city dwellers. Another system are the green valleys. They are mainly used for drainage in rainy areas. Depending on the design they can be activated by programmes. Landscape design, parks, sport fields, playgrounds and more increase the use for the people and improve the quality of the green system. Green strips along rivers have the highest potential for successful recreational areas. When activated with programmes, they can be qualitative, local recreation areas for all city dwellers. Green systems have an impact on our perception of the city. They increase the perceived quality of life and increase the attractiveness of the location. In the competition for the most livable city and the resulting influx of talented workers, they have an economic impact as well.

und Gastronomie. Die Art des Straßennetzwerks hat einen direkten Einfluss auf die Lebensqualität innerhalb der urbanen Zelle.

Die Industrie bildet einen weiteren wichtigen Bestandteil jedes urbanen Wesens. Stirbt ein Industriezweig, wie in Detroit, trägt auch das urbane Wesen großen Schaden. Ohne Arbeit gibt es weder Güter noch Menschen. Die urbanen Nährstoffe, die die Stadt am Leben erhalten, schwinden. Welcher Industriezweig eine Stadt am Leben erhält, hängt von vielen Faktoren ab. Politische Entscheidungen, natürliche Ressourcen, Spezialisierung und Arbeitskräfte sind nur ein paar Beispiele. Die Lage der Industriegebiete folgt jedoch einer gewissen Logik. Produzierende Industrien müssen ihre Güter bewegen und liegen idealerweise in der unmittelbaren Nähe zu Zuggleisen, Autobahnen, Flüssen, Häfen und Flughäfen. Werden sie dezentral im urbanen Wesen verteilt, verringert sich der Weg für die Arbeiter. Kurze Distanzen schaffen Lebensqualität für die Menschen und eine direkte Anbindung an eine starke Nährstoffader begünstigt die Industrie. Ziel einer gerechten Stadt sollte es sein, beiden Anforderungen zu gerecht zu werden.

Grüne Systeme

Viele urbane Wesen besitzen keine großen grünen Systeme. Sie sind eine Option, die der Stadt zusätzliche Qualitäten verleihen kann. Je nach Typ erfüllen sie wenige oder viele Funktionen. Am einfachsten sind Waldflächen innerhalb der Stadt. Sie spenden frische Luft und werden auch als Lunge einer Stadt bezeichnet. Meist bieten sie wenige Aktivitäten für die Bewohner der Stadt. Ein weiterer Typ ist das grüne Tal. Es dient vor allem in regenreichen Gebieten der Entwässerung. Je nach Ausführung kann es durch Programme aktiviert werden. Landschaftsgestaltung, Parks, Sportflächen, Spielplätze und mehr erhöhen die Nutzung für den Menschen und steigern die Qualität. Das höchste Potenzial hat der Grünstreifen entlang eines Flusses. Wird er durch Programme aktiviert, kann er zum qualitativen Naherholungsbereich

Megacities

The anatomy and its influence on the quality of the city become more important with the rapid growth of megacities. By 2050, an estimated 70 % of the world population will live in such megacities, exceeding a population of 10 million people. Targeted urban planning can counteract some problems of these megacities.

The most obvious problem in megacities is the traffic. Urban mobility is an independent research and strongly linked to the development of technology. Self-driving cars optimise traffic flows and have the potential to create new traffic arteries. The ideal course of these new traffic arteries is closely linked with the principles of the road network. Mobility is also an important factor for sustainability. Fewer emissions and short distances reduce the environmental impact. Sufficient green areas also have a cleaning function. They benefit the environment and increase the quality of life and attractiveness. The influx of people supports economic growth. At the same time, social problems can be counteracted. The equitable city relates to the needs of all residents and counteracts social inequality. Even crime can be reduced. Roads with much of commerce are busier, brighter and more secure at night. The structure can help to improve the quality of megacities. The megacities of the future are the hotspots of cultural, social, technological and economic development. In a globalised world, the location becomes less important, while the quality of the city is getting more significant. The quality determines where a megacity positions itself in the global context.

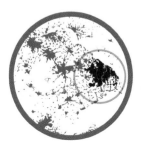

für alle Stadtbewohner werden. Grüne Systeme haben einen Einfluss auf unsere Wahrnehmung. Sie steigern die gefühlte Lebensqualität und erhöhen die Attraktivität. Im Wettbewerb um die lebenswerteste Stadt und den damit verbundenen Zuzug talentierter Arbeitskräfte bekommen sie auch eine wirtschaftliche Bedeutung.

Megastädte

Die Anatomie und ihr Einfluss auf die Qualität der Stadt gewinnen durch das rasante Wachstum der Megastädte an Bedeutung. Bis 2050 werden geschätzte 70 % der Weltbevölkerung in Megastädten mit über 10 Millionen Einwohnern leben. Eine gezielte Stadtplanung kann einigen Problemen dieser Megastädte entgegenwirken.

Am offensichtlichsten ist das Verkehrschaos. Urbane Mobilität ist ein eigenständiger Forschungsbereich und stark mit der Entwicklung der Technik verknüpft. Selbstständig fahrende Autos optimieren den Verkehrsfluss und haben das Potenzial, neue Verkehrsadern zu schaffen. Der ideale Verlauf dieser neuen Verkehrsadern folgt den Prinzipien des Straßennetzwerks. Mobilität ist auch ein wichtiger Faktor in der Nachhaltigkeit. Weniger Abgase und kurze Distanzen schonen die Umwelt. Ausreichende Grünflächen haben zudem eine säubernde Funktion. Was der Umwelt zugutekommt, steigert auch die Lebensqualität und Attraktivität. Der Zuzug der Menschen unterstützt das wirtschaftliche Wachstum. Aber auch sozialen Problemen kann entgegengewirkt werden. Eine gerechte Stadt bezieht die Bedürfnisse aller Bewohner mit ein und wirkt sozialer Ungleichheit entgegen. Selbst Kriminalität kann teilweise verhindert werden. Straßen mit viel Kommerz sind belebter, heller und haben eine erhöhte Sicherheit. Die Struktur der Stadt kann dazu beitragen, die Qualität von Megastädten zu steigern. Die Megastädte der Zukunft sind die Hotspots kultureller, sozialer, technologischer und wirtschaftlicher Entwicklung. In einer globalisierten Welt verliert die Lage an Bedeutung, während die Qualität der Stadt wichtiger wird. Sie entscheidet, wo sich eine Megastadt im globalen Gefüge positioniert.

Urban Being

Typologies

highly condensed
hochverdichtet

fried egg
Spiegelei

uncondensed
unverdichtet

condensed
verdichtet

tentacle
Tentakel

scattered
verstreut

highly condensed
hochverdichtet

Santiago de Chile

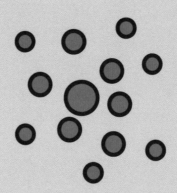

scattered
verstreut

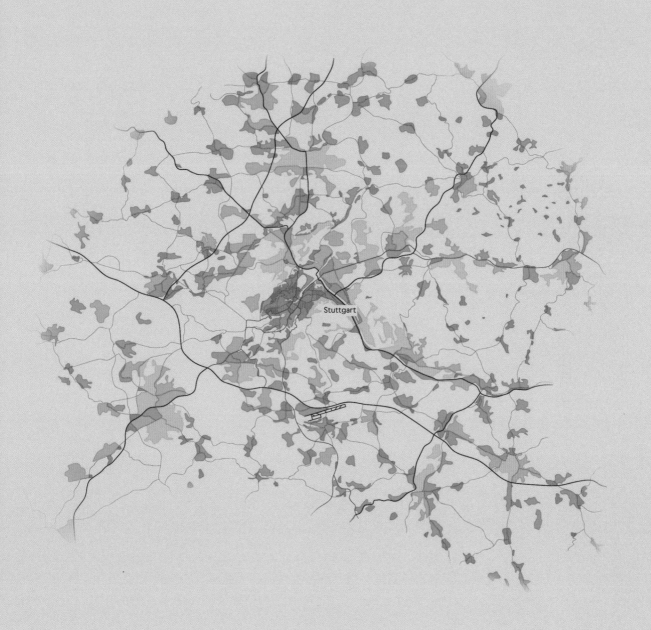

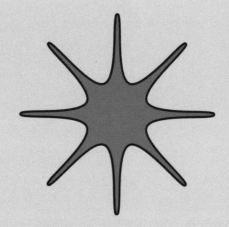

tentacle
Tentakel

Rio de Janeiro

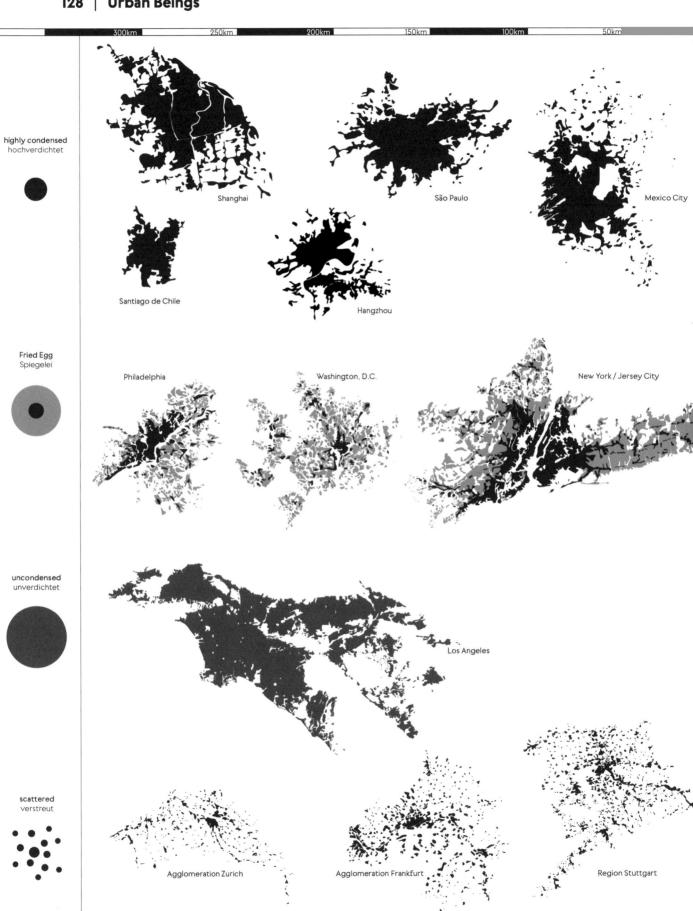

300km　　250km　　200km　　150km　　100km　　50km

highly condensed
hochverdichtet

Shanghai

São Paulo

Mexico City

Santiago de Chile

Hangzhou

Fried Egg
Spiegelei

Philadelphia

Washington, D.C.

New York / Jersey City

uncondensed
unverdichtet

Los Angeles

scattered
verstreut

Agglomeration Zurich

Agglomeration Frankfurt

Region Stuttgart

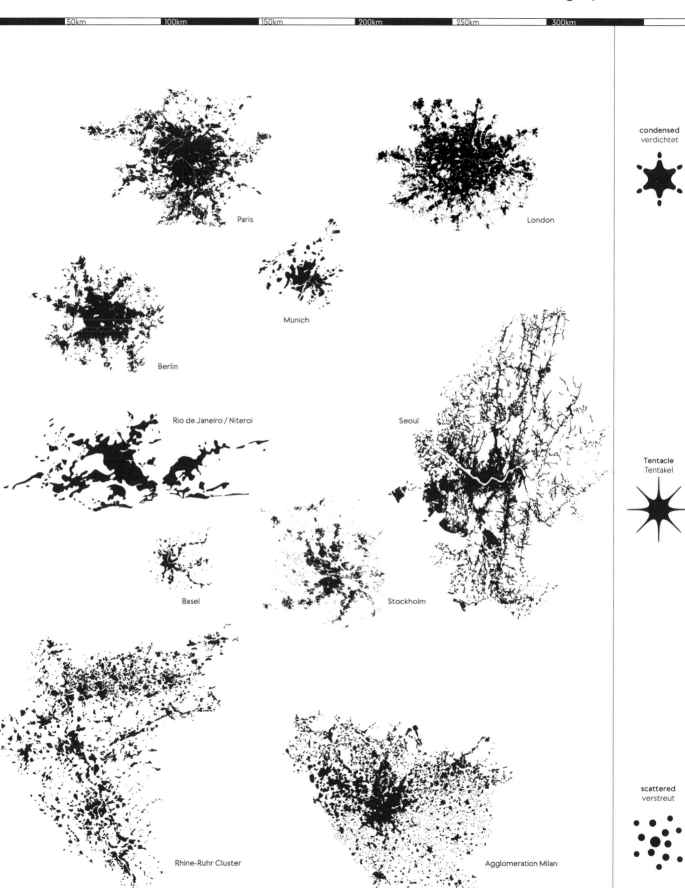

50km 100km 150km 200km 250km 300km

Paris

London

Munich

Berlin

Rio de Janeiro / Niteroi

Seoul

Basel

Stockholm

Rhine-Ruhr Cluster

Agglomeration Milan

condensed
verdichtet

Tentacle
Tentakel

scattered
verstreut

Urban Being

Urban Nutrition Arteries

highway ~120 km/h
Autobahn ~120 km/h

urban freeway ~60 km/h
Stadtautobahn ~60 km/h

main roads ~50 km/h
Hauptstraßen ~50 km/h

capillary streets ~30 km/h
Kapillarstraßen ~30 km/h

Munich is a classic ring city that responds to the different speeds of the car. The outer ring road has an average speed of about 120 km/h without interruption. The ring is open to the southwest, due to the little traffic coming from the mountains. The *Middle Ring* is a typical urban freeway with an average speed of about 60 km/h and no interruptions. The middle ring defines the Urban Nucleus of Munich, similar to the torso of the city, and serves as its bypass. The inner ring is a main artery with an average speed of 50 km/h and traffic lights that interrupt the flow of traffic. Each ring defines the limit of a certain speed towards the centre, meaning it has only slower speeds within.

Similarly, the public transport system is divided into different speeds. The fastest transport is the *S-Bahn* (MRT), which extends far beyond the edges of the Urban Being. The metro is slower and its stops are closer together. It is limited to the Urban Being. But the slowest is the tram. It stops every few hundred meters and reaches only just beyond the Urban Nucleus. The river *Isar* is not a navigable water and not an urban nutrition artery. It is mainly used for recreational purposes. Without a waterway and industry, the river is kept very clean.

In total, Munich has a very coherent and well-functioning transport system. The main problem is its limited capacity. The overload of too many people causes regular gridlock, congesting the traffic in a similar way to an infarction in a blood vein. Furthermore, the timing of the traffic light causes obstructions and some exits of the urban freeways are short, which intensifies the problem. The congestion occurs mostly along the *Middle Ring* and the arterial roads.

München ist eine klassische Ringstadt, die auf die unterschiedlichen Geschwindigkeiten der Autos eingeht. Der äußere Autobahnring hat eine durchschnittliche Geschwindigkeit von circa 120 km/h, ohne Unterbrechungen. Da von den Bergen im Südwesten relativ wenig Verkehr kommt, ist der Ring dort geöffnet. Weiter Richtung Zentrum liegt der Mittlere Ring. Er ist eine typische Stadtautobahn mit einer Durchschnittsgeschwindigkeit von circa 60 km/h und ebenfalls ohne Unterbrechungen. Der *Mittlere Ring* definiert den Stadtkern von München und dient als dessen Umfahrung. Der Innere Ring, auch Altstadtring genannt, ist eine Hauptverkehrsader mit einer durchschnittlichen Geschwindigkeit von 50 km/h und Unterbrechungen in Form von Ampeln. Jeder Ring bildet eine Geschwindigkeitsgrenze, besitzt also in seinem Inneren nur langsamere Geschwindigkeiten.

Auch der öffentliche Nahverkehr ist auf verschiedene Geschwindigkeiten aufgeteilt. Am schnellsten ist die S-Bahn, die weit über das urbane Wesen hinausreicht. Die U-Bahn hat näher beieinanderliegende Haltestellen und eine langsamere Geschwindigkeit. Sie beschränkt sich auf das urbane Wesen. Am langsamsten ist jedoch die Tram. Ihre Haltestellen liegen dicht beieinander und sie reicht nur ein Stück über den Stadtkern hinaus. Der Fluss *Isar* ist nicht schiffbar und daher keine urbane Nährstoffader. Er dient hauptsächlich der Naherholung der Bewohner. Ohne den Schiffsverkehr und die Industrie ist der Fluss sehr sauber.

Im Gesamten hat München ein sehr stimmiges und gut funktionierendes Verkehrskonzept. Das Hauptproblem ist, dass es für weit weniger Menschen ausgelegt wurde. Durch die Überlastung kommt es immer wieder zu Verkehrsinfarkten, also Stauungen oder Behinderungen. Eine verkehrsbehindernde Ampelschaltung und kurze Abfahrten der Stadtautobahn verschärfen das Problem an manchen Stellen sogar. Dadurch treten die meisten Stauungen im Bereich des *Mittleren Rings* und den Ausfallstraßen auf.

Outer Ring

Middle Ring

River Isar

Inner Ring

Middle Ring

Outer Ring

train / metro   highway   river

The metropolitan area of Stuttgart has big problems in its traffic management, which causes the small city with low density to suffer under extreme traffic congestion.

The town centre is clearly defined by the topography of the valley. Unlike most major cities, the traffic is not directed on a freeway around the nucleus, but right through it. As a consequence, the city centre is cut off from the rest of the nucleus by comparatively large streets with high amounts of traffic. As the air circulates inside the valley, the contamination of the cars cannot escape and pollutes the air in the city. A freeway ring on the edge of the valley, basically a bypass road around the Urban Nucleus, would solve these problems.

Even the outer highway ring is way too close to the centre. In the northeast it runs along the Urban Nucleus, cutting through the city. The highway ring ideally directs the traffic around the city with an average speed of 120 km/h without interruption. The unconventional routing in Stuttgart reduces the speed to 50 km/h with interruptions. The consequence is extreme traffic congestion.

The basic principle of the Stuttgart traffic routing forces the traffic to a few streets in the city centre and then slows it down. This principle has disadvantages for all city users. The car traffic flow is disabled. The busy streets endanger cyclists. The highways act as strong boundaries for pedestrians. The residents suffer from noise and air pollution.

Bypass roads with different speeds could resolve many problems of the city, but such an endeavour would require the political will and the understanding of the population.

Der Großraum Stuttgart hat große Probleme in seiner Verkehrsführung, wodurch die kleine Großstadt mit niederer Dichte unter extremen Staus leidet.

Der Stadtkern ist durch die Topografie des Tals klar definiert. Anders als in den meisten Großstädten wird der Verkehr jedoch nicht auf einer Stadtautobahn um den Kern herumgeleitet, sondern mitten hindurch. Als Konsequenz wird die Innenstadt durch vergleichsweise große Straßen vom Rest des Stadtkerns abgeschnitten und leidet unter einem sehr hohen Verkehrsaufkommen. Da die Luft innerhalb des Kessels zirkuliert, können auch die Abgase nicht abziehen und verschmutzen die Luft der Innenstadt stark. Ein Kesselrandring, also eine Umgehungsstraße des Stadtkerns, würde diese Probleme lösen.

Auch der Autobahnring liegt viel zu innerstädtisch. Im Nordosten verläuft er entlang des Stadtkerns praktisch durch die Stadt hindurch. Der Autobahnring leitet den Verkehr idealerweise um die Stadt herum und besitzt eine Geschwindigkeit von 120 km/h ohne Unterbrechungen. Durch den eigenwilligen Verlauf verringert sich seine Geschwindigkeit auf 50 km/h mit Unterbrechungen. Die Folgen sind auch hier extreme Stauungen.

Das Grundprinzip der Stuttgarter Verkehrsführung zwingt den Verkehr auf ein einige wenige Straßen in der Innenstadt und bremst ihn dann aus. Dieses Prinzip hat Nachteile für alle Stadtbenutzer. Der Autoverkehr wird in seinem Fluss behindert. Die verkehrsreichen Straßen gefährden Fahrradfahrer. Die Autostraßen wirken als starke Grenze für Fußgänger. Die Anwohner leiden unter Lärm und Luftverschmutzung.

Umgehungsstraßen mit unterschiedlichen Geschwindigkeiten könnten viele Probleme der Stadt beheben, jedoch braucht es dafür den politischen Willen und das Verständnis der Bevölkerung.

Pragsattel

City Centre

Neckar Valley

5km   10km   15km   20km   25km   30km   35km

train / metro   highway   river

Paris has an extremely strongly defined ring around the Urban Nucleus. It consists of a highway and an urban freeway. The highway reaches too far into the Urban Being and cuts off the core from the rest of the city. The highway is a strong division within the city. The ideal location of the beltway would be around 30 kilometers further outside, to direct the traffic around the Urban Being. But the *belt of asphalt* is based on the political boundary.

Another feature that was found in the analysis is the high number of main artery roads. They result in a high number of comparatively small Urban Cells.

Paris hat einen extrem stark definierten Ring um den Stadtkern. Er besteht aus einer Autobahn und einer Stadtautobahn. Die Autobahn dringt zu weit in das urbane Wesen hinein und schneidet den Kern vom Rest der Stadt ab. Sie besitzt eine starke teilende Wirkung. Idealerweise würde der Autobahnring circa 30 Kilometer weiter außerhalb den Verkehr um das urbane Wesen herumleiten. Der *Gürtel aus Asphalt* verläuft jedoch um die politische Stadtgrenze.

Eine weitere Besonderheit aus der Analyse ist die hohe Anzahl von Hauptverkehrsadern. Durch sie entsteht eine Vielzahl von vergleichsweise kleinen urbanen Zellen.

90km 80km 70km 60km 50km 40km 30km 20km 10km

Paris

◯ train / metro　◯ highway　⬤ river

data of the drawing | street length: ~9,600 km

London's beltway has a comparatively large distance from the centre, to reduce the heavy vehicular traffic in the Urban Being. Two more rings with the quality of an urban freeway additionally help to minimise traffic within the city centre. The three rings provide sufficient alternative routes around the central area of London. A high number of main artery roads further support this effect.

London Congestion Charge introduced in 2003 is an additional measure. Cars in the city centre have to pay a fee. This reduces the amount of traffic passing through the city centre.

London besitzt einen vergleichsweise weit außen liegenden Autobahnring, um den starken Autoverkehr im urbanen Wesen zu reduzieren. Zwei weitere Ringe mit der Qualität einer Stadtautobahn helfen zusätzlich, den Verkehr im Stadtkern zu minimieren. Die drei Ringe bieten ausreichend Alternativen, um die Innenstadt zu umfahren. Eine hohe Anzahl von Hauptverkehrsadern unterstützt diesen Effekt weiter.

Eine zusätzliche Maßnahme ist die 2003 eingeführte *Staugebühr*. Für Autos im Stadtzentrum ist eine Gebühr fällig, um den Verkehr so weit wie möglich aus der Innenstadt rauszuhalten.

train / metro   highway   river

data of the drawing | street length: ~8,300 km

For a megacity with over 21 million inhabitants in the metropolitan area, New Delhi has very few highways. An outer beltway is completely missing and the speed on the main roads, except for the southern ones, is slowed down by crossing main thoroughfares. The lack of highways and the slow speed result in high levels of congestion.

The nearby satellite towns are not common at all. New Delhi lies in one of the most densely populated regions of the world, the *Indo-Gangetic* plain. It has a city densification similar to the *Po Valley.*

Für eine Megastadt mit über 21 Millionen Einwohnern in der Metropolregion besitzt Neu-Delhi sehr wenige Autobahnen. Ein äußerer Autobahnring fehlt komplett und die Geschwindigkeit auf den Ausfallstraßen, mit Ausnahme der südlichen, wird durch kreuzende Hauptverkehrsadern verlangsamt. Durch die fehlenden Autobahnen und die geringere Geschwindigkeit entsteht eine Überlastung der Straßen.

Auffällig sind auch die nahe gelegenen Satellitenstädte. Neu-Delhi liegt in einer der am dichtesten besiedelten Regionen der Welt, der *Indus-Ganges-Ebene*. Sie besitzt eine Stadtverdichtung ähnlich der *Po-Ebene* in Norditalien.

train / metro   highway   river

Moscow is a city with a clearly pronounced ring system. There are eight rings in total. The four inner rings have a clear gradation of speeds. The innermost ring encloses the *Kremlin* and the *Red Square*. The fourth ring has the speed of a highway and defines the Urban Nucleus, followed by a rail ring and another highway. The two outermost rings lie about 50 kilometers and 100 kilometers from the centre.

For a city the size of Moscow there are quite few main artery roads. With over 15 million inhabitants Moscow is the second largest agglomeration in Europe.

Moskau ist eine Stadt mit einem stark ausgeprägten Ringsystem. Insgesamt gibt es acht Ringe. Die inneren vier haben eine klare Abstufung nach Geschwindigkeiten. Der innerste Ring umschließt den *Kreml* und den *Roten Platz*. Der vierte Ring hat die Geschwindigkeit einer Autobahn und definiert den Stadtkern. Danach folgen ein Schienenring und ein weiterer Autobahnring. Gute 50 Kilometer und 100 Kilometer außerhalb des Zentrums verlaufen die zwei äußersten Ringe.

Auffällig sind die vergleichsweise wenigen Hauptverkehrsadern für eine Stadt der Größe von Moskaus. Mit über 15 Millionen Menschen ist Moskau die zweitgrößte Agglomeration Europas.

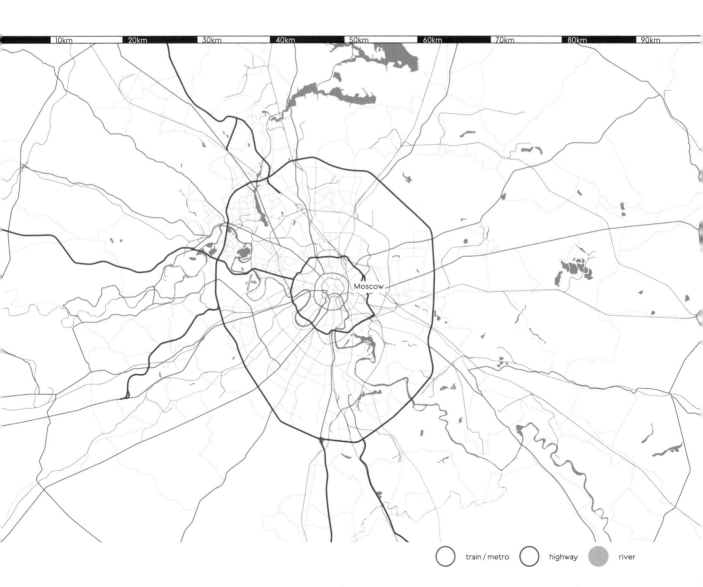

train / metro   highway   river

data of the drawing | street length: ~3,100 km

As a former British colony, Melbourne has a very rectangular street grid. The main streets run mostly straight through the entire Urban Being. The size of the city can be estimated quite accurately by the densification of the main thoroughfares. The straight main roads facilitate the orientation within the city.

The highways have a less clear structure. There is no ring around the Urban Nucleus. The core is only recognizable through the densification of the main streets at the mouth of the *Yarra River*. Within the CBD (Central Business District), the streets almost condense to a block cell structure and favour the formation of a financial district.

Als ehemalige britische Kolonie besitzt Melbourne ein sehr rechtwinkliges Straßenraster. Vor allem die Hauptstraßen ziehen sich größtenteils gerade durch das gesamte urbane Wesen. An ihrer Verdichtung lässt sich die Größe der Stadt relativ exakt ablesen. Die geraden Hauptstraßen erleichtern die Orientierung innerhalb der Stadt.

Die Autobahnen haben eine weniger klare Struktur. Ein Ring um den Stadtkern existiert nicht. Allein durch die Verdichtung der Hauptstraßen wird der Kern an der Mündung des *Yarra-Flusses* erkennbar. Innerhalb des *CBD (Central Business District)* verdichten sich die Straßen fast zu einem Blockzellenverband und begünstigen die Bildung eines Finanzviertels.

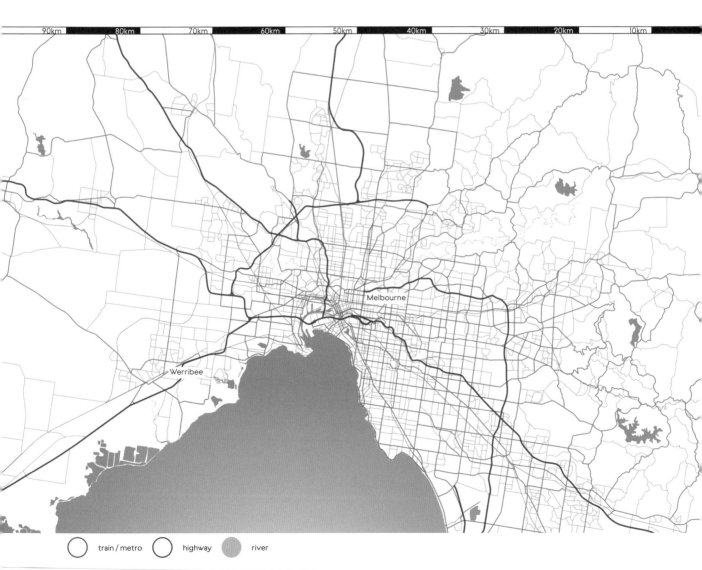

train / metro　　highway　　river

data of the drawing | street length: ~5,300 km

Los Angeles is the absolute car city. The low density results in large distances, so the residents are dependent on their cars. The plan favours the use of cars, which is why there are many of them. The consequence is extreme traffic congestion .

The enormous urban freeways are condensed around the small Urban Nucleus. Even the main artery roads are very close together within the urban core and form a block cell structure. The financial district of the city is located in this structure. Outside the core the main artery roads extend in a uniform grid and shape cells of similar size.

Los Angeles ist die Autostadt schlechthin. Die niedere Dichte hat große Distanzen zur Folge, weswegen die Bewohner auf ihr Auto angewiesen sind. Die Planung bevorzugt die Nutzung des Autos, weswegen es viele davon gibt. Als Konsequenz enstehen extreme Stauungen.

Die enorm großen Stadtautobahnen verdichten sich um den kleinen Stadtkern. Auch die Hauptverkehrsadern liegen innerhalb des Stadtkerns sehr nah beieinander und formen einen Blockzellenverband. Hier befindet sich das Finanzviertel der Stadt. Außerhalb des Kerns verlaufen die Hauptverkehrsadern in einem gleichmäßigen Raster und formen ähnlich große Zellen.

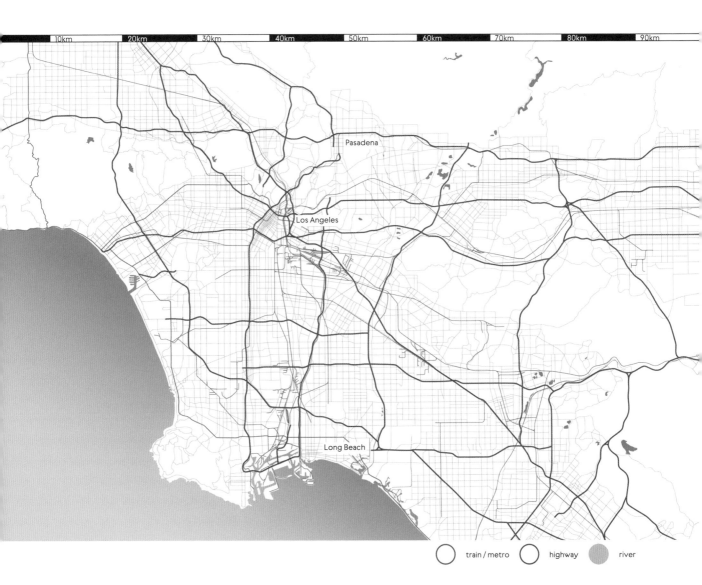

train / metro   highway   river

data of the drawing | street length: ~8,500 km

Rio de Janeiro has a unique topography, which can be recognised in the road network. The highways pass through the valleys and passes, because of the numerous mountains, which makes the creation of a ring road impossible. The main arteries follow the same principle. The Urban Nucleus is difficult to recognise in the road network. Originally, the city grew in the interior, where the bridge across the bay is located. Today the Urban Nucleus is situated directly near the sea, west of the mouth of the bay. The famous city extensions *Copacabana* and *Ipanema* have caused this shift. The origin of the city lies in the nucleus, next to the *Sugarloaf*.

Rio de Janeiro hat eine einzigartige Topografie, die auch im Straßennetzwerk erkennbar ist. Wegen der vielen Berge werden die Autobahnen durch die Täler und über die Pässe geleitet, weswegen eine Ringbildung unmöglich ist. Auch die Hauptverkehrsadern folgen diesem Prinzip. Der Stadtkern ist nur schwer im Straßennetzwerk erkennbar. Ursprünglich wuchs die Stadt weiter im Landesinneren, wo sich die Brücke über die Bucht befindet. Heute liegt der Stadtkern direkt am Meer, westlich der Mündung der Bucht. Die bekannten Stadterweiterungen *Copacabana* und *Ipanema* haben diese Verschiebung bewirkt. Ihren Ursprung fand die Stadt im heutigen Stadtkern, neben dem *Zuckerhut*.

train / metro   highway   river

Dubai has grown intensively during the last decades. But its original nucleus is still visible in the road network. It is located on a peninsula at the mouth of the *Dubai Creek*. The new downtown area has shifted further south, to the beginning of the very same creek. It is not recognizable in the road network.

The immense highways running through the city are located parallel to the beach. They are very difficult to cross for pedestrians and cut the city into linear pieces. With just around 2.5 million people in the Urban Being, the city has a huge dimension.

Dubai ist in den letzten Jahrzehnten stark gewachsen. Der ursprüngliche Stadtkern ist jedoch immer noch im Straßennetzwerk sichtbar. Er befindet sich auf einer Halbinsel an der Mündung des *Dubai Creek*. Das neue Stadtzentrum hat sich weiter nach Süden verschoben, an den Beginn desselben Kanals. Es ist nicht im Straßennetzwerk erkennbar.

Die immensen Stadtautobahnen verlaufen parallel zum Strand. Sie sind für Fußgänger sehr schwer zu überqueren und schneiden die Stadt in längliche Stücke. Mit nur 2,5 Millionen Einwohnern im urbanen Wesen besitzt Dubai eine enorme Ausdehnung.

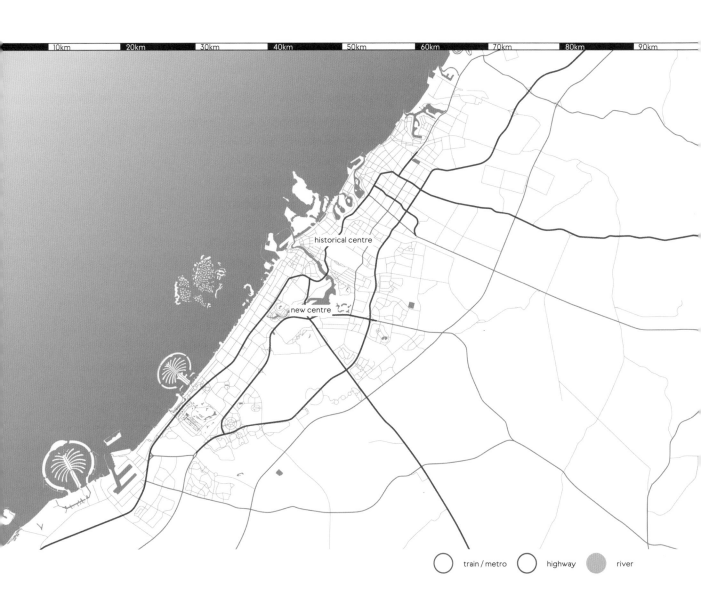

train / metro   highway   river

data of the drawing | street length: ~2,500 km

The metropolitan area of Tokyo has a very dense road network. With over 10,000 kilometers of freeways and main thoroughfares, it is significantly longer than Los Angeles or Paris. The inner city train network is even the longest in the world.

The urban nutrition arteries have a ring structure with large radial roads. The city centre is bordered by the *Arakawa* river and an urban freeway. The car-free, imperial palace can be recognised at its centre.

The Urban Being Tokyo is located within a city cluster, together with Yokohama to the southwest. In this direction the traffic arteries also maintain their fine mesh width.

Die japanische Metropolregion besitzt ein sehr dichtes Straßennetzwerk. Mit über 10.000 Kilometern Autobahnen und Hauptverkehrsadern ist es deutlich länger als das von Los Angeles oder Paris. Das innerstädtische Zugnetz ist sogar das längste der Welt.

Grundsätzlich haben die urbanen Nährstoffadern einen ringförmigen Aufbau mit großen Radialstrecken. Der Stadtkern wird vom Fluss *Arakawa* und einer Stadtautobahn begrenzt. In seinem Zentrum ist der autofreie Kaiserliche Palast zu erkennen.

Das urbane Wesen Tokio liegt in einem Stadtverband mit dem südwestlich gelegenen Yokohama. In dieser Richtung behalten auch die Verkehrsadern ihre feine Maschenweite bei.

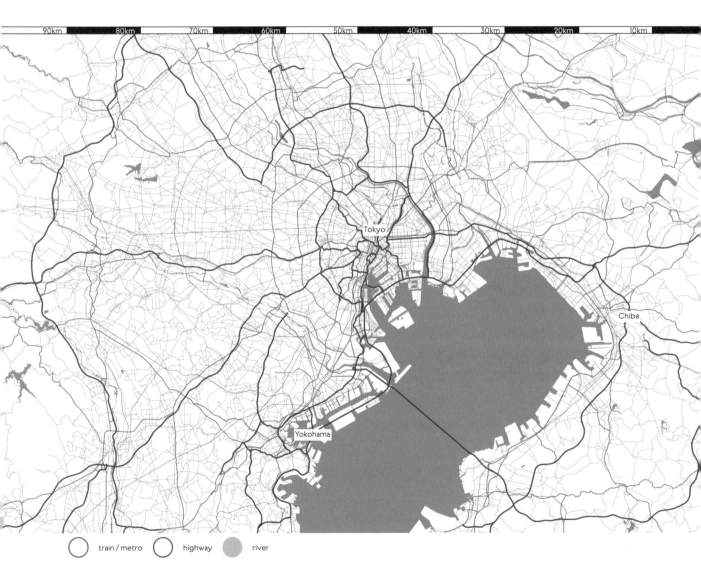

train / metro　　highway　　river

data of the drawing | street length: ~10,200 km

The former division of the city is still visible in the road network today. Berlin has two Urban Nuclei, which are located directly next to each other. The historic core lies in the east and the newly formed core in the west. Both meet in the area of the *Brandenburg Gate*, the former border. The western core is delimited by the A100 freeway, which was planned as a ring road during the division of the city. The two cores support the typical variety of sub-centres in Berlin.

The building of the outer beltway began even before the destruction of the city in the 1930s. Through its deformation in the southwest, the satellite city Potsdam is included.

Am Straßennetzwerk lässt sich die ehemalige Teilung der Stadt bis heute ablesen. Berlin besitzt zwei Stadtkerne, die direkt nebeneinanderliegen: der historische Stadtkern im Osten und der neu geformte Kern im Westen. Beide treffen sich im Bereich des *Brandenburger Tors*, der ehemaligen Grenze. Der westliche Kern wird von der Stadtautobahn A100 begrenzt, die während der Teilung der Stadt als Ringautobahn konzipiert wurde. Der doppelte Kern unterstützt die für Berlin typische Vielfalt von Subzentren.

Mit dem Bau des äußeren Autobahnrings wurde bereits vor der Zerstörung der Stadt in den 1930er Jahren begonnen. Durch die Deformierung des Ringes im Südwesten wird die Satellitenstadt Potsdam mit eingeschlossen.

data of the drawing | street length: ~4,400 km

Urban Being

Cellular Structure

centre - big cell
Zentrum - große Zelle

sub-centre - linear cell
Subzentrum - lineare Zelle

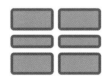

**residential district - small /
medium cells**
Wohnviertel - kleine / mittlere
Zellen

business district - small block cells
Finanzviertel - kleine Blockzellen

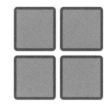

industrial park - big cells
Industriepark - große Zellen

30km 25km 20km 15km 10km 5km

Novo Iguaçu

Duque de Caxias

Tijuca National Park

Barra da Tijuca

small cell   medium cell   big cell

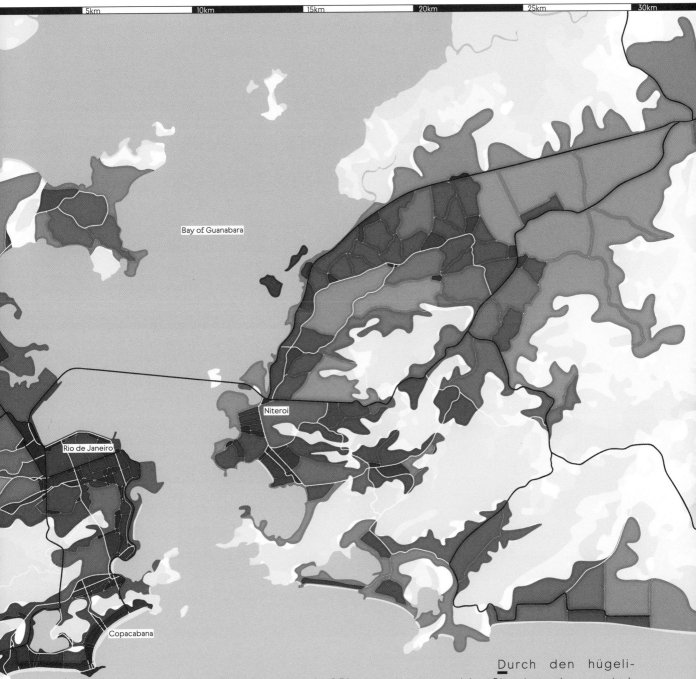

5km   10km   15km   20km   25km   30km

Bay of Guanabara

Niteroi

Rio de Janeiro

Copacabana

The hilly ground of Rio has shaped a very organic cell structure. Notable are the densifications of cells in the centres and sub-centres. Rio de Janeiro, Duque de Caixas, Novo Iguacu and Niteroi possess these densifications. Even sub-centres like *Copacabana* and *Botafogo* have this small-scale cell structure. The western city expansion *Barra da Tijuca* consists of large cells. This neighbourhood has little urban life and is colloquially known as *the highway*.

Durch den hügeligen Untergrund hat Rio eine sehr organisch geformte Zellstruktur. Auffällig sind die Verdichtungen in den Zentren und Subzentren. Rio de Janeiro, Duque de Caixas, Novo Iguacu und Niteroi besitzen diese Verdichtungen. Auch Subzentren wie *Copacabana* und *Botafogo* weisen diese kleinteilige Zellstruktur auf. Die westliche Stadterweiterung *Barra da Tijuca* besteht aus großen Zellen. Dieses Viertel hat wenig städtisches Leben und wird scherzhaft *die Autobahn* genannt.

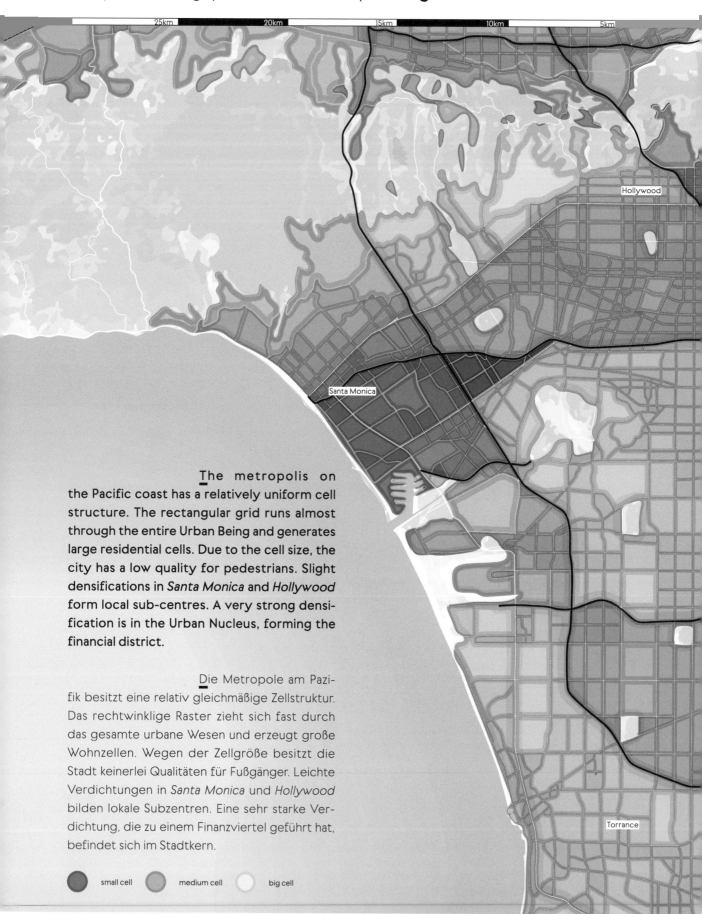

The metropolis on the Pacific coast has a relatively uniform cell structure. The rectangular grid runs almost through the entire Urban Being and generates large residential cells. Due to the cell size, the city has a low quality for pedestrians. Slight densifications in *Santa Monica* and *Hollywood* form local sub-centres. A very strong densification is in the Urban Nucleus, forming the financial district.

Die Metropole am Pazifik besitzt eine relativ gleichmäßige Zellstruktur. Das rechtwinklige Raster zieht sich fast durch das gesamte urbane Wesen und erzeugt große Wohnzellen. Wegen der Zellgröße besitzt die Stadt keinerlei Qualitäten für Fußgänger. Leichte Verdichtungen in *Santa Monica* und *Hollywood* bilden lokale Subzentren. Eine sehr starke Verdichtung, die zu einem Finanzviertel geführt hat, befindet sich im Stadtkern.

small cell   medium cell   big cell

30km   25km   20km   15km   10km   5km

The centre of Paris has a large number of small Urban Cells that contribute to the urban qualities of the city. The small cells, the high density and pedestrian-friendly streets enhance the quality and lead to a bustling downtown.

Im Pariser Stadtkern gibt es eine Vielzahl kleiner urbaner Zellen, die die städtischen Qualitäten maßgeblich bestimmen. Die kleinen Zellen, die hohe Dichte und die fußgängerfreundlichen Straßen steigern die Lebensqualität für den Menschen und führen zu einer belebten Innenstadt.

small cell   medium cell   big cell

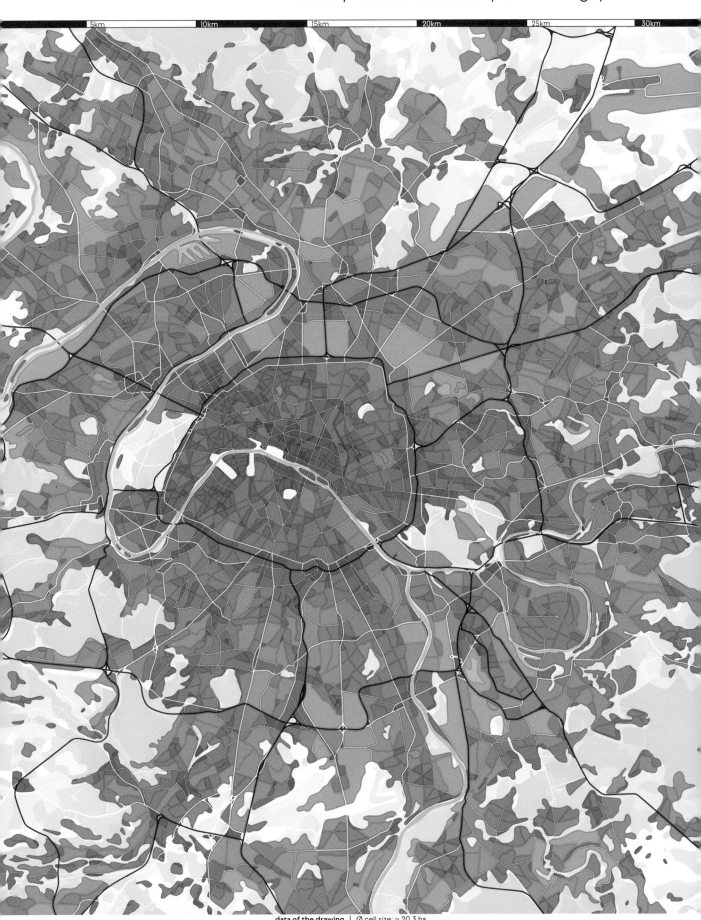

5km 10km 15km 20km 25km 30km

Urban Being

Industrial Organs

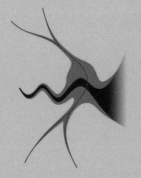

canals
Kanäle

train tracks
Zuggleise

industry
Industrie

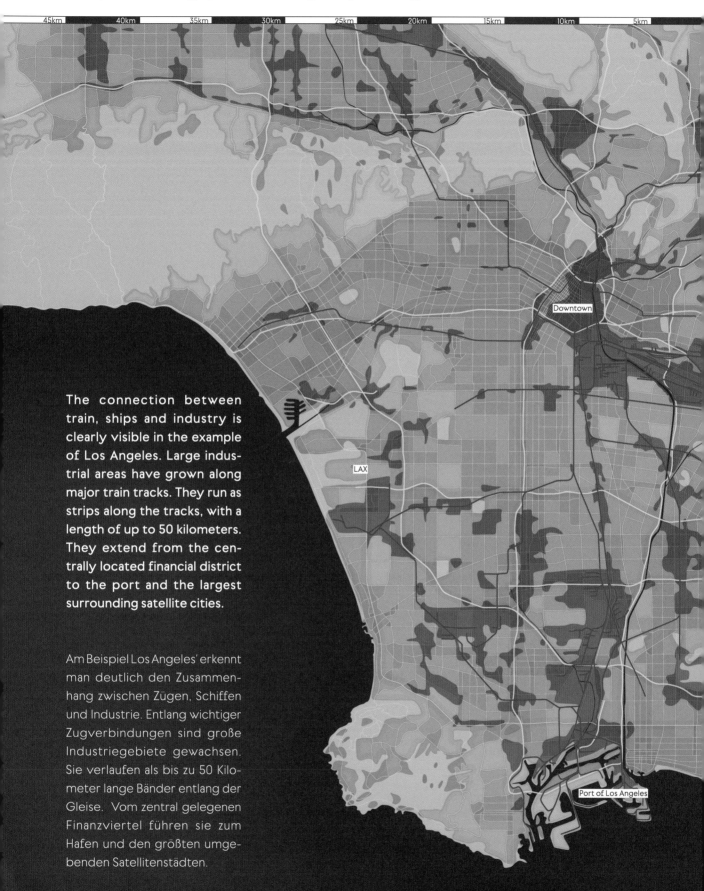

45km 40km 35km 30km 25km 20km 15km 10km 5km

Downtown

LAX

Port of Los Angeles

The connection between train, ships and industry is clearly visible in the example of Los Angeles. Large industrial areas have grown along major train tracks. They run as strips along the tracks, with a length of up to 50 kilometers. They extend from the centrally located financial district to the port and the largest surrounding satellite cities.

Am Beispiel Los Angeles' erkennt man deutlich den Zusammenhang zwischen Zügen, Schiffen und Industrie. Entlang wichtiger Zugverbindungen sind große Industriegebiete gewachsen. Sie verlaufen als bis zu 50 Kilometer lange Bänder entlang der Gleise. Vom zentral gelegenen Finanzviertel führen sie zum Hafen und den größten umgebenden Satellitenstädten.

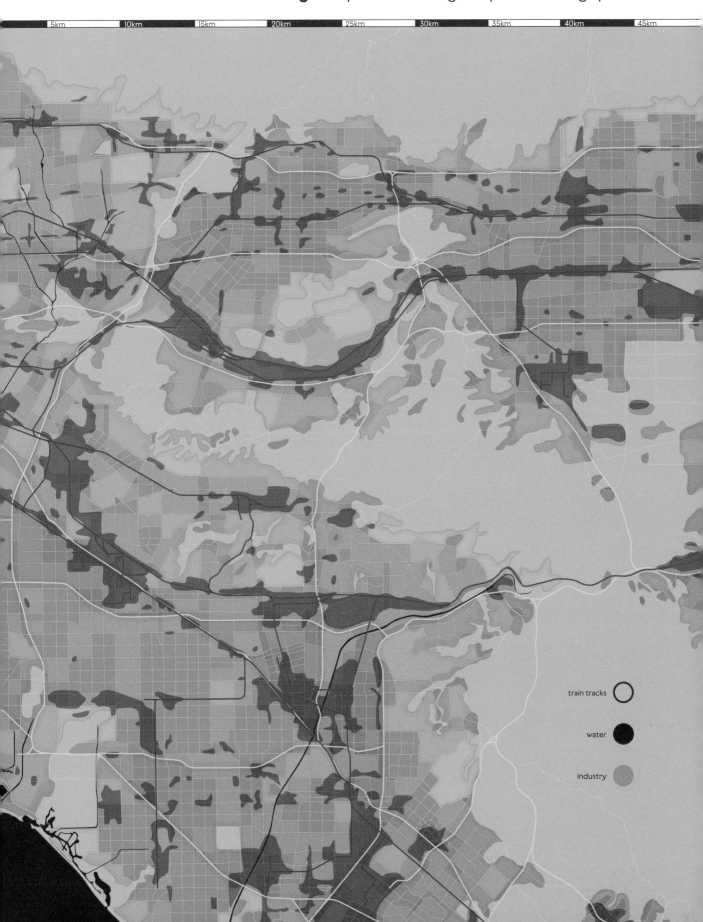

train tracks ◯

water ⬤

industry ⬤

The industry in *London* has settled between the mouth of the *Thames* and the Urban Nucleus. The high accessibility of cargo ships has led to the city's strong growth. The recent shift towards a financial industry transformed the former dock lands into a financial district.

The finely woven rail network and the international airport *Heathrow* have produced plenty of industry in the western part of the city as well.

Die Industrie hat sich in London vor allem zwischen der Mündung der *Themse* und dem Stadtkern niedergelassen. Die hohe Erreichbarkeit mit dem Frachtschiff hat zu dem starken Wachstum der Stadt geführt. Mittlerweile hat sich eine Verschiebung in Richtung Finanzindustrie vollzogen, weswegen sich die ehemaligen Hafengebiete zu einem Finanzviertel gewandelt haben.

Das feinmaschige Schienennetz und der internationale Flughafen *Heathrow* haben auch im Westen der Stadt viel Industrie hervorgebracht.

O   train tracks   ● water   ● industry

75km   50km   25km

Edmonton is primarily known for its oil and gas industry. Oil and gas are the urban nutrients that help the city to grow. They are mainly transported on rail, which is why the industrial areas extend along the tracks. The geographical location of the city supports the function as a cross-regional transport hub, increasing the importance of the train tracks.

As a financial centre Edmonton has a CBD (Central Business District), also known as Downtown. It is where the financial industry and other office-based businesses are located.

Edmonton ist vor allem für seine Öl- und Gasindustrie bekannt. Öl und Gas sind die urbanen Nährstoffe, die der Stadt zum Wachstum verhelfen. Sie werden hauptsächlich über den Schienenverkehr transportiert, weswegen die Industriegebiete entlang der Gleise verlaufen. Durch die geografische Lage ist die Stadt ein wichtiger Verkehrsknoten. Dadurch erlangen die Gleise eine weitere Bedeutung.

Als Finanzzentrum besitzt Edmonton ein *CBD (Central Business District)*, auch Downtown genannt. Hier befinden sich die Finanzindustrie und andere bürobasierte Unternehmen.

○ train tracks ● water ● industry

Urban Being

Green Systems

green systems
grüne Systeme

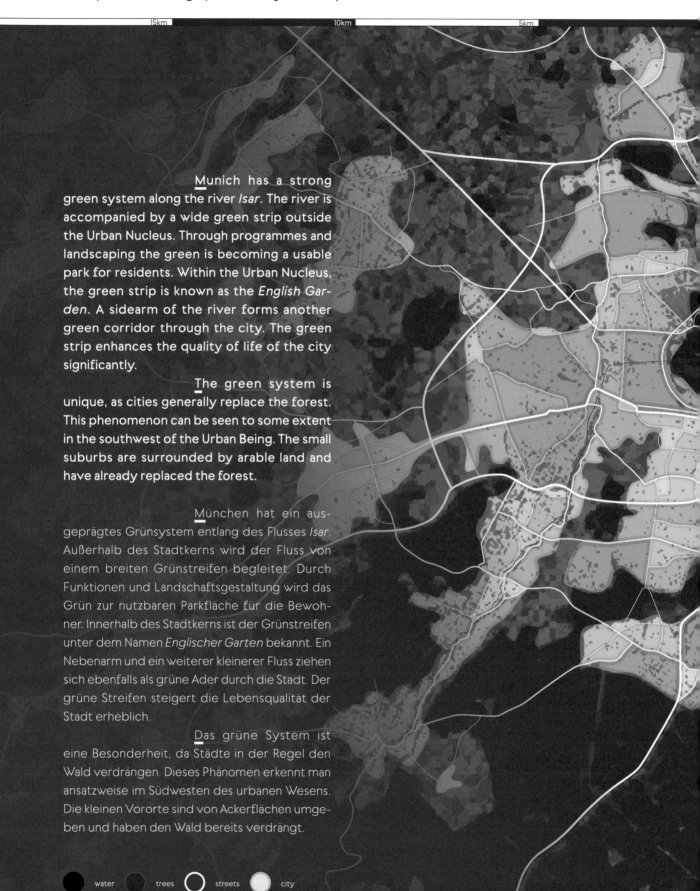

15km   10km   5km

Munich has a strong green system along the river *Isar*. The river is accompanied by a wide green strip outside the Urban Nucleus. Through programmes and landscaping the green is becoming a usable park for residents. Within the Urban Nucleus, the green strip is known as the *English Garden*. A sidearm of the river forms another green corridor through the city. The green strip enhances the quality of life of the city significantly.

The green system is unique, as cities generally replace the forest. This phenomenon can be seen to some extent in the southwest of the Urban Being. The small suburbs are surrounded by arable land and have already replaced the forest.

München hat ein ausgeprägtes Grünsystem entlang des Flusses *Isar*. Außerhalb des Stadtkerns wird der Fluss von einem breiten Grünstreifen begleitet. Durch Funktionen und Landschaftsgestaltung wird das Grün zur nutzbaren Parkfläche für die Bewohner. Innerhalb des Stadtkerns ist der Grünstreifen unter dem Namen *Englischer Garten* bekannt. Ein Nebenarm und ein weiterer kleinerer Fluss ziehen sich ebenfalls als grüne Ader durch die Stadt. Der grüne Streifen steigert die Lebensqualität der Stadt erheblich.

Das grüne System ist eine Besonderheit, da Städte in der Regel den Wald verdrängen. Dieses Phänomen erkennt man ansatzweise im Südwesten des urbanen Wesens. Die kleinen Vororte sind von Ackerflächen umgeben und haben den Wald bereits verdrängt.

water   trees   ○ streets   ● city

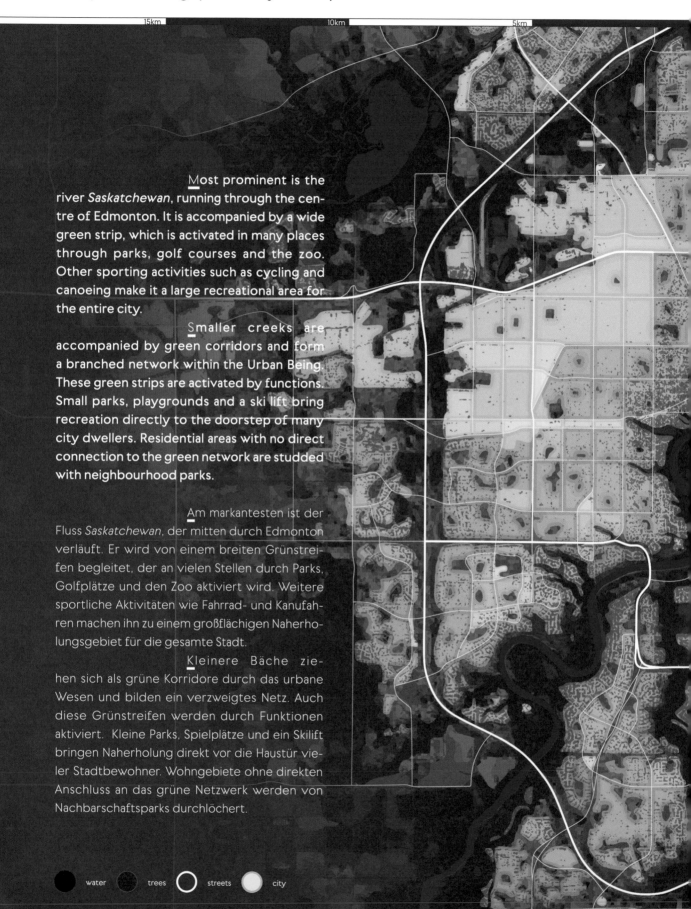

15km 10km 5km

Most prominent is the river *Saskatchewan*, running through the centre of Edmonton. It is accompanied by a wide green strip, which is activated in many places through parks, golf courses and the zoo. Other sporting activities such as cycling and canoeing make it a large recreational area for the entire city.

Smaller creeks are accompanied by green corridors and form a branched network within the Urban Being. These green strips are activated by functions. Small parks, playgrounds and a ski lift bring recreation directly to the doorstep of many city dwellers. Residential areas with no direct connection to the green network are studded with neighbourhood parks.

Am markantesten ist der Fluss *Saskatchewan*, der mitten durch Edmonton verläuft. Er wird von einem breiten Grünstreifen begleitet, der an vielen Stellen durch Parks, Golfplätze und den Zoo aktiviert wird. Weitere sportliche Aktivitäten wie Fahrrad- und Kanufahren machen ihn zu einem großflächigen Naherholungsgebiet für die gesamte Stadt.

Kleinere Bäche ziehen sich als grüne Korridore durch das urbane Wesen und bilden ein verzweigtes Netz. Auch diese Grünstreifen werden durch Funktionen aktiviert. Kleine Parks, Spielplätze und ein Skilift bringen Naherholung direkt vor die Haustür vieler Stadtbewohner. Wohngebiete ohne direkten Anschluss an das grüne Netzwerk werden von Nachbarschaftsparks durchlöchert.

 water   trees   ○ streets   ● city

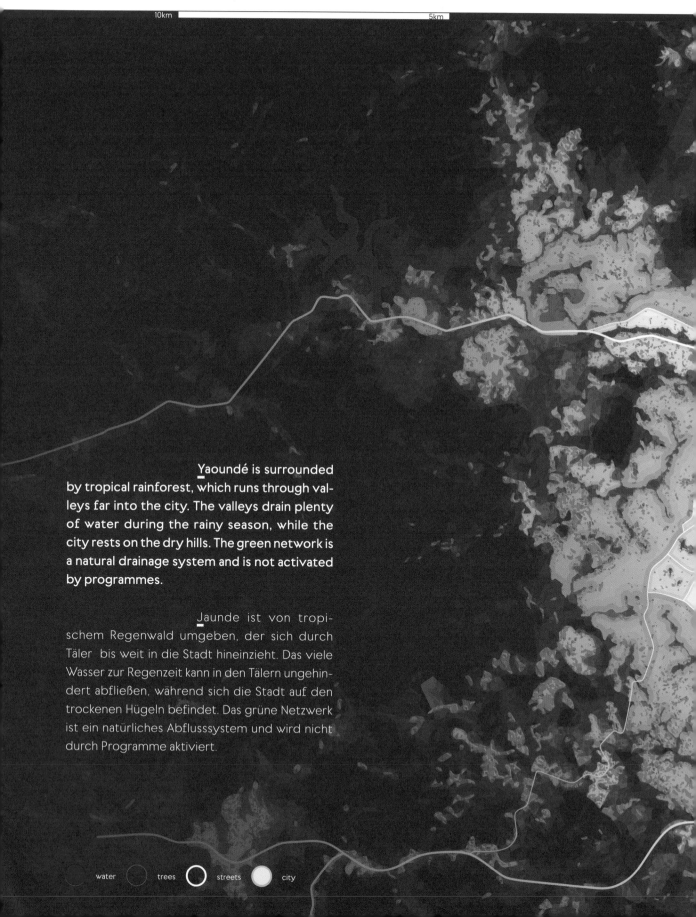

10km   5km

Yaoundé is surrounded by tropical rainforest, which runs through valleys far into the city. The valleys drain plenty of water during the rainy season, while the city rests on the dry hills. The green network is a natural drainage system and is not activated by programmes.

Jaunde ist von tropischem Regenwald umgeben, der sich durch Täler bis weit in die Stadt hineinzieht. Das viele Wasser zur Regenzeit kann in den Tälern ungehindert abfließen, während sich die Stadt auf den trockenen Hügeln befindet. Das grüne Netzwerk ist ein natürliches Abflusssystem und wird nicht durch Programme aktiviert.

water ○ trees ○ streets ○ city

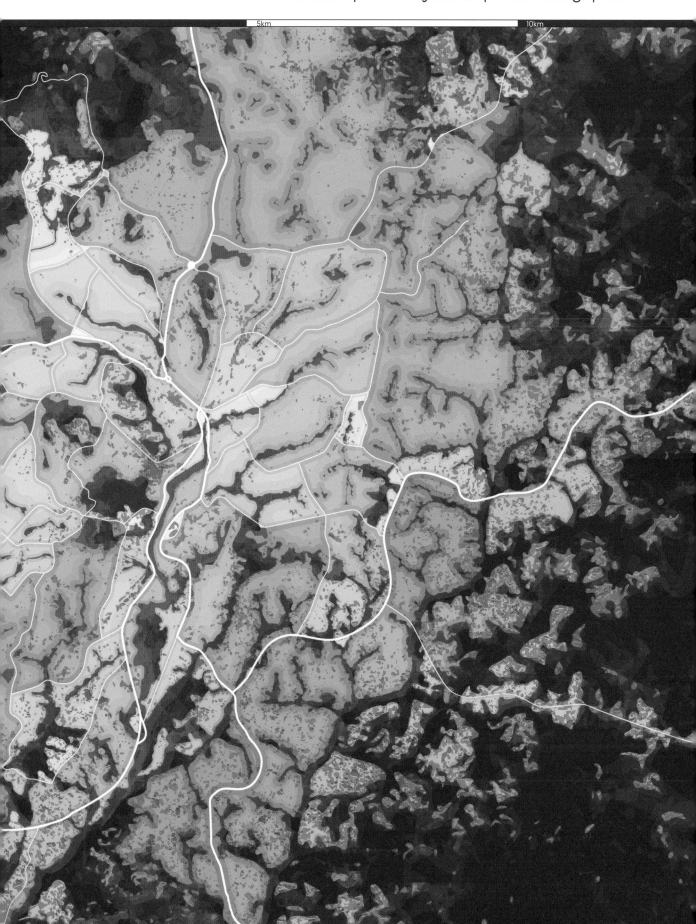

5km 10km

Urban Being

Megacities

megacities with over 10 million people
Megastädte mit mehr als 10 Millionen Einwohnern

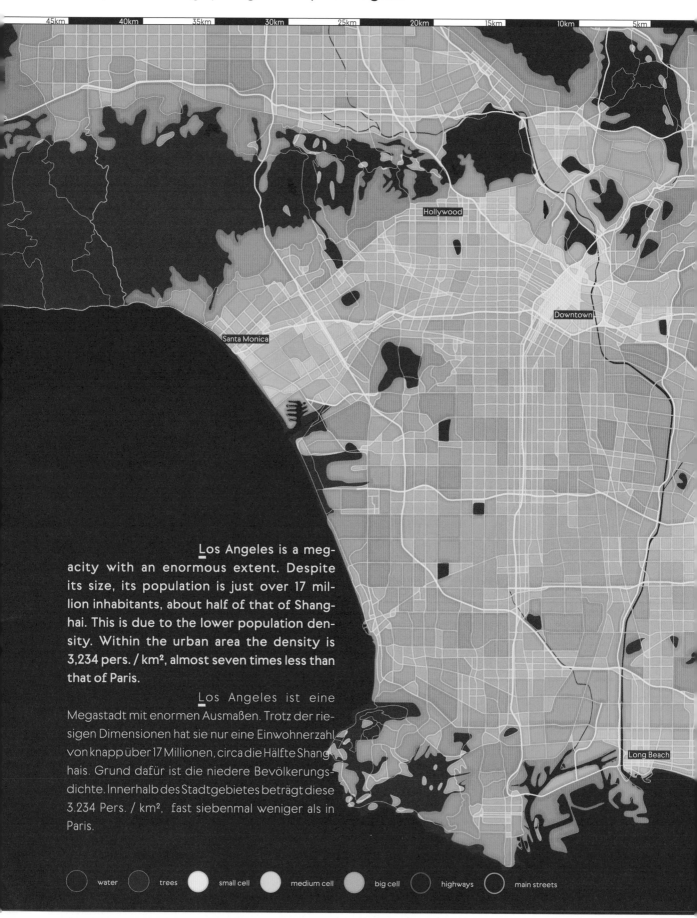

45km 40km 35km 30km 25km 20km 15km 10km 5km

Hollywood

Downtown

Santa Monica

Long Beach

Los Angeles is a megacity with an enormous extent. Despite its size, its population is just over 17 million inhabitants, about half of that of Shanghai. This is due to the lower population density. Within the urban area the density is 3,234 pers. / km², almost seven times less than that of Paris.

Los Angeles ist eine Megastadt mit enormen Ausmaßen. Trotz der riesigen Dimensionen hat sie nur eine Einwohnerzahl von knapp über 17 Millionen, circa die Hälfte Shanghais. Grund dafür ist die niedere Bevölkerungsdichte. Innerhalb des Stadtgebietes beträgt diese 3.234 Pers. / km², fast siebenmal weniger als in Paris.

water   trees   small cell   medium cell   big cell   highways   main streets

45km 40km 35km 30km 25km 20km 15km 10km 5km

In terms of area, Shanghai is a small Urban Being, but with many of residents. Nowadays, around 34 million people live in the metropolitan area, 10 million more than in the whole of *Australia*. Shanghai and its surrounding cities form the largest city cluster in the world. A remarkable density is achieved due to the many high-rise buildings. In the central districts, the population density lies between 40,000 - 47,000 pers./ km².

Densely populated city blocks with a size of about 4 hectares and a population of over 10,000 inhabitants are not uncommon. Due to the high population density, the streets are used by more people, making the city very lively. However, the overcrowding has a dark side as well. High levels of air pollution, water pollution and contaminated food are a normal part of life within this megacity.

Shanghai ist flächenmäßig ein kleines urbanes Wesen, jedoch mit sehr vielen Einwohnern. In der Metropolregion leben mittlerweile 34 Millionen Menschen und damit 10 Millionen mehr als in ganz Australien. Mit den umgebenden Städten bildet Shanghai den größten Stadtverband der Welt.

Durch die vielen Hochhäuser entsteht eine bemerkenswerte Dichte. In den zentralen Stadtbezirken beträgt die Bevölkerungsdichte zwischen 40.000 und 47.000 Pers./ km². Dicht besiedelte Straßenblocks mit einer Größe von circa 4 Hektar und einer Bevölkerung von über 10.000 Einwohnern sind keine Seltenheit. Durch die hohe Bevölkerungsdichte werden die Straßen von mehr Menschen genutzt. Dadurch wirkt die Stadt sehr belebt. Die Überbevölkerung hat jedoch auch eine Schattenseite: Starke Luftverschmutzung, Wasserverschmutzung und damit verseuchte Lebensmittel gehören in der Megastadt zum Alltag. Mit der Größe der Stadt wächst die Notwendigkeit für einen nachhaltigen Lebensstil exponentiell.

water   trees   small cell   medium cell   big cell   highways   main streets

5km 10km 15km 20km 25km 30km 35km 40km 45k

Yangtze river

outer ring

Pudong

Puxi

Hongqiao airport

outer ring

Pudong airport

data of the drawing | ∅ cell size: ~ 183.3 ha | street length: ~ 3,100 km

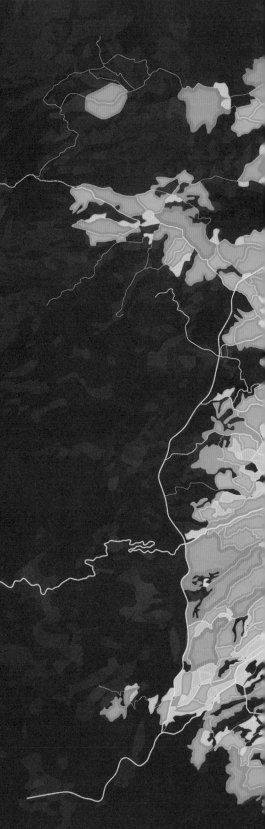

40km | 35km | 30km | 25km | 20km | 15km | 10km | 5km

With a population of about 20 million, Mexico City is the most populated metropolitan area in North America. The surrounding mountains cut off the Urban Being from the surrounding satellite cities and prevent a contiguous city cluster.

The location in the valley densifies the city. The topography shapes organically formed cells in the west. The Urban Nucleus is situated on the former *Lake Texcoco*, which was drained by the Spaniards in the 18th century, leaving behind a soft and fertile ground. Today's central cell was formerly on an island. The link between the flat surface and a rectilinear and small-scale cell structure is clearly visible.

The urban freeways respond to the ground as well. In the west, the outer ring, *Anillo Periferico*, jumps back to the Inner Ring, *Circuito Interior*, to avoid the hills.

Mit circa 20 Millionen Einwohnern ist Mexiko-Stadt die am stärksten bevölkerte Metropolregion Nordamerikas. Die umgebenden Berge schneiden das urbane Wesen von den umgebenden Satellitenstädten ab und verhindern einen zusammenhängenden Stadtverband.

Die Lage im Tal komprimiert die Stadt. Durch die Topografie sind im Westen organisch geformte Zellen entstanden. Der Stadtkern liegt auf dem ehemaligen *Texcoco-See*, der durch die Spanier im 18. Jahrhundert trockengelegt wurde. Dadurch entstand ein relativ flacher und weicher Untergrund. Die heutige zentrale Zelle befand sich früher auf einer Insel. Deutlich erkennbar ist der Zusammenhang zwischen dem flachen Untergrund und einem geradlinigen und kleinteiligen Zellverband.

Auch die Stadtautobahn reagiert auf den Untergrund. Der äußere Ring, *Anillo Periferico*, springt im Westen auf den Inneren Ring, *Circuito Interior*, zurück, um die Hügel zu umgehen.

water | former Texcoco lake | trees | small cell | medium cell | big cell | highways | main streets

5km 10km 15km 20km 25km 30km 35km 40km 45km

Ecatepec

Anillo Periférico

Central Cell

sque de Chapultepec

Neza

Circuito Interior

Anillo Periférico

Xochimilco

45km 40km 35km 30km 25km 20km 15km 10km 5km

Harrow

Heathrow Airport

Croydon

With more than 13 million people in the metropolitan area, London is one of the largest cities in Europe. The population density in the inner regions is approximately 10,000 pers. / km² and is thus in the upper mid range.

Mit über 13 Millionen Menschen in der Metropolregion gehört London zu den größten Städten Europas. Die Bevölkerungsdichte beträgt in den inneren Bereichen circa 10.000 Pers. / km² und liegt damit im höheren Mittelfeld.

water   trees   small cell   medium cell   big cell   highways   main streets   trains / metro

data of the drawing | Ø cell size: ~ 21.5 ha | street length: ~ 8.300 km

45km 40km 35km 30km 25km 20km 15km 10km 5km

Yokohama

Imperial Palace

Chiba

The Urban Being of Tokyo is one of the largest in the world, with a population of about 35 million people. With 14,800 pers. / km² in the core, the city has a high population density.

Das urbane Wesen Tokio gehört mit circa 35 Millionen Menschen zu den größten der Welt. Mit 14.800 Pers. / km² im Kern hat die Stadt eine hohe Bevölkerungsdichte.

water   trees   small cell   medium cell   big cell   highways   main streets   trains / metro

data of the drawing | Ø cell size: ~ 25.4 ha | street length: ~ 10.200 km

Urban Nucleus

Urban Nucleus

Definition

The Urban Nucleus is the core of the Urban Being, limited by physical boundaries.

Der Stadtkern bildet den Kern des urbanen Wesens, der durch physische Grenzen definiert wird.

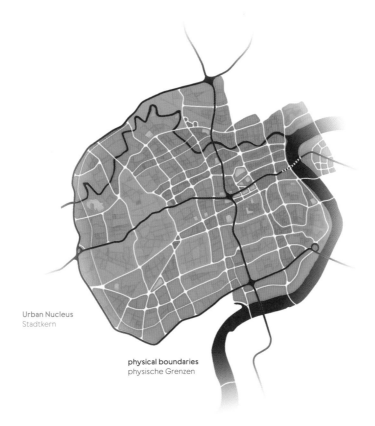

Urban Nucleus
Stadtkern

physical boundaries
physische Grenzen

London

Berlin

Shanghai

Stuttgart

Santiago de Chile

Rio de Janeiro

Munich

Mexico City

Urban Nucleus

Descriptive Essay

The Urban Nucleus is the central area of a city. It has a geographical and historical significance. Depending on the cultural area, it has different names. In China it is known as the *Urban Core*, in northern America it is called *Downtown*, in Australia it is known as *CBD (Central Business District)*, in the Netherlands it is the *Binnenstad* or *Stadcentrum* (inner city or city centre), in Germany it is the *City Core*. The different names already indicate different functions. Some cores fulfill all the social, political and cultural functions of a city. Other cores contain only a part of the functions. But the nuclei also differ greatly in size. There are large cities with small nuclei and small cities with large nuclei. Other cities have a core in a core and some have a twin core. The core is defined by physical and mental boundaries.

Physical and Mental Boundaries

The Urban Nucleus is defined by different boundaries, depending on the location and type of the city. The strongest barrier for humans is water. This physical and mental boundary is clearly visible in the Urban Nucleus of New York. Manhattan is located on an island between two rivers. The water distinctly divides the core from the surrounding city, much like Strasbourg. In Shanghai, the river

Der Stadtkern ist der zentrale Bereich einer Stadt. Er hat eine geografisch und historisch bedeutende Lage. Je nach Kulturbereich ist er unter verschiedenen Namen bekannt. In China ist es der *urbane Kern*, im Nördlichen Amerika heißt er *Downtown*, in Australien kennt man ihn unter *CBD (Central Business District)*, in den Niederlanden ist es die *Binnenstad* oder das *Stadcentrum*, in Deutschland der *Stadtkern*. Die verschiedenen Bezeichnungen deuten bereits auf unterschiedliche Funktionen hin. Manche Kerne erfüllen alle sozialen, politischen und kulturellen Funktionen einer Stadt. Andere Kerne beinhalten nur einen Teil der Funktionen. Aber auch in der Größe unterscheiden sich die Kerne stark. Es gibt große Städte mit kleinen Kernen und kleine Städte mit großen Kernen. Andere Städte besitzen einen Kern im Kern, wieder andere haben einen Doppelkern. Definiert wird der Kern über physische und mentale Grenzen.

Physische und mentalen Grenzen

Je nach Lage und Art der Stadt wird der Stadtkern durch unterschiedliche Grenzen definiert. Die stärkste Barriere für den Menschen ist das Wasser. Diese physische und mentale Grenze ist deutlich am Stadtkern von New York erkennbar. Manhattan liegt auf einer Insel zwischen zwei Flüssen. Das Wasser grenzt

Huanpu forms the eastern boundary of the core. The Urban Nucleus of Amsterdam is dense and defined by several rings of canals. In Stockholm, the water divides the core into a northern part, the old town and a southern part. In most cities, however, the nucleus is limited by urban freeways. These freeways direct a large part of the traffic around the core. Their constant flow of traffic makes them physical and mental boundaries for humans. Nevertheless, they are easier to cross than rivers and therefore form less strict boundaries. Their border effect is determined by the width and traffic intensity. Large and busy urban freeways severely cut the core from the rest of the city of Los Angeles. Other cities distribute traffic across several rings. This causes a core-in-core structure. Moscow, with its numerous ring roads, has such a structure. Shanghai and London also work according to this principle. A much rarer type is the twin nucleus. The long-term division of Berlin has created such a twin nucleus. A ring road has emerged in both parts of the city during the separation. Ring roads, as well as rivers, form a strongly defined border. They are obstacles that are difficult to overcome. Topography, on the other hand, is a much softer boundary. The further a person has to climb a hill, the more it becomes an obstacle and thus a boundary.

Topography as a boundary is rare, since cities mainly grow in flat areas. A well-known example is Rio de Janeiro. In the middle of the city lies a mountain, on which the famous *Corcovado* statue is perched. The Urban Nucleus winds around the mountain, on the narrow strip between the topography and the sea. Numerous landfills have extended this flat strip and have produced the famous districts of *Copacabana* and *Ipanema*. The Urban Nucleus is not located in the physical centre of the Urban Being, but at the coast. This is a typical feature of coastal cities. The core is defined by topography and water. The Urban Nucleus of Stuttgart is also defined by topography. It is situated in a basin and is surrounded by hills on almost all sides.
Functions of the Urban Nucleus

den Kern deutlich von der umgebenden Stadt ab, ähnlich wie in Straßburg. In Shanghai bildet der Fluss *Huanpu* ebenfalls den östlichen Abschluss des Kerns. Der Amsterdamer Stadtkern wird durch mehrere Ringe aus Grachten komprimiert und bestimmt. In Stockholm gliedert das Wasser den Kern in einen Nordteil, die Altstadt und einen Südteil. In den meisten Städten wird der Kern jedoch von Stadtautobahnen begrenzt. Diese Stadtautobahnen leiten einen Großteil des Verkehrs um den Kern herum. Ihr konstanter Verkehrsfluss macht sie zu physischen und mentalen Grenzen für den Menschen. Trotzdem sind sie einfacher zu überqueren als Flüsse und bilden daher weniger intensive Grenzen. Ihre Grenzwirkung wird durch die Breite und Verkehrsintensität bestimmt. Große und viel befahrene Stadtautobahnen wie in Los Angeles schneiden den Kern stark vom Rest der Stadt ab. Andere Städte verteilen den Verkehr auf mehrere Ringe. Dadurch entsteht eine Kern-im-Kern-Struktur. Moskau mit seinen zahlreichen Ringstraßen besitzt solch eine Struktur. Auch Shanghai und London funktionieren nach diesem Prinzip. Deutlich seltener ist der Doppelkern, also zwei Kerne nebeneinander. In Berlin ist durch die langjährige Teilung der Stadt solch ein Doppelkern entstanden, da in beiden Stadthälften eine Ringstraße entstanden ist. Sowohl Ringstraßen als auch Flüsse bilden eine klar definierte Grenze, da sie schwer überwindbare Hindernisse sind.

Topografie hat hingegen eine sanfte Grenzwirkung. Je höher ein Mensch einen Hügel erklimmen muss, umso mehr wird dieser zum Hindernis und damit zur Grenze. Da Städte bevorzugt in flachen Gebieten wachsen, ist Topografie als Grenze eher selten. Ein bekanntes Beispiel ist Rio de Janeiro. In der Mitte des Stadtkerns liegt ein Berg, auf dem die bekannte Christusstatue thront. Der Stadtkern schlängelt sich auf dem schmalen Streifen am Meer um den Berg. Zahlreiche Landaufschüttungen haben diesen flachen Streifen verbreitert und unter anderem die Stadtviertel *Copacabana* und *Ipanema* hervorgebracht. Wie bei den meisten Städten am Meer befindet sich auch in Rio der Stadtkern an der Küste. Der Kern wird durch Topografie

The Urban Nucleus differs functionally from the surrounding city. The boundaries create a special and privileged location. The core is comparable to the torso of a large organism. The essential and extraordinary functions of a city lie within. The city government, as an organizational institution, lies not only in the core, but mostly in the central cell. Cultural programmes such as operas, theaters and museums are almost invariably to be found within the core. These programmes constitute the cultural soul of the city and are an important part of its attractiveness. In addition to culture, the city fulfills a number of important tasks, which are largely located in the core. Education is part of these important tasks, which is why universities traditionally have a central location. Other institutes and social institutions also take advantage of this location. Entertainment and commerce have always been one of the advantages of the city. Collections of shops and restaurants, as well as nightlife, have historically played a central role in the city.

The core also differs by a higher density from the rest of the city. Functions with high space requirements are therefore outside. These include large university campuses, large hospitals and airports. The limited space leads to higher rents, which is why the core would simply be too expensive for such functions. Houses with gardens or the manufacturing industries have an increased space requirement as well and are located outside the core.

The core is particularly affordable for the financial industry and management. The Australian Central Business District or the American Downtown is much more oriented towards business than the European city core. An extreme can be observed in Los Angeles. The core is a strictly financial and industrial district. It is very small and contains hardly any other functions, which is one reason why L.A. is a city without a centre. These nuclei have a strong focus on trade and commerce. In contrast, many Asian urban cores have imperial palaces. In Tokyo, Beijing and Bangkok, they bear witness to the political past. Cities are often

und Wasser definiert. Der Stuttgarter Stadtkern wird ebenfalls durch Topografie definiert. Er liegt in einem Talkessel und ist auf fast allen Seiten von Hügeln umgeben.

Funktionen des Stadtkerns

Der Stadtkern unterscheidet sich von der umgebenden Stadt vor allem funktional. Durch die Abgrenzung hat er eine besondere und bevorzugte Lage. Er ist vergleichbar mit dem Torso eines großen Organismus. In ihm befinden sich oft die überlebensnotwendigen und außergewöhnlichen Funktionen, die eine Stadt ausmachen. Die Stadtregierung als ordnende und organisatorische Einheit liegt nicht nur im Kern, sondern meistens sogar in der zentralen Zelle. Auch kulturelle Angebote wie Oper, Theater und Museen sind fast ausnahmslos innerhalb des Kerns anzutreffen. Diese Funktionen bilden die kulturelle Seele der Stadt und sind wichtiger Bestandteil für ihre Attraktivität. Neben der Kultur erfüllt die Stadt eine Reihe von wichtigen Aufgaben, die sich größtenteils im Kern befinden. Bildung gehört zu diesen wichtigen Aufgaben, weswegen traditionelle Universitäten oft eine zentrale Lage haben. Auch andere Institute und soziale Einrichtungen nutzen diesen Vorteil. Unterhaltung und Kommerz gehören seit jeher zu den Vorzügen der Stadt. Ansammlungen von Läden und Gastronomie sowie Orte des Nachtlebens liegen daher ebenfalls im Kern.

Der Kern unterscheidet sich auch durch eine höhere Dichte vom Rest der Stadt. Funktionen mit hohem Platzbedarf liegen eher außerhalb. Dazu zählen neue Universitätsstädte, große Krankenhäuser und Flugplätze. Der geringe Platz führt zu höheren Mieten, weswegen der Kern für solche Funktionen schlichtweg zu teuer wäre. Auch Wohnhäuser mit Gärten oder die verarbeitende Industrie haben einen erhöhten Platzbedarf und liegen außerhalb des Kerns.

Bezahlbar ist der Kern vor allem für die Finanzindustrie und Geschäftsführungen. Der australische *Central Business District* oder die amerikanische *Downtown* ist im

religious centres. Important temples, churches and mosques are located in the nucleus as well. A well-known example is the Vatican in Rome.

The identity of the city arises mainly through these extraordinary functions. They reflect the achievements of the city. This can be seen in tourist maps. They show almost exclusively the core of the city. The attractions mostly considered to be worth visiting are not found in the outskirts, but in the core.

Urban Freeways

Depending on the traffic layout, the urban freeway can have a different influence on the quality of the nucleus. The ring around the core is the most widespread. It directs the traffic around the city centre. The lack of traffic provides space for possible qualities for humans. If urban freeways pass through the core, it gets divided. The individual areas are isolated from each other. A high amount of traffic makes the movement of the pedestrians more difficult and leads to reduced urban qualities. Increased noise and air pollution are further consequences. For high-density cities, urban freeways are necessary within the core. Elevated highways, by their nature, do not constitute physical obstacles to humans. They are impressive orientation aids and help divide the core into zones. In combination with linear parks, they can become high-quality, urban traffic arteries.

Vergleich zum europäischen Stadtkern verstärkt auf Büroflächen ausgerichtet. Ein Extrem ist in Los Angeles zu beobachten. Der Kern ist ein reines Finanz- und Industrieviertel. Er ist sehr klein und beinhaltet kaum andere Funktionen, weswegen L.A. als Stadt ohne Zentrum bezeichnet wird. Diese Stadtkerne haben einen ausgeprägten Fokus auf Handel und Kommerz. In asiatischen Städten befinden sich häufig kaiserlich Paläste im urbanen Kern. In Tokio, Peking und Bangkok zeugen sie von der politischen Vergangenheit. Städte sind oft auch religiöse Zentren. Wichtige Tempel, Kirchen und Moscheen liegen im Stadtkern. Ein bekanntes Beispiel ist der Vatikanstaat in Rom.

Die Identität der Stadt entsteht hauptsächlich durch diese außergewöhnlichen Funktionen. Sie spiegeln die Errungenschaften der Stadt wider. Erkennbar ist dies an Touristenkarten. Sie zeigen fast ausnahmslos den Kern der Stadt. Die für den Besucher lohnenswerten Attraktionen liegen nicht in den Randbereichen, sondern im Kern.

Stadtautobahnen

Je nach Verkehrsführung kann die Stadtautobahn unterschiedliche Einflüsse auf die Qualität des Stadtkerns haben. Der Ring um den Stadtkern ist am weitesten verbreitet. Seine Funktion ist es, den Verkehr um den Kern zu leiten. Der Verkehr macht Platz für mögliche Qualitäten für den Menschen. Verlaufen die Stadtautobahnen durch den Kern, wird er zerschnitten. Die einzelnen Bereiche werden voneinander isoliert. Das hohe Verkehrsaufkommen erschwert die Bewegung der Fußgänger und mindert dadurch die städtischen Qualitäten. Erhöhte Lärmbelästigung und Luftverschmutzung sind weitere Folgen. Bei hochverdichteten Städten sind Stadtautobahnen innerhalb des Kerns notwendig. Als aufgeständerte Stadtautobahnen bilden sie keine physischen Hindernisse für den Menschen. Sie sind eindrucksvolle Orientierungshilfen und zonieren den Kern. In Verbindung mit linearen Parks können sie zu qualitätvollen städtischen Verkehrsadern werden.

Green Lungs

Grüne Lungen

Green lungs have a dimension between green systems, which permeate the entire Urban Being, and neighbourhood parks. They form large green areas, which provide additional qualities to the Urban Nucleus.

The lack of large green areas, as in Shanghai for example, is often criticised by the inhabitants. The basic function of a green lung is the production of fresh air. The type of accessibility and the number of programmes can add additional qualities to the green lung. Wild green areas are barely used. They mostly consist of forested mountains within the city. In Rio de Janeiro they are used for hiking and climbing. Santiago de Chile activates the forested hill *San Cristobal* through designated public barbeque areas. Park-like green areas have a higher quality. They can be used more diversely by the residents. Broadly speaking, there are two factors that determine the success of a large green park, accessibility and usable programmes, such as lawns, water surfaces, play or sports facilities. Parks with easy access are highly used. Parks with moderate use are normally cut off through big roads or railways. The central location of *Central Park* in New York City makes it easy to reach and easily accessible. In combination with several programmes, it became a high-quality, green lung. The ring-shaped park in Adelaide surrounds the CBD and is surrounded by large streets. It has few programmes and is used moderately. It isolates the business-oriented core from the rest of the city. The relevance of accessibility can be seen in the comparison between parks in Munich and Stuttgart. Both city cores have large, central parks with numerous programmes. The easily accessible *English Garden* in Munich is highly used, while the difficult-to-reach *Schlossgarten* in Stuttgart, with its main entrances on the narrow sides of the park is only used moderately.

Grüne Lungen befinden sich von der Größe her zwischen den grünen Systemen, die das gesamte urbane Wesen durchziehen, und den Nachbarschaftsparks. Sie bilden große Grünflächen, die dem Stadtkern zusätzliche Qualitäten verleihen.

Das Fehlen großer Grünflächen, wie im Beispiel Shanghai, wird von den Bewohnern oft bemängelt. Die grundlegende Funktion einer grünen Lunge ist die Produktion von Frischluft. Die Art der Zugänglichkeit und die Anzahl der Funktionen können der grünen Lunge zusätzliche Qualitäten verleihen. Wilde Grünflächen werden kaum genutzt. Sie bestehen meist aus bewaldeten Bergen innerhalb der Stadt. In Rio de Janeiro werden sie nur zum Wandern und Klettern genutzt. Santiago de Chile aktiviert den bewaldeten Hügel *San Cristobal* durch öffentliche Grillplätze. Qualitativ hochwertiger sind parkähnliche Grünflächen. Sie können von den Bewohnern vielfältiger genutzt werden. Grundsätzlich gibt es zwei Faktoren, die den Erfolg einer großen Parkfläche bestimmen. Zum einen spielen nutzbare Funktionen wie Rasen- und Wasserflächen, Spiel- und Sportplätze eine Rolle, zum anderen ist die Zugänglichkeit von Bedeutung. Große Parks, die durch Autostraßen oder Zuggleise von der Stadt abgeschnitten sind, werden weniger genutzt als leicht zugängliche Parkflächen. Durch die zentrale Lage ist der *Central Park* in New York City leicht erreichbar und zudem einfach zugänglich. In Kombination mit mehreren Funktionen wird er zur qualitativ hochwertigen grünen Lunge. Der ringförmige Park in Adelaide umgibt den Stadtkern und ist von großen Autostraßen umgeben. Er besitzt wenige Funktionen und wird mäßig genutzt. Er isoliert den auf Büros ausgerichteten Kern vom Rest der Stadt. Am Vergleich München-Stuttgart wird die Bedeutung der Zugänglichkeit sichtbar: Beide Stadtkerne besitzen große, zentrale Parkflächen mit Funktionen. Der leicht zugängliche *Englische Garten* in München wird stark genutzt, während der schwer zugängliche *Schlossgarten* in Stuttgart nur mäßig besucht wird. Der schlauchartige *Schlossgarten* hat seine Hauptzugänge an den schmalen Seiten.

Cell Structure

Urban Cells are the areas between the main traffic arteries. Their main features are their size and shape. These features allow their classification into typologies, which occur frequently, but not necessarily every time.

Many cities have a central cell. It is usually located in the centre and is significantly larger than the surrounding cells. In many cases, it marks the birthplace of the city. In combination with pedestrian zones, a distinctive, commercial network develops within it. Linear cells usually are one or two roadblocks wide and lie between a divided main artery road. With the right road section and the appropriate traffic management, they become important sub-centres. These simple measures can stimulate the potential of every linear cell. Most of the popular inner city residential areas consist of middle-sized and small cells. The reason is their proximity to commerce and public transport, which both run alongside the main roads. The quieter streets in the interior of the cell provide residential qualities. The financial and office districts are predominantly in a structure made up of block cells. This cell typology is suitable for high-rise buildings and their increased amount of traffic.

Through cell typology, desired functions within the city can be favoured. Simple measures can enhance existing neighbourhoods, but also new plans. A good mixture of cell typologies supports a multifunctional city.

Zellstruktur

Die urbane Zelle ist der Bereich zwischen Hauptverkehrsadern. Ihre wichtigsten Merkmale sind ihre Größe und ihre Form. Dadurch lässt sie sich in Typologien einordnen, die häufig, jedoch nicht zwingend auftreten.

Viele Städte besitzen eine zentrale Zelle. Sie befindet sich meist im Zentrum und ist deutlich größer als die umgebenden Zellen. Sie markiert in vielen Fällen die Geburtsstelle der Stadt. In Kombination mit Fußgängerzonen entwickelt sich in ihrem Inneren ein ausgeprägtes kommerzielles Netzwerk. Lineare Zellen bestehen hingegen meist nur aus ein bis zwei Straßenblocks in der Breite und liegen innerhalb einer geteilten Hauptverkehrsader. Mit dem richtigen Straßenschnitt und der entsprechenden Verkehrsführung werden sie zu wichtigen Subzentren. Diese einfachen Maßnahmen können das Potenzial jeder linearen Zelle stimulieren. Vergleicht man beliebte innerstädtische Wohnviertel, bestehen sie oft aus mittleren und kleineren Zellen. Grund dafür ist die Nähe zum Kommerz und öffentlichen Nahverkehr, die an und auf den Hauptstraßen verlaufen. Die beruhigten Straßen im Inneren bieten hingegen Wohnqualitäten. Finanz- und Büroviertel liegen überwiegend in einer Struktur aus Blockzellen. Diese Zelltypologie eignet sich für Hochhäuser und ihrem erhöhtes Verkehrsaufkommen.

Durch die Zelltypologie können gewollte Funktionen innerhalb der Stadt begünstigt werden. Einfache Maßnahmen können existierende Viertel, aber auch neue Planungen aufwerten. Die Mischung aus Zelltypologien unterstützt eine multifunktionale Stadt.

Urban Nucleus

Typologies

defined by freeways
definiert durch Stadtautobahnen

defined by water
definiert durch Wasser

defined by topography
definiert durch Topografie

standard
Standard

divided
geteilt

twin core
Doppelkern

core in core
Kern im Kern

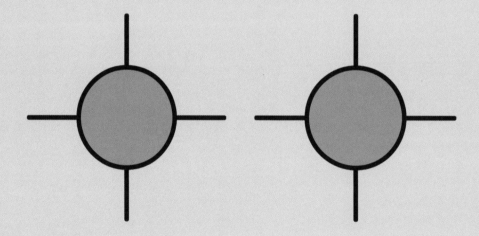

defined by freeways
definiert durch Stadtautobahnen

standard
Standard

City Centre, Munich

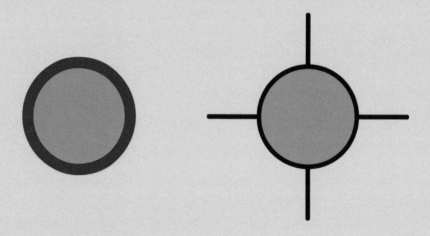

defined by water
definiert durch Wasser

standard
Standard

Central Park, New York City

defined by topography
definiert durch Topografie

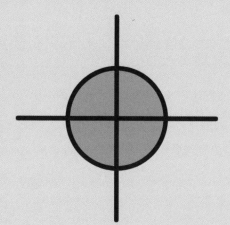

divided
geteilt

City Centre, Stuttgart

27km 24km 21km 18km 15km 12km 9km 6km 3km

Stuttgart

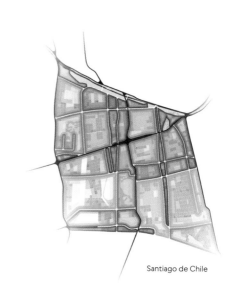

Santiago de Chile

Los Angeles

Adelaide

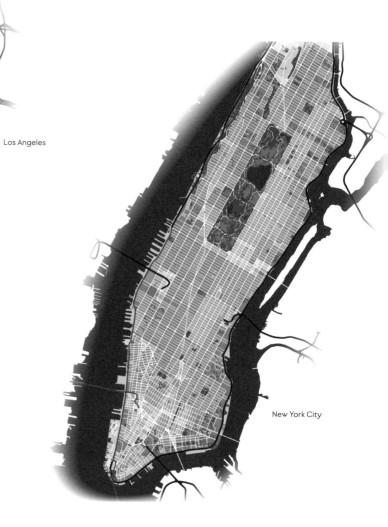

New York City

3km 6km 9km 12km 15km 18km 21km 24km 27km

Munich

Rio de Janeiro

Amsterdam

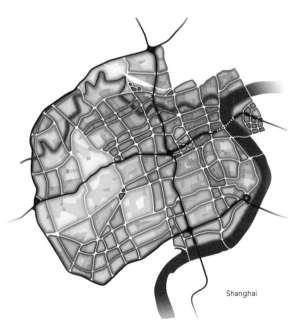

Shanghai

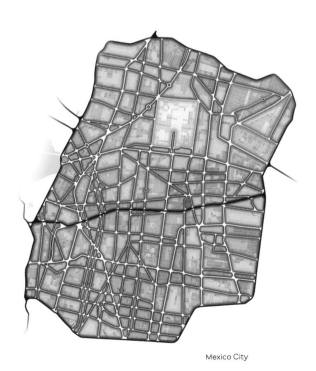

Mexico City

Urban Nucleus

Freeways

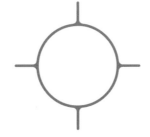

throughpass road
divided nucleus

bypass road
united nucleus

elevated throughpass road
zoned nucleus

Durchgangsstraße
geteilter Kern

Umgehungsstraße
zusammenhangender Kern

aufgeständerte
Durchgangsstraße
zonierter Kern

Despite the size of Shanghai, it is very easy to find one's way within the Urban Nucleus. This is due to the elevated highways. They divide the core into four zones and provide highly visible guidance. The five-storey intersection of the two freeways is an important transport hub and a landmark within the city. This benefits drivers and cyclists in particular. If you are in one quadrant, you can move freely within it until you come to an elevated highway. There you follow its course until you reach the desired street. The traffic flow on the bridges is undisturbed and without traffic lights. Below is enough space for cars and cyclists. Therefore the highways are the fastest connections for all traffic participants within the city. The areas under the bridges are flooded with light and have a pleasant character. The accompanying parks and high bridges allow enough light to enter. Because of the elevation, the freeways do not have a dividing effect. Pedestrians can cross the road easily at the traffic lights.

Trotz der Größe Shanghais ist es sehr einfach, sich innerhalb des Stadtkerns zu orientieren. Grund dafür sind die aufgeständerten Autobahnen. Zum einen zonieren sie den Kern in vier Teile, zum anderen sind sie unübersehbare Orientierungshilfen. Die fünfgeschossige Kreuzung der beiden Stadtautobahnen stellt einen wichtigen Verkehrsknoten und Orientierungspunkt innerhalb der Stadt dar. Das kommt vor allem Auto- und Fahrradfahrern zugute. Befindet man sich in einem Quadranten, kann man sich frei in ihm bewegen, bis man auf eine Autobahn trifft. Dort folgt man ihrem Verlauf bis an die gewünschte Straße. Während der Autoverkehr ungestört auf den Brücken fließt, befindet sich darunter Platz für Auto- und Fahrradfahrer. Das macht die Autobahnen zu den schnellsten Verbindungen für alle Verkehrsteilnehmer innerhalb der Stadt. Der Bereich unter den Brücken hat eine angenehme Wirkung. Die begleitenden Parks und die hohen Brücken lassen viel Licht einfallen. Wegen der Aufständerung hat die Stadtautobahn keine teilende Wirkung. An den Ampeln können Fußgänger die Straße einfach überqueren.

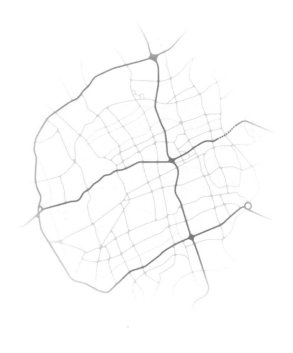

freeway ⬭ artery ⬭ capillary

Munich has a clearly defined and very functional bypass road around the Urban Nucleus. It is known as the *Middle Ring* far beyond the city limits and directs the through traffic of the Urban Being around the city core. The urban freeway has an average speed of 60 km/h with no interruptions. The ring avoids intersections with major arterial roads by passing over bridges and through tunnels. The continuous ring keeps the traffic out of the city core and facilitates orientation. The city becomes structured, easy to move in and neat.

Despite the exemplary traffic routing, Munich suffers frequent congestion. Short access roads and obstructive traffic lights are the reason. The departing traffic is stopped directly, creating a tailback. This congests the traffic on the ring road. A few weak points are able to paralyse the whole functional traffic network.

München besitzt einen klar definierten und sehr funktionalen Stadtkernring. Er ist unter dem Namen *Mittlerer Ring* bis über die Stadtgrenzen hinaus bekannt und leitet den internen Durchgangsverkehr des urbanen Wesens um den Stadtkern herum. Die Stadtautobahn hat eine mittlere Geschwindigkeit von 60 km/h und besitzt keine Unterbrechungen. Der Ring vermeidet Kreuzungen mit größeren Ausfallstraßen, indem er sie über Brücken und durch Tunnel umgeht. Der durchgängige Ring hält den Verkehr aus der Innenstadt heraus und erleichtert die Orientierung. Er strukturiert die Stadt auf einfache Weise und macht sie sehr bewegungsfreundlich und übersichtlich.

Trotz der beispielhaften Verkehrsführung kommt es zu häufigen Stauungen. Kurze Zubringerstraßen und eine verkehrsbehindernde Ampelschaltung sind der Grund dafür. Der abfahrende Verkehr wird direkt gestoppt, wodurch eine Rückstauung entsteht. Diese stoppt den Verkehrsfluss auf dem Ring und verstopft ihn. Durch wenige Schwachstellen wird so das funktionale Verkehrsnetz lahmgelegt.

○ freeway ○ artery ○ capillary

The Urban Nucleus in Stuttgart suffers from heavy traffic. A total of five major freeways and wide train tracks cut the city core into several pieces. The controversial *Stuttgart 21* railway project moves at least the tracks under ground and gives access to the large park next to it. Almost all traffic of the Urban Being is led around the central cell, right through the Urban Nucleus. The urban freeways reduce the speed to 40 km/h with interrupting traffic lights. As a result, the relatively small metropolis suffers from extreme traffic jams and stressed drivers. The timing of the traffic light is obstructive, worsening the situation. Furthermore, the pollution from the roads circulate within the valley. One possible solution would be a ring road on the valley edge, basically, a bypass around the Urban Nucleus. This would keep the traffic, as well as the pollution out of the city centre. It would mainly require political will and the understanding of the residents to implement a project like this.

Stuttgart hat eine vom Verkehr geplagte Innenstadt. Insgesamt fünf große Stadtautobahnen sowie breite Gleisanlagen zerschneiden den Stadtkern. Das umstrittene Bahnprojekt *Stuttgart 21* verlegt zumindest die Gleise unter die Erde und ermöglicht den Zugang zum großen Park daneben. Fast der gesamte Autoverkehr des urbanen Wesens wird jedoch um die zentrale Zelle herum mitten durch den Stadtkern geleitet. Die Stadtautobahnen verringern ihre Geschwindigkeit auf 40 km/h mit unterbrechenden Ampeln. So kommt es in der relativ kleinen Großstadt zu extremen Verkehrsstauungen und gestresste Autofahrer. Eine verkehrsbehindernde Ampelführung verschärft die Situation weiter, während die Abgase innerhalb des Talkessels zirkulieren. Eine mögliche Lösung wäre ein Kesselrandring, im Prinzip eine Umgehungsstraße um den Stadtkern. Diese würde sowohl den Verkehr, als auch die Abgase aus der Innenstadt heraushalten. Dazu braucht es vor allem politischen Willen sowie das Verständnis der Bevölkerung.

Stuttgart today
Stuttgart heute

Stuttgart 21
Stuttgart 21

fictitious bypass road
fiktiver Stadtkernring

 freeway artery ⭘ capillary

Urban Nucleus

Green Lungs

no green - not used
keine Grünflächen - nicht genutzt

wild green areas - barely used
wilde Grünflächen - kaum genutzt

difficult access - moderately used
schwer zugänglich - mäßig genutzt

easy access - highly used
leicht zugänglich - stark genutzt

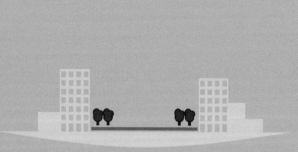

easy access - highly used
leicht zugänglich - stark genutzt

The most famous park in the world is located in the heart of the island of Manhattan. With an area of about 330 hectares, it is located in the upper middle of the large green areas. Its elongated shapecreates a long park edge. This attractive location is maximised and fully utilised by high buildings. The middle of the park is easily accessible due to the narrow width of just over 800m.

Central Park is bordered on all sides by main or secondary roads. There are no urban freeways nearby. This makes the park easily accessible and strongly accepted by the city dwellers. A variety of functions increase the quality. Numerous sports facilities on the water surfaces and large meadows activate the park. Programmes for young and old, noisy and quieter areas, as well as public and private corners support the diverse nature of the park.

Der wohl bekannteste Park der Welt liegt im Herzen der Insel *Manhattan*. Mit einer Fläche von circa 330 Hektar befindet er sich im oberen Mittelfeld der großen Grünflächen. Durch seine längliche Form entsteht ein langer Parkrand. Diese attraktive Lage wird maximiert und durch hohe Gebäude voll ausgenutzt. Auch die Mitte des Parks ist durch die schmale Breite von knapp über 800 Metern schnell erreichbar.

Der *Central Park* wird an allen Seiten von Haupt- oder Nebenstraßen begrenzt. In seiner Nähe befinden sich keinerlei Stadtautobahnen. Dadurch ist der Park leicht zugänglich und wird gut von den Stadtbewohnern angenommen. Eine Vielzahl von Funktionen steigert die Qualität. Zahlreiche Sportmöglichkeiten auf den Wasserflächen und großen Wiesen aktivieren den Park. Programme für Jung und Alt, laute und ruhigere Bereiche sowie öffentliche und privatere Ecken unterstützen die Vielschichtigkeit des Parks.

Central Park

Times Square

Madison Square

trees   park   water

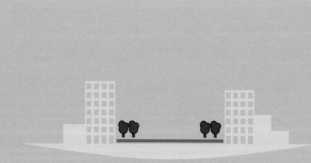

easy access - highly used
leicht zugänglich - stark genutzt

Schloss Nymphenburg

Munich has a huge variety of large green areas. Best known is the English Garden, which extends from the centre to the north. It runs along the river *Isar* and is crossed by a few branches of the river. Houses protect the park from street noise and it is easy to access from all sides. It has a variety of very different programmes. In addition to the beer gardens and restaurants, the lawns and water areas are highly used.

The *English Garden* is part of a green system along the river. In the south, the park expands at a rapid rate. Again, it is easily accessible and highly used by people.

The *Olympic Park* offers many sporting events and concerts. In addition to the water surface and gastronomy, the Olympic buildings attract many people.

Nymphenburg Palace is located a bit outside and is less accessible. It has fewer programmes and is less used.

München besitzt eine Vielzahl große Grünflächen. Am bekanntesten ist der *Englische Garten*, der sic vom Zentrum in Richtung Norden zieht. Er verläuft entlang de Flusses *Isar* und wird von einigen Nebenarmen durchzogen. De Park wird durch Häuser vom Autoverkehr geschützt und ist übe all leicht zugänglich. Er besitzt eine Vielzahl ganz unterschiedliche Funktionen. Neben den Biergärten und Restaurants werden vo allem die Liegewiesen und Wasserflächen stark frequentiert.

Der *Englische Garten* ist Teil eines Grün zugs entlang des Flusses. Im Süden weitet sich der Park an eine Stromschnelle auf. Auch hier ist er leicht zugänglich und wird gu von den Bewohnern der Stadt genutzt.

Der *Olympiapark* bietet viele Sportverar staltungen und Konzerte. Neben der Wasserfläche und der Gas ronomie ziehen vor allem die Olympiabauten Menschen an.

Das *Schloss Nymphenburg* liegt etwa außerhalb und ist schlechter zugänglich. Es hat weniger Funktio nen und wird auch weniger genutzt.

English Garden

Olympia Park

English Garden

Marienplatz

Wiesn

Flaucher

trees   park   water

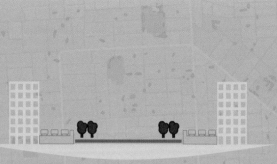

difficult access - moderately used
schwer zugänglich - mäßig genutzt

The Urban Nucleus of Adelaide is surrounded by a ring-shaped park. Furthermore, there is a wide urban freeway around the park. The freeway also incorporates North Adelaide, a separate residential area on the northern side of the river.

The wide urban freeway shields the park from the surrounding city and makes it difficult to access. The park distictly separates the city centre from the surrounding city. At its centre is the CBD, a typical Australian financial district. Due to the strong demarcation, the centre is only active on working days during the week. Weekend activities mainly take place outside the green ring. The low number of active programmes, such as sports and play facilities, reduce the use of the park further.

Der Stadtkern von Adelaide wird von einem ringförmigen Park umschlossen. Um den Park herum verläuft zudem eine breite Stadtautobahn. Die Stadtautobahn schließt auch *North Adelaide* mit ein, ein separates Wohngebiet auf der nördlichen Flussseite.

Die breite Stadtautobahn schirmt den Park von der umgebenden Stadt ab und macht ihn schwer zugänglich. Der Park grenzt den Stadtkern stark von der umgebenden Stadt ab. Im Zentrum befindet sich der für Australien typische *CBD (Central Business District)*, das Finanzviertel. Durch die starke Abgrenzung ist das Zentrum nur an Arbeitstagen unter der Woche belebt. Die Wochenendaktivitäten finden hauptsächlich außerhalb des grünen Rings statt. Die wenigen aktiven Programme wie Sport- und Spielmöglichkeiten mindern die Nutzung des Parks zusätzlich.

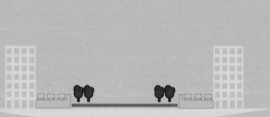

difficult access - moderately used
schwer zugänglich - mäßig genutzt

The largest park network in the Urban Nucleus of Stuttgart is known as the *Green U*. It stretches from the *Schlossplatz* in the centre, over the *Schlossgarten* to the river, where it bends to the north and extends over the *Rosensteinpark* up to the *Killesberg*.

Inside the central cell, the parks are highly used. This does not apply to the *Schlossgarten*. This park is squeezed between a big freeway and train tracks and very difficult to access. Despite its central location, the use of the park is comparatively moderate. A positive effect of the new train station, is the improved accessibility to the park.

The big green areas on the edge of the Urban Nucleus are mostly wild forests and therefore rarely used. An exception is the *Killesberg*. It is highly used thanks to appealing programmes, such as animals, a playground, a lawn, an observation tower and a carnival.

Das größte Parknetzwerk im Stuttgarter Stadtkern ist unter dem Namen *Grünes U* bekannt. Es zieht sich vom *Schlossplatz* im Zentrum über den *Schlossgarten* in Richtung Fluss. Dort knickt der Park nach Norden ab und verläuft über den *Rosensteinpark* bis zum *Killesberg*.

Während der Park in der zentralen Zelle stark genutzt wird, nimmt die Nutzung im *Schlossgarten* rapide ab. Der Park ist zwischen einer großen Stadtautobahn und Zuggleisen eingepfercht und nur sehr schwer zugänglich. Dadurch wird der zentral gelegene Park vergleichsweise mäßig genutzt. Ein positiver Effekt des geplanten Bahnhofs ist die stark verbesserte Zugänglichkeit zum Park.

Die Grünflächen am Rande des Stadtkerns sind weitgehend wilde Wälder und werden daher kaum genutzt. Eine Ausnahme bildet der *Killesberg*. Durch attraktive Funktionen wie einige Tiere, einen Spielplatz, eine Liegewiese, ein Aussichtsturm und einen Jahrmarkt wird er gut angenommen.

Killesberg

Wilhelma

Rosensteinpark

Neckar

Schlossgarten

Villa Berg

Schlossplatz

trees   park   water

San Cristobal

Parque Forestal

Plaza Italia

Cerro Santa Lucia

trees park water

© Juan Pablo Scarafia

Plaza Italia

Parque Forestal

The largest big green area is the *San Cristobal* hill. The steep slopes are undeveloped. Due to its topography, it counts as a wild green area, but with many programmes. The main attractions are the zoo and a small cog railway. The view and restaurants enliven the park as well. The *Mapocho River* winds through the city south of the hill. It is accompanied by a long green vein, the *Parque Forestal*. This green vein runs through the entire city for several kilometers.

Die größte innerstädtische Grünfläche ist der Hügel *San Cristobal*. Seine steilen Hänge sind unbebaut. Durch seine Topografie gehört er zu den wilden Grünflächen, jedoch mit zahlreichen Nutzungen. Neben dem Zoo ist vor allem die kleine Zahnradbahn eine Attraktion. Auch die Aussichtspunkte und Gastronomie beleben den Park. Südlich des Hügels windet sich der Fluss *Mapocho* durch die Stadt. Er wird von einer langen grünen Ader, dem *Parque Forestal*, begleitet. Diese grüne Ader zieht sich über mehrere Kilometer durch die gesamte Innenstadt.

San Cristobal

Shanghai
~2 % green area

urban area: ~5,350 ha
green area: ~125 ha

 trees   park   water

Rio de Janeiro
~ 33 % green area

urban area: ~2,525 ha
green area: ~1,275 ha

trees   park   water   beach

Urban Nucleus

Cellular Structure

centre - big cell
Zentrum - große Zelle

sub-centre - linear cell
Subzentrum - lineare Zelle

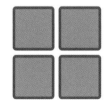

**residential district - small /
medium cells**
Wohnviertel - kleine / mittlere
Zellen

business district - small block cells
Finanzviertel - kleine Blockzellen

industrial park - big cells
Industriepark - große Zellen

12km	11km	10km	9km	8km	7km	6km	5km	4km	3km	2km	1km

centre

sub-centre

Mexico City

Providencia, Santiago de Chile

Munich

Flamengo, Laranjeiras, Catete, Rio de Janeiro

Stuttgart

Botafogo, Rio de Janeiro

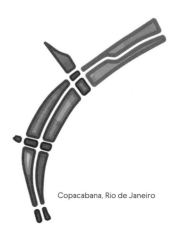

Copacabana, Rio de Janeiro

1km 2km 3km 4km 5km 6km 7km 8km 9km 10km 11km 12km

residential

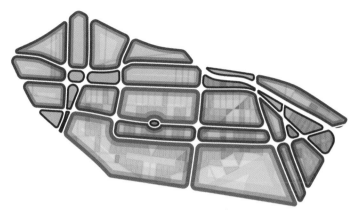

Polanco, Mexico City

business

Pudong, Shanghai

Stuttgart West

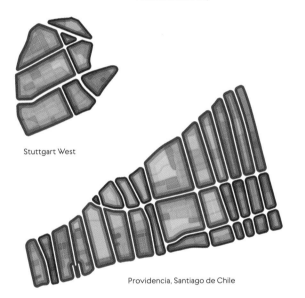

Providencia, Santiago de Chile

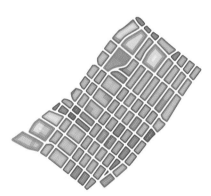

Downtown, Los Angeles

industrial

Downtown, Los Angeles

Schwabing, Munich

sub-centre
Flamengo, Laranjeiras, Catete

The unique topography of Rio has created a special Urban Nucleus. An abundance of mountains separate it into several districts. The largest united cell structure is the city centre in the north. The first sub-centre lies south of it, in the districts *Flamengo*, *Laranjeiras* and *Catete*. Each of these neighbourhoods has a linear cell, which meet in a block cell. This block cell forms the central point of the sub-centre. Further south, a linear cell structure runs through the valley of *Botafogo*. The cells densify towards the bay and again form the central point of the sub-centre. Even *Copacabana* consists of linear cells, which are grouped around a block cell. This block cell has the highest commercial density and is again an important point of the district.

The numerous and strongly developed sub-centres are quite peculiar. They are a strong competition for the centre and include not only the typical residences, but also commerce, gastronomy and offices. The linear cells bundle the traffic flow and concentrate it in the block cell. The high concentration of people, cars and public transport is an important condition for the sub-centres survival.

sub-centre
Botafogo

Die einzigartige Topografie Rios hat einen besonderen Stadtkern entstehen lassen. Durch die vielen Berge wird er in mehrere Viertel zergliedert. Der größte zusammenhängende Zellverband liegt im Norden, in der Stadtmitte. Daran schließt sich südlich das Subzentrum aus *Flamengo*, *Laranjeiras* und *Catete* an. Jedes dieser Stadtviertel besitzt eine lineare Zelle. Die linearen Zellen treffen sich in einer Blockzelle. Diese Blockzelle bildet den zentralen Punkt des Subzentrums. Weiter südlich zieht sich eine lineare Zellstruktur durch das Tal von *Botafogo*. Zur Bucht hin verdichten sich die Zellen, wodurch auch hier wieder der zentrale Punkt ausgeformt wird. Auch das Subzentrum *Copacabana* besteht aus linearen Zellen, die sich um eine Blockzelle gruppieren. Die Blockzelle hat die höchste Dichte an Läden und bildet auch hier einen wichtigen Punkt des Subzentrums.

Auffällig sind die zahlreichen und stark ausgeformten Subzentren. Sie bilden eine starke Konkurrenz zum Zentrum und beinhalten neben dem klassischen Wohnen viel Kommerz, Gastronomie und Büros. Die linearen Zellen bündeln den Verkehrsstrom und konzentrieren ihn in den Blockzellen. Die hohe Konzentration an Personen, Auto- und öffentlichem Nahverkehr ist eine wichtige Voraussetzung für das Überleben der Subzentren.

sub-centre
Copacabana

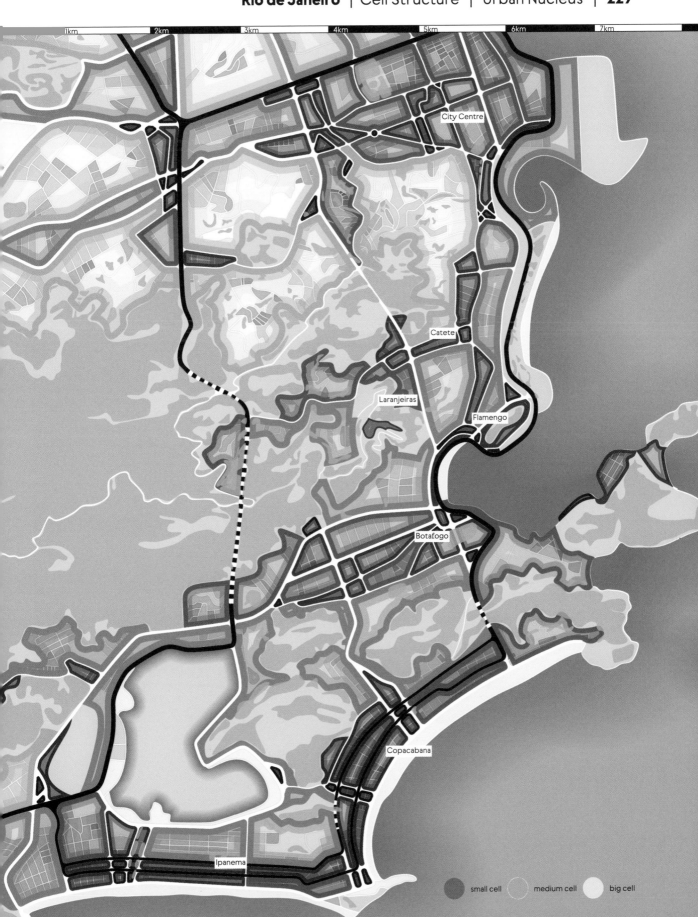

1km 2km 3km 4km 5km 6km 7km

City Centre

Catete

Laranjeiras

Flamengo

Botafogo

Copacabana

Ipanema

small cell   medium cell   big cell

central cell

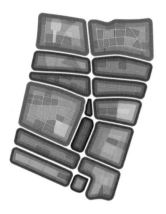

residential cells
Maxvorstadt, Schwabing

residential cells
Lehel

The largest Urban Cell in the nucleus is the central cell, which is located in the physical centre of the city. It is a commercial cell with high pedestrian traffic. Several major axes were converted to pure pedestrian areas, resulting in the large size of the cell. It is surrounded by much smaller cells, with the exception of the cell in the north, including the park.

The size of the Urban Cells of the popular residential district of *Schwabing* and *Maxvorstadt* is also interesting. The residential cells have a small to medium size of about 20 to 30 hectares. Two small cells are located almost in the middle. They have increased commerce and gastronomy. East of the centre lies *Lehel*, another popular residential area with small Urban Cells.

Die größte urbane Zelle im Stadtkern ist die zentrale Zelle. Sie befindet sich in der physischen Mitte der Stadt und ist eine kommerzielle Zelle mit hohem Fußgängeranteil. Mehrere Hauptachsen wurden in reine Fußgängerzonen umgewandelt, wodurch ihre Größe entstanden ist. Sie wird von weit kleineren Zellen umgeben, mit Ausnahme der Zelle im Norden, die den Park beinhaltet.

Interessant ist auch die Zellgröße der beliebten Wohnviertel *Schwabing* und *Maxvorstadt*. Die Wohnzellen haben eine kleine bis mittlere Größe von circa 20 bis 30 Hektar. Relativ mittig befinden sich zwei kleine Zellen, die einen erhöhten Anteil an Kommerz und Gastronomie besitzen. Östlich des Zentrums liegt der *Lehel*, ebenfalls ein beliebtes Wohnviertel mit kleinen urbanen Zellen.

1km 2km 3km 4km 5km 6km 7km

Schwabing

City Centre

Lehel

small cell   medium cell   big cell

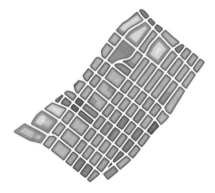

financial district

The Urban Nucleus of Los Angeles is very small in relation to the Urban Being. It is limited by the typical multi-lane freeways and consists mainly of two cell structures. To the west is a rectangular block cell structure. These cells contain all high-rise buildings of the Urban Nucleus. It is the location of the financial district and the city government.

The eastern part of the core is crossed by the *Los Angeles River*. It is bordered by train tracks. The cells are far bigger than in the west of the core and highly industrialised. There are almost no residential areas within the nucleus. Only the northeast edge has a narrow strip of residential development.

industrial park

Der Stadtkern in Los Angeles ist im Verhältnis zum urbanen Wesen sehr klein. Er wird durch die für Los Angeles typischen mehrspurigen Stadtautobahnen begrenzt und setzt sich hauptsächlich aus zwei Zellverbänden zusammen. Im Westen liegt ein rechtwinkliger Blockzellenverband. Innerhalb dieses Verbandes stehen alle Hochhäuser des Stadtkerns. Hier befindet sich neben dem Finanzviertel auch die Regierung der Stadt.

Der Osten des Kerns wird vom Los Angeles River durchzogen. Er ist von Bahngleisen gesäumt. Die Zellen sind um ein Vielfaches größer als im Westen des Kerns und stark industriell geprägt. Wohnviertel gibt es im Stadtkern fast gar nicht. Nur der nordöstliche Rand besitzt einen schmalen Streifen mit Wohnbebauung.

1km 2km 3km 4km 5km 6km 7km

Financial District

Arts District

Fashion District

small cell   medium cell   big cell

Amsterdam has a highly dense Urban Nucleus. With a length of about three kilometers, it is one of the smallest in the world. The canals are the reason for this. They form strong barriers for pedestrians and cars. There is little space in the small nucleus, which is why the bicycle has become the main means of transport for the residents.

The core is divided into two areas. The inner part forms the commercial centre, while the canals in the outer area are mostly used for residences. The main traffic arteries run radially outwards in the residential areas. They have increased commerce and gastronomy. The streets along the canals are quieter and suitable as residential streets.

The centre is divided into two areas. The shopping streets lie to the west, which attracts people during the day. The red light district is located in the geometric centre, which is particularly lively at night. The strong densification results in an extremely high density of commerce and gastronomy. The high density and the day and night functions make Amsterdam the city that really never sleeps.

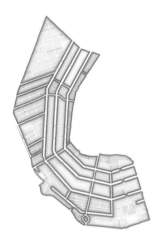

residential area

Amsterdam hat einen stark komprimierten Stadtkern. Mit einer Länge von circa drei Kilometern gehört er zu den kleinsten weltweit. Grund dafür sind die Grachten. Sie bilden starke Barrieren für Fußgänger und Autos. In dem kleinen Stadtkern gibt es wenig Platz, weswegen das Fahrrad zum Hauptverkehrsmittel für die Bewohner geworden ist.

Der Kern gliedert sich in zwei Bereiche: Der innere Teil bildet das kommerzielle Zentrum, während der Bereich um die Grachten überwiegend zum Wohnen benutzt wird. In den Wohnbereichen verlaufen die Hauptverkehrsadern radial nach außen. Sie haben erhöhten Kommerz und Gastronomie. Die Straßen entlang der Grachten sind ruhiger und eignen sich als Wohnstraßen.

commercial centre

Das Zentrum gliedert sich in zwei Bereiche: Im Westen liegen die Einkaufsstraßen, die tagsüber Menschen anziehen. In der geometrischen Mitte liegt das Rotlichtviertel, das vor allem nachts belebt ist. Durch die starke Komprimierung entsteht eine extrem hohe Dichte an Kommerz und Gastronomie. Die hohe Dichte und die Tag- und Nachtfunktionen machen Amsterdam zu der Stadt, die wirklich niemals schläft.

1km 2km 3km 4km 5km 6km 7km

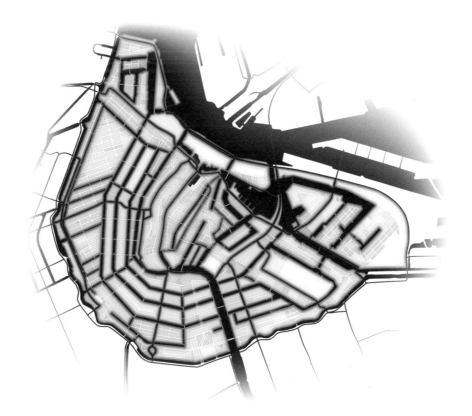

small cell   medium cell   big cell

Urban Cell

Urban Cell

Definition

The Urban Cell is the area between the main artery roads within the city.

Die urbane Zelle ist der Bereich zwischen den Hauptverkehrsadern innerhalb der Stadt.

Urban Cell
Urbane Zelle

main artery roads
Hauptverkehrsadern

Urban Cell

Descriptive Essay

Cells are the smallest living units of any organism. They form a system that can sustain itself. Within the Urban Being, the Urban Cell is the unit in which individual resident can sustain themselfs. Simple cells have few functions such as living, working and shopping. Cells with a highly developed structure have further functions such as public transport, gastronomic offerings, commerce, parks, squares or street hierarchies. Urban Cells are neighbourhoods, as well as organizational units, in which the everyday life of the resident takes place. They are defined by main artery roads, sometimes by train tracks, canals or green corridors. Different cell typologies emerge, depending on traffic management, size and use.

Origin and Benefits of the Urban Cell

The basic idea of the Urban Cell is based on the *LTAs (Local Transport Areas)* by Christopher Alexander. In his book, *A Pattern Language*, he describes areas in the city that have no through traffic, containing only local traffic. The areas with local traffic, the local transport areas, form the basis for the Urban Cell. In his approach, Alexander describes main artery roads as physical and mental boundaries. City residents tend to move within the *LTA*, or the Urban Cell as it is called in this book.

Zellen sind die kleinsten lebenden Einheiten eines jeden Organismus. Sie bilden ein System, das sich selbst erhalten kann. Innerhalb des urbanen Wesens ist die urbane Zelle die Einheit, in der ein Bewohner selbstständig überleben kann. Einfache Zellen besitzen wenige Funktionen wie Wohnen, Arbeiten und Einkaufsmöglichkeiten. Zellen mit einer höher entwickelten Struktur haben weitere Funktionen wie ÖPNV, Gastronomie, Kommerz, Parks, Plätze oder Straßenhierarchien. Urbane Zellen sind Nachbarschaften, aber auch Organisationseinheiten, in denen sich der Alltag der Bewohner abspielt. Sie werden meistens von Hauptverkehrsadern, manchmal auch von Gleisen, Kanälen oder Grünzügen begrenzt. Je nach Verkehrsführung, Größe und Nutzung entstehen verschiedene Zelltypologien.

Ursprung und Vorzüge der urbanen Zelle

Der Grundgedanke der urbanen Zelle basiert auf den *LTAs (Local Transport Areas)* von Christopher Alexander. In seinem Buch *A Pattern Language* beschreibt er Bereiche in der Stadt, durch die kein Durchgangsverkehr verläuft. In ihnen bewegt sich nur lokaler Verkehr. Die Bereiche mit lokalem Verkehr, die *Local Transport Areas*, bilden die Grundlage für die urbane Zelle. In seinem Ansatz beschreibt

The understanding of a neighbourhood or urban quarter depends on the perception of people. How big is it? Are city centres neighbourhoods as well? Is an industrial area an urban quarter? A scientific approach on the necessities of urban quarters is impossible without a distinct definition of the term. The benefit of Urban Cells is their clear definition. Main artery roads or other borders clearly define the areas in between. A categorisation into several typologies becomes possible. Industrial cells have a different structure from central or residential cells. Comparing cells of the same type allows determination of the ideal cell size, programmes and structure, as well as their disadvantages. Successful residential cells, for example, have similar sizes. But, there is another benefit that makes the Urban Cell a strong planning tool. Main artery roads around the cell feature fast traffic and have a limiting effect on pedestrians. They are part of the city of cars. The Urban Cell has slow traffic and is part of the city of humans. Due to the boundary effect, the everyday life of the residents takes place within the cell. This determines the need for programmes. Residential cells, for example, have a need for kindergartens and supermarkets.

Every cell typology follows a certain structural logic. This structure can be applied to retrofit or enhance existing cells. It also can achieve intended urban qualities in newly planned quarters. Dysfunctional new districts are often the result of a wrong combination of structure and use. For example, if offices are forced into a central cell typology, the district needs a long time to develop urban qualities. The slow development of qualities therefore is an indicator of dysfunctionality.

Alexander Hauptverkehrsadern als physische und mentale Grenzen. Bewohner der Stadt tendieren also dazu, sich innerhalb der *LTA* bzw. der urbanen Zelle zu bewegen.

Die Begriffe Nachbarschaft oder Stadtquartier werden je nach Wahrnehmung der Menschen ganz unterschiedlich interpretiert. Wie groß sind sie? Ist die Innenstadt eine Nachbarschaft? Sind industrielle Gebiete Stadtquartiere? Eine wissenschaftliche Untersuchung der Bedürfnisse eines Stadtquartiers ist ohne eine einheitliche Definition unmöglich. Der Vorteil der urbanen Zelle ist ihre einheitliche Definition. Der Bereich zwischen Hauptverkehrsadern und anderen Grenzen ist klar definiert. Eine Kategorisierung in verschiedene Typologien wird möglich. Zum Beispiel unterscheiden sich Industriezellen strukturell von zentralen Zellen. Durch den Vergleich mehrerer Zellen derselben Typologie lassen sich Struktur, Funktionen und ideale Zellgröße ermitteln. Erfolgreiche Wohnzellen haben ähnliche Größen. Es gibt jedoch noch einen weiteren Vorteil, der die urbane Zelle zu einem starken stadtplanerischen Instrument macht. Hauptverkehrsadern um die Zelle haben schnellen Verkehr und einen begrenzenden Effekt auf Fußgänger. Sie sind Teil der Stadt der Autos. Die urbane Zelle hat langsamen Verkehr und ist Teil der Stadt der Menschen. Durch den Grenzeffekt spielt sich der Alltag der Bewohner vorwiegend in der Zelle ab. Dadurch lässt sich der Bedarf der Funktionen bestimmen. Wohnzellen zum Beispiel benötigen einen Kindergarten und einen Supermarkt.

Jede Zelltypologie folgt einer gewissen strukturellen Logik. Diese Struktur lässt sich auf existierende Zellen anwenden, um sie nachzurüsten oder zu verbessern. Sie kann auch gewollte städtische Qualitäten in neu geplanten Stadtvierteln erzeugen. Disfunktionale neue Stadtviertel sind meistens das Resultat einer falschen Kombination aus Struktur und Nutzung. Werden zum Beispiel Büros in eine zentrale Zelltypologie gezwungen, werden sich städtische Qualitäten erst über einen langen Zeitraum entwickeln. Das notwendige „Einleben" eines neuen Stadtviertels ist ein Indikator für Dysfunktionalität.

Typologies

Typologien

The cell typologies are mainly determined by the size and street hierarchy. Their qualities are influenced by urban programmes.

The smallest cell consists of only one block. This block cell is surrounded by main traffic arteries. An assembly of these block cells is suitable for financial districts. The best known example is *Manhattan*, but also the financial districts of Los Angeles, Melbourne, Taipei or Shanghai have this cell structure. Their main roads are busy and fast, similar to the use of the district. They are not suitable for neighbourhood parks and other quieter functions. The street noise does not affect the use of the offices. In addition, the single block can easily be accessed from all sides, making it ideal for high-rise buildings. A concentration of high-rise buildings causes a high volume of traffic during rush hours. The large roads can transport many people. Block cells always have an increased traffic flow. This characteristic renders them ideal in their function as a sub-centre. If a block cell is combined with linear cells, the traffic and the pedestrian frequency increases. The public transport stations become closer and commerce starts to grow. The sub-centre becomes enlivened. Linear cells have the same effect and can be used as a sub-centres as well. They work perfectly within a divided main artery road. If a main artery is divided into two one-way streets, a linear cell emerges in between. They unfold their potential through a width of one to two blocks. The divided traffic causes thinner streets, which can be easily crossed. Therefore, the streets are used more by people and commerce arises. The linear cell in *Copacabana*, a sub-centre of the city, has more shops per kilometer than the main shopping street in central Munich. Public transport, sufficient space for pedestrians and segregated vehicular traffic are necessary to make a linear cell a sub-centre.

The residential cell should offer quiet living areas, but also be connected to the active functions of the city. Unlike

Die Zelltypologien werden vor allem durch die Straßenhierarchie und die Größe bestimmt. Ihre Qualitäten werden durch die städtischen Programme beeinflusst.

Die kleinsten Zellen bestehen aus nur einem Straßenblock. Dieser Straßenblock ist von Hauptverkehrsadern umgeben. Ein Verband aus diesen Blockzellen eignet sich für Finanzviertel. Am bekanntesten ist Manhattan, aber auch die Finanzviertel in Los Angeles, Melbourne, Taipeh oder Shanghai besitzen diesen Blockzellenverband. Die Hauptstraßen sind geschäftig und schnell, wie auch die Nutzung des Viertels. Sie eignen sich nicht für Nachbarschaftsparks und andere ruhigere Funktionen. Der Straßenlärm beeinträchtigt die Nutzung der Büros nicht. Hinzukommt, dass der Straßenblock von allen Seiten erschlossen werden kann, eine ideale Voraussetzung für Hochhäuser. Eine Konzentration von Hochhäusern hat auch einen hohen Verkehrsfluss zu den Stoßzeiten zur Folge. Durch die großen Straßen können viele Menschen transportiert werden. Blockzellen haben immer einen erhöhten Verkehrsfluss. Diese Eigenschaft kommt ihnen in der Funktion als Subzentrum entgegen. Wird eine Blockzelle mit linearen Zellen kombiniert, verdichtet sich der Verkehr und die Fußgängerfrequenz erhöht sich. Dadurch liegen die Haltestellen des öffentlichen Nahverkehrs näher beieinander und es entstehen Läden. Das Subzentrum wird belebt. Auch lineare Zellen haben diesen Effekt und bilden mit der richtigen Struktur starke Subzentren. Sie funktionieren ideal innerhalb einer geteilten Hauptverkehrsader. Wird eine Hauptverkehrsader in zwei Einbahnstraßen geteilt, entsteht dazwischen die lineare Zelle. Sie entfaltet ihr Potenzial bei einer Breite von ein bis zwei Straßenblocks. Durch die Separation des Verkehrs sind die halbierten Straßen einfach zu überqueren. Daher werden die Straßen stärker von den Menschen angenommen und Kommerz entsteht. Die lineare Zelle in Copacabana, ein Subzentrum der Stadt, hat mehr Läden pro Kilometer als die Haupteinkaufsstraße im Münchener Zentrum. Öffentlicher

the city's edge cell, it is the cell typology for inner-city living. The road hierarchy, or the quality of the urban nutrition arteries, has a great influence. A well-structured residential cell should include slow traffic streets. The Woonerf system describes such measures. Traffic noise is avoided and safety increases. The slow traffic and the traffic at rest, the parking, should be close together. They do not interfere with each other. Providing the parking inside the cell makes sense, since it is located close to the housing, where it is needed. The slow speed gives the streets the potential to be used by people. This works best with simple programmes. Simple sports equipment, a bench, a small playground or some water are enough. Up to a point, the quality of living in the neighbourhood increases with a higher amount of features in the road. Trees have a positive effect as well. They provide shade and fresh air and increase the privacy between houses. The quality of the residential cell or the neighbourhood can be increased by further programmes. A central park offers opportunities for recreation, sporting activities and social encounters. A supermarket, cafes and restaurants, a school and kindergartens, a medical centre and pharmacies, culture and office space increase the quality of the cell and thus the quality of life of the residents. The main roads and their public transport connect the cell quickly to the rest of the city. In residential cells, the public transport is mostly located on the main traffic arteries. The public transport brings in many pedestrians. Wide sidewalks offer space for those pedestrians and strongly support the formation of a commercial network. Shops and public transport add value to the quality of the residential cell, when they are in walkable distance to the housing. The ideal size of a residential cell is about 400 m to 800 m, based on the analysed neighbourhoods. Popular residential areas like *Schwabing* in Munich, *Polanco* in Mexico City, *Providencia* in Santiago de Chile or *Stuttgart West* all consist of medium and small cells. The smaller cells often form a slight sub-centre.
Central cells also have a street hierarchy with slower capillary streets.

Nahverkehr, ausreichend Platz für Fußgänger und ein geteilter Verkehrsfluss sind notwendig, um ein Subzentrum in der linearen Zelle entstehen zu lassen.

Die Wohnzelle sollte ruhige Wohnqualitäten bieten, aber auch an die aktiven Bereiche der Stadt angebunden sein. Anders als die Stadtrandzelle ist sie die Zelltypologie für innerstädtisches Wohnen. Die Straßenhierarchie, also die Qualität der urbanen Nährstoffadern, hat einen großen Einfluss. Eine qualitative Wohnzelle hat stark verkehrsberuhigte Straßen im Inneren. Das Woonerf System beschreibt genau solche Maßnahmen. Dadurch wird Verkehrslärm vermieden und die Sicherheit erhöht. Der langsame Verkehr und der stehende Verkehr, das Parken, sollten beieinanderliegen, da sie sich nicht behindern. Befinden sich die Parkplätze im Zellinneren, liegen sie auch in der Nähe der Wohnungen. Dort werden sie gebraucht. Durch die langsame Geschwindigkeit erhällt die Straße das Potenzial von den Menschen genutzt zu werden. Dies funktioniert am besten mit Funktionen: Ein paar Sportgeräte, eine Sitzbank, ein kleiner Spielplatz oder etwas Wasser genügen schon. Bis zu einem Punkt erhöht sich die Wohnqualität der Zelle, je mehr die Straße bietet. Auch Bäume haben eine positive Wirkung. Sie spenden Schatten und frische Luft und sind gleichzeitig Sichtschutz zwischen den Häusern. Die Qualität der Wohnzelle bzw. der Nachbarschaft lässt sich durch Programme erhöhen: Ein zentraler Park bietet Möglichkeiten zur Naherholung, zu sportlicher Betätigung und sozialen Aktivitäten. Ein Supermarkt, Cafés und Restaurants, eine Schule und Kindergärten, ein Ärztehaus und Apotheken, Kultur und Büroflächen erhöhen die Qualität der Zelle zusätzlich und damit die Lebensqualität der Bewohner. Über die Hauptstraßen wird die Zelle schnell an den Rest der Stadt angebunden und auch der öffentliche Nahverkehr sollte bei einer Wohnzelle auf den Hauptstraßen verlaufen. In Kombination mit ausreichend breiten Gehwegen und Arkaden entwickeln sie viel Kommerz. All diese Nutzungen werten die Qualität der Wohnzelle auf, wenn sie in geringer Distanz zu diesen Wohnungen liegt. Wohnzellen sollten

Their slowest streets are bustling pedestrian zones. Not all cities have a central cell, but when they do exist, they have similarities. Mostly, it is the largest cell in the Urban Nucleus and lies in the physical centre. The cell is often the birthplace of the city and hence its oldest part. It is the heart of the city. Following the advent of the car, many major axes in the central cells were converted back to pure pedestrian areas. The tendency towards several pedestrian areas in the central cell can be observed worldwide. In general, the cell contains many features and is visited by many people. Although the speed inside it is slow, the cell is very active. Public transport should bring people exactly to the centre. The high pedestrian frequency results in a strong commercial network. Its central location also attracts offices and cultural establishments. The central cell is therefore a commercial and cultural cell.

Well-connected large cells are suited for industry. These cell types offer plenty of room and can be further divided depending on the requirements. The proximity to large urban nutrition arteries such as highways, railroads or rivers are beneficial. Connection via public transport gives workers a sustainable alternative to the car.

daher eine mittlere Größe von circa 400 bis 800 Metern haben. Beliebte Wohnviertel wie *Schwabing* in München, *Polanco* in Mexiko-Stadt, *Providencia* in Santiago de Chile oder *Stuttgart West* bestehen alle aus mittleren und kleinen Zellen. Die kleinen Zellen bilden dabei oft ein leichtes Subzentrum.

Auch zentrale Zellen haben eine Straßenhierarchie mit langsameren Kapillarstraßen. Ihre langsamsten Straßen sind geschäftige Fußgängerzonen. Nicht jede Stadt besitzt eine zentrale Zelle, doch wenn es diese Zellen gibt, haben sie Ähnlichkeiten. Meist ist die Zelle sie die größte im Stadtkern und befindet sich in der physischen Mitte. Die Zelle ist oft der Geburtsort der Stadt und daher auch ihr ältester Teil. Sie ist sozusagen das Herz der Stadt. Zuerst kam der Siegeszug der Autos. Danach wurden viele Hauptbewegungsachsen im Inneren dieser Zellen wieder zu reinen Fußgängerzonen umgewandelt. Die Tendenz zu einem ausgeprägten Fußwegenetz in der zentralen Zelle ist weltweit zu beobachten. In der Regel besitzt die Zelle viele Funktionen und wird von sehr vielen Menschen besucht. Obwohl es im Inneren eine langsame Geschwindigkeit gibt, ist die Zelle sehr geschäftig. Der öffentliche Nahverkehr bringt die Menschen idealerweise genau in die Mitte. Die hohe Fußgängerfrequenz hat ein stark verdichtetes kommerzielles Netzwerk zur Folge. Ihre zentrale Lage zieht auch Büros und Kultur an. Die zentrale Zelle ist also eine kommerzielle und kulturelle Zelle.

Für Industrie eignen sich gut angebundene große Zellen. Diese Zelltypen bieten genug Platz und lassen sich je nach Anforderungen weiter unterteilen. Die Nähe zu großen urbanen Nährstoffadern wie Autobahnen, Zuggleisen oder Flüssen ist von erheblichem Vorteil. Eine Anbindung über den öffentlichen Nahverkehr ermöglicht den Arbeitern eine nachhaltige Alternative zum Auto.

Urban Nutrition Arteries

Urbane Nährstoffadern

On the scale level of the Urban Cell, the roads are the most important nutrition arteries. The most common roads can be roughly divided into two types, the fast main arteries and slow capillary streets.

The purpose of the main artery is to keep the traffic moving as quickly as possible. They are used for longer distances within the city. The different speeds of the traffic participants should be physically separated to keep the traffic flow consistent. A separate lane for buses will benefit both buses and cars. Trams and traffic lights should disrupt traffic as little as possible. At major intersections, where traffic lights are needed, the foot traffic can cross at ground level. Otherwise, bridges or tunnels are of advantage. Parked cars considerably slow down the fast traffic and should be avoided. Bike paths are best protected by small walls or trees. The slower bikes don't interfere with the cars and cycling becomes safer. Pedestrians should be given sufficient space too. Many pedestrians move on the main artery roads because of the public transport. Therefore, the main arteries have a high potential for commerce. A weather protected arcade supports the commercial network at all times. Green strips along these roads provide shade and visual enhancement. Commerce, public transport and fast traffic are the main components of these arteries.

Capillary streets function the opposite way. Their purpose is to slow down the traffic to pedestrian speed. Parked cars, crossing pedestrians and cyclists in the middle of the streets have just that effect. A continuous pavement, a winding road layout and other traffic calming measures are suitable for these streets. The slow traffic streets work well in combination with trees, linear parks, as well as gastronomic offerings and sporting programmes. They have an intimate character and are mainly used in residential cells.

Auf der Maßstabsebene der urbanen Zelle sind vor allem die Straßen die wichtigsten Nährstoffadern. Die häufigsten Straßen lassen sich grob in zwei Typen unterscheiden: die schnellen Hauptverkehrsadern und die langsamen Kapillarstraßen.

Die Aufgabe der Hauptverkehrsadern ist es, den Verkehr so schnell wie möglich vorwärts zu bringen. Sie werden für größere Distanzen innerhalb der Stadt genutzt. Um den Verkehrsfluss nicht zu behindern, sollten die unterschiedlichen Geschwindigkeiten räumlich getrennt sein. Eine eigene Spur für den Busverkehr kommt Bus und Autos zugute. Auch die Tram und Ampeln sollten den Autoverkehr so wenig wie möglich stören. An großen Kreuzungen, wo Ampeln nötig sind, kann auch der Fußverkehr ebenerdig passieren. Ansonsten sind Brücken oder Tunnel von Vorteil. Parkende Autos bremsen den Verkehr stark aus und sollten unbedingt vermieden werden. Fahrradwege werden am besten durch kleine Mauern oder Bäume geschützt. Dadurch wird das Radfahren sicher und der langsamere Radverkehr kommt den Autos nicht in die Quere. Auch für Fußgänger sollte ausreichend Platz sein. Da sich der öffentliche Nahverkehr oft auf Hauptstraßen befindet, bewegen sich dort auch viele Menschen. Daher haben Hauptverkehrsadern ein hohes Potenzial für Kommerz. Verläuft der Gehweg unter einer Arkade, ist dieser Effekt bei jedem Wetter spürbar. Grünstreifen entlang dieser Straßen dienen hauptsächlich der Verschattung und dem visuellen Eindruck. Kommerz, öffentlicher Personennahverkehr und schneller Verkehr sind die Hauptbestandteile dieser Verkehrsadern.

Kapillarstraßen funktionieren auf gegensätzliche Weise. Sie sollten den Verkehr auf Fußgängergeschwindigkeit ausbremsen. Parkende Autos, überquerende Fußgänger und Radfahrer in der Mitte der Straßen haben eben diesen Effekt. Ein durchgängiger Bodenbelag, eine gewundene Straßenführung und andere verkehrsberuhigende Maßnahmen eignen sich für diese Straßen. Die langsamen

Parks

A good park improves the quality of an Urban Cell significantly. It serves as a social gathering place throughout the neighbourhood, provides space for sporting and cultural activities and influences the microclimate in a positive way.

The ideal size of a neighbourhood park for an Urban Cell is about 200 to 400 meter. The intensity of how a park is used by the residents differs depending on several factors. An important factor for the quality of the park is its location in relation to the main artery roads. If a park is enclosed by main thoroughfares, it is barely used by the people. Since the roads are difficult to cross, the park is difficult to reach. Instead of passing through the park, it is easier to get around it. People do not arrive in the park by chance, but need to make a conscious decision to go to it. Within the park, the traffic noise can be heard from all sides. A park is usually associated with rest and relaxation. Traffic noise is perceived as disturbing. The park cell is therefore the worst location for a park. If the park is located in a larger cell, but next to a main thoroughfare, its use increases. The side towards the main street has less people, while the side towards the cell centre is more lively. The better the park is protected from the road, the more it is used. The ideal location of the park is therefore at the centre of the cell. There is no unpleasant traffic noise, only the noise of the park users. There are several strategies to activate parks further. The coincidental use has a very high potential. The *Parque Mexico* is located in the middle of a residential cell. On one side is a large supermarket, on the other public transport. The residents of the cell cross the park on a daily basis. The coincidental use increases. A plaza is located at the main axis of movement through the park. Small markets and concerts activate this plaza. The residents automatically pass by these social events and use them. The combination of coincidental use and a functioning programme, the plaza, activates the park. Pleasant walkways and a few water areas with benches enliven the park

Straßen funktionieren gut in Kombination mit Bäumen, linearen Parks, aber auch mit Gastronomie und sportlichen Funktionen. Die Straßen haben einen intimen Charakter und werden vor allem in Wohnzellen verwendet.

Parks

Ein guter Park kann die Qualität einer urbanen Zelle erheblich verbessern. Er dient als sozialer Treffpunkt der gesamten Nachbarschaft, bietet Raum für sportliche und kulturelle Aktivitäten und beeinflusst das Mikroklima auf positive Weise.

Um als Nachbarschaftspark für eine urbane Zelle zu dienen, sollte der Park eine Größe von circa 200 bis 400 Metern haben. Wie gut ein Park von den Bewohnern angenommen wird, ist jedoch sehr unterschiedlich. Ein wichtiger Faktor für die Qualität des Parks ist seine Lage in Bezug auf die Hauptverkehrsadern. Wird ein Park von Hauptverkehrsadern umschlossen, wird er wenig von den Menschen genutzt. Wie eine Blockzelle wird auch die Parkzelle von Autostraßen umgeben. Da die Straßen schwer zu überqueren sind, ist auch der Park schwer zu erreichen. Statt den Park zu durchqueren, ist es meist einfacher, ihn zu umgehen. Man gelangt nicht zufällig in den Park, sondern muss die bewusste Entscheidung treffen, ihn aufzusuchen. Innerhalb des Parks ist von allen Seiten Verkehrslärm zu hören. Da ein Park mit Erholung und Entspannung verbunden wird, wirkt dieser Lärm störend. Die Parkzelle ist damit die schlechteste Lage für einen Park. Liegt der Park in einer größeren Zelle, jedoch an einer Hauptverkehrsader, wird er schon mehr genutzt. Die Seite, die an der Autostraße liegt, ist oft menschenleer, während die Seite zur Zellmitte belebter ist. Je besser der Park vor der Straße geschützt ist, um so eher wird er genutzt. Die ideale Lage des Parks ist daher in der Mitte der Zelle. Es gibt keinen unangenehmen Verkehrslärm, sondern nur den Freizeitlärm der Parknutzer. Um Parks weiter zu aktivieren, gibt es einige Strategien: Die zufällige Nutzung hat ein sehr großes Pozential. Der *Parque Mexico* liegt in der Mitte einer Wohnzelle. Auf einer

further. These very simple programmes result in a higher acceptance of the park by the residents. It is a small neighbourhood park, which cannot be compared with large green areas. It does not serve the entire city, but mainly the Urban Cell. It has an extremely high frequency of use by the interaction of these factors. It is used almost daily by every resident. The *Schlossplatz* in Stuttgart downtown is located in the centre of the cell as well. It is another example of a highly used park within the Urban Cell. Because of its location within the central cell, it is used by the residents of the entire Urban Being.

The location of the park and the type of activation decide whether a park is a decorative green or a social meeting place for a neighbourhood.

Seite befindet sich ein großer Supermarkt, auf der anderen der öffentliche Nahverkehr. Die Bewohner der Zelle durchqueren den Park daher täglich. Die zufällige Nutzung erhöht sich. An der Hauptbewegungsachse durch den Park liegt ein Platz. Auf ihm finden kleine Märkte und Konzerte statt. Die vorbeigehenden Bewohner laufen an diesen sozialen Veranstaltungen vorbei und nutzen sie. Die Kombination aus zufälliger Nutzung und einem funktionierenden Programm, dem Platz, belebt den Park stark. Um den Platz befinden sich Wege zum Laufen und ein paar Wasserflächen mit Bänken. Durch diese sehr einfachen Funktionen wird der Park noch besser von den Bewohnern angenommen. Er ist ein kleiner Nachbarschaftspark, der sich nicht mit großen Grünflächen vergleichen lässt. Er dient nicht der gesamten Stadt, sondern hauptsächlich der urbanen Zelle. Durch das Zusammenspiel der genannten Faktoren hat er eine extrem hohe Nutzungsfrequenz. Er wird täglich von den Bewohnern genutzt. Auch der *Schlossplatz* in der Stuttgarter Innenstadt liegt in der Mitte der Zelle. Er ist ein weiteres Beispiel eines stark genutzten Parks in der Zellmitte. Durch die Lage in der zentralen Zelle wird er von allen Bewohnern des urbanen Wesens genutzt.

Die Lage des Parks und die Art der Aktivierung entscheiden, ob ein Park ein dekoratives Grün oder ein sozialer Treffpunkt der Nachbarschaft wird.

Residential and Park Cell, Mexico City ©Benedikt Fahlbusch

Commerce

Stores grow naturally in areas with high levels of pedestrian traffic. That's why they emerge on road edges with high pedestrian frequencies. Pedestrian areas and shops form commercial networks. Broadly speaking, there are two types of commercial networks, those along busy pedestrian areas and those on main roads with public transport.

Central cells have many pedestrian zones. They have the highest footfall and the highest density of stores. The central cells of Stuttgart and Munich reveal the connection between commerce and pedestrian zones. The commercial network concentrates exclusively on the pedestrian areas. A small exception is the central cell in Munich. It has a main road with public transport and wide sidewalks, where an increased density of stores has developed. This relationship becomes clear in linear cells and residential cells. The linear cells in Rio de Janeiro and Santiago de Chile feature public transport and wide sidewalks. There is a large number of shops along these main roads. In the aforementioned residential cell in Mexico City, commerce is developed according to the same principle.

If a planner understands the movement pattern of the people, the perfect location for commerce can be easily found. Roads with high pedestrian frequencies should be provided with retail space on the ground floor. Underground subway stations have an enormous potential for commercial networks. Walls, fences or office facades should be avoided. Even the movement pattern can partially be controlled. Narrow and unfriendly sidewalks usually prevent the foot traffic and thus commerce. Pedestrian-friendly streets, however, can support commercial networks.

Kommerz

Läden entstehen auf natürliche Weise durch hohe Laufkundschaft, weswegen sie sich an Straßenkanten mit hoher Fußgängerfrequenz verdichten. Fußgängerbereiche und Läden bilden so kommerzielle Netzwerke. Grundsätzlich gibt es zwei Typen von kommerziellen Netzwerken: entlang belebter Fußgängerzonen und an Hauptstraßen mit öffentlichem Personennahverkehr.

Zentrale Zellen besitzen viele Fußgängerzonen. Sie haben die höchste Laufkundschaft und gleichzeitig die höchste Ladendichte. In den zentralen Zellen von Stuttgart und München wird der Zusammenhang zwischen Kommerz und Fußgängerzonen deutlich. Das kommerzielle Netzwerk konzentriert sich ausschließlich auf die Fußgängerzonen. Eine kleine Ausnahme bildet die zentrale Zelle in München. Sie besitzt eine Hauptstraße mit öffentlichem Nahverkehr und breiten Gehwegen. An ihr hat sich ebenfalls eine erhöhte Ladendichte gebildet. Dieser Zusammenhang wird bei linearen Zellen und Wohnzellen deutlich. Die linearen Zellen in Rio de Janeiro und Santiago de Chile haben öffentlichen Personennahverkehr und breite Gehwege. An diesen Hauptverkehrsadern befindet sich ein Großteil der Läden. In der untersuchten Wohnzelle in Mexiko-Stadt entsteht der Kommerz nach dem gleichen Prinzip.

Versteht man als Planer das Bewegungsmuster der Menschen, lässt sich der ideale Ort für Kommerz einfach herausfinden. So sollte man darauf achten, an fußgängerreichen Straßen im Erdgeschoss mögliche Ladenflächen anzubieten. Unterirdische Metrostationen haben zum Beispiel ein enormes Potenzial für kommerzielle Netzwerke. Mauern, Zäune, geschlossene Wände oder Bürofassaden sollten unbedingt vermieden werden. Auch das Bewegungsmuster lässt sich ein Stück weit steuern. Schmale und unfreundliche Gehwege verhindern meist den Fußverkehr und somit den Kommerz. Fußgängerfreundliche Straßen können hingegen kommerzielle Netzwerke hervorbringen.

Gastronomy

Gastronomy is located in every possible location and its success relies heavily on its culinary offerings. But urban planning conditions have an impact as well. Regardless of culture, certain conditions foster agglomerations of gastronomy. The intimacy of the place plays a major role. A medium pedestrian frequency is another condition. Outdoor seating areas have a positive impact too. Gastronomy cannot be forced, only be favoured.

The intimacy of the place is probably the most important parameter. Short streets, self-contained plazas and other intimate areas are excellent. Intimacy can be achieved by simple structural measures. A row of trees or half-height planters are already enough to increase the quality of the outdoor areas. It is important that the seating areas do not form the centre of attention. The intimacy is connected to the medium pedestrian frequency. Restaurants at busy plazas or shopping streets usually have a very sheltered seating area. Intimate streets with fewer pedestrians have their seating areas mostly unprotected in the public realm. Fewer pedestrians means fewer customers and the gastronomy only survives by its reputation.

Not every restaurant has outdoor seating areas, but every agglomeration of gastronomy has. Urban planners and architects should consciously offer these areas.

Gastronomie

Gastronomie gibt es in jeder erdenklichen Lage und ihr Erfolg basiert stark auf ihrem kulinarischen Angebot. Aber auch stadtplanerische Gegebenheiten haben einen Einfluss. Unabhängig von der Kultur lassen Verdichtungen von Gastronomie auf die idealen Voraussetzungen schließen. Zum einen spielt die Intimität des Ortes eine große Rolle, zum anderen ist eine mittlere Fußgängerfrequenz von Bedeutung. Sitzmöglichkeiten im Freien haben ebenfalls einen positiven Einfluss.

Die Intimität des Ortes ist wahrscheinlich am wichtigsten. Kurze Straßen, in sich geschlossene Plätze und andere intime Bereiche eignen sich hervorragend. Die Intimität kann aber auch durch einfache bauliche Maßnahmen erreicht werden: Eine Baumreihe oder halbhohe Pflanzenkübel genügen schon, um die Qualität der Außenbereiche zu steigern. Wichtig ist, dass sich die Sitzbereiche in der beobachtenden Position befinden und nicht selbst das Zentrum der Aufmerksamkeit bilden. Die Intimität hängt mit der mittleren Fußgängerfrequenz zusammen. Restaurants an stark belebten Plätzen und Einkaufsstraßen haben meistens einen sehr geschützten Sitzbereich. Intimere Straßen mit weniger Fußgängern haben ihre Sitzbereiche hingegen meist ungeschützt im öffentlichen Raum. Zu wenige Fußgänger bedeuten wiederum fehlende Kundschaft und die Gastronomie überlebt nur durch ihren Ruf.

Nicht jedes Restaurant hat Sitzbereiche im Freien, aber jede Verdichtung von Gastronomie besitzt sie. Als Stadtplaner und Architekt sollte man bewusst darauf achten, diese Bereiche anzubieten.

Urban Cell

Typologies

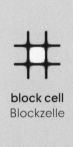

block cell
Blockzelle

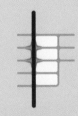

city edge cell
Stadtrandzelle

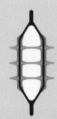

linear cell
lineare Zelle

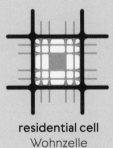

residential cell
Wohnzelle

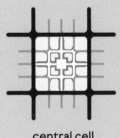

central cell
zentrale Zelle

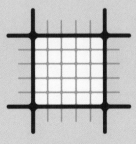

industrial cell
Industriezelle

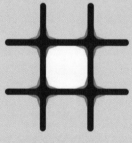

block cell
Blockzelle

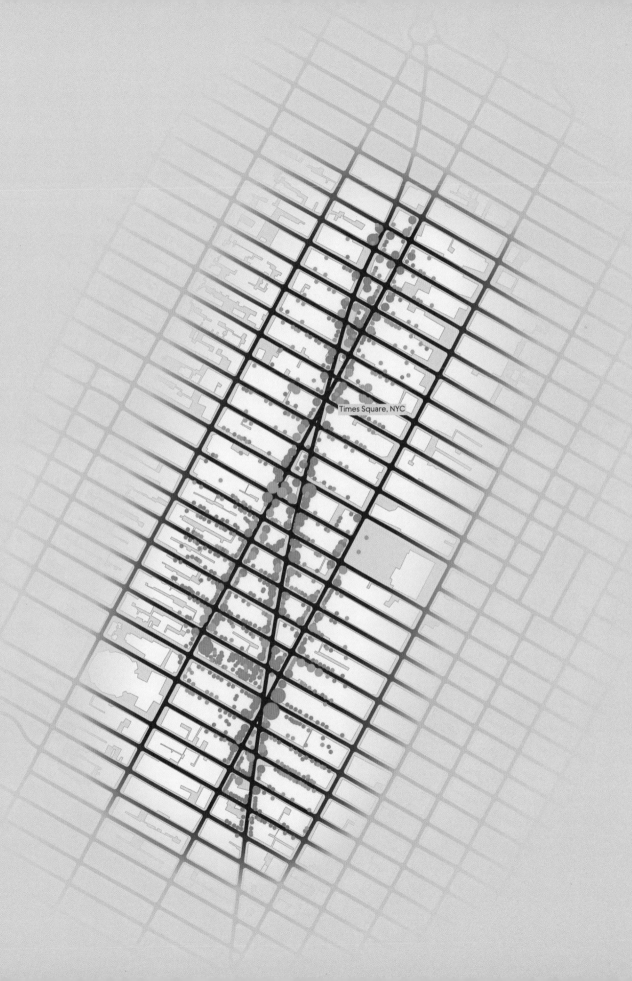
Times Square, NYC

linear cell
lineare Zelle

Pedro de Valdivia, Santiago de Chile

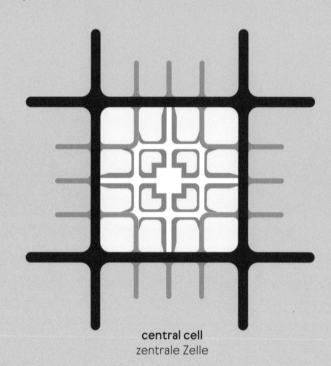

central cell
zentrale Zelle

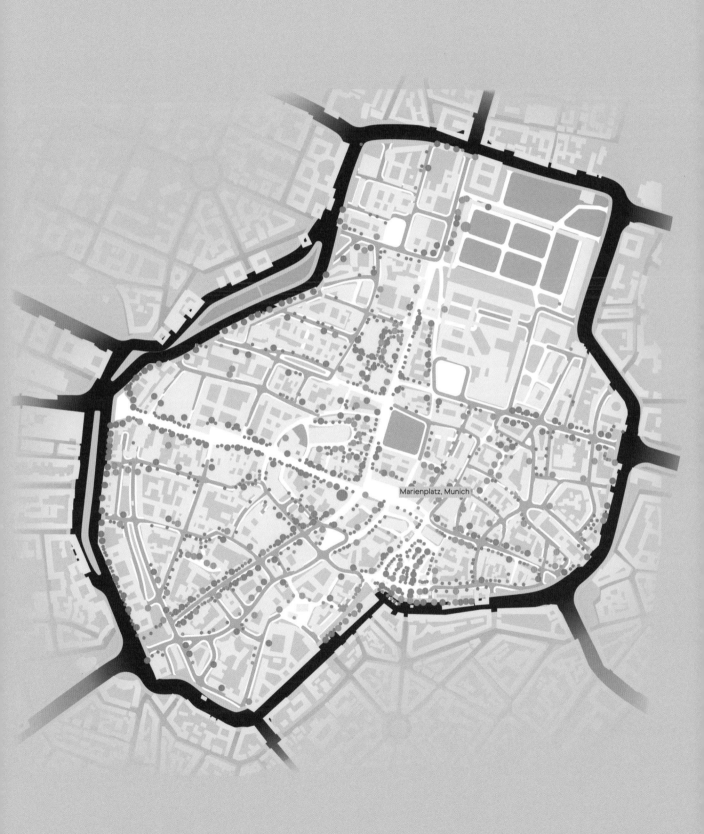

Marienplatz, Munich

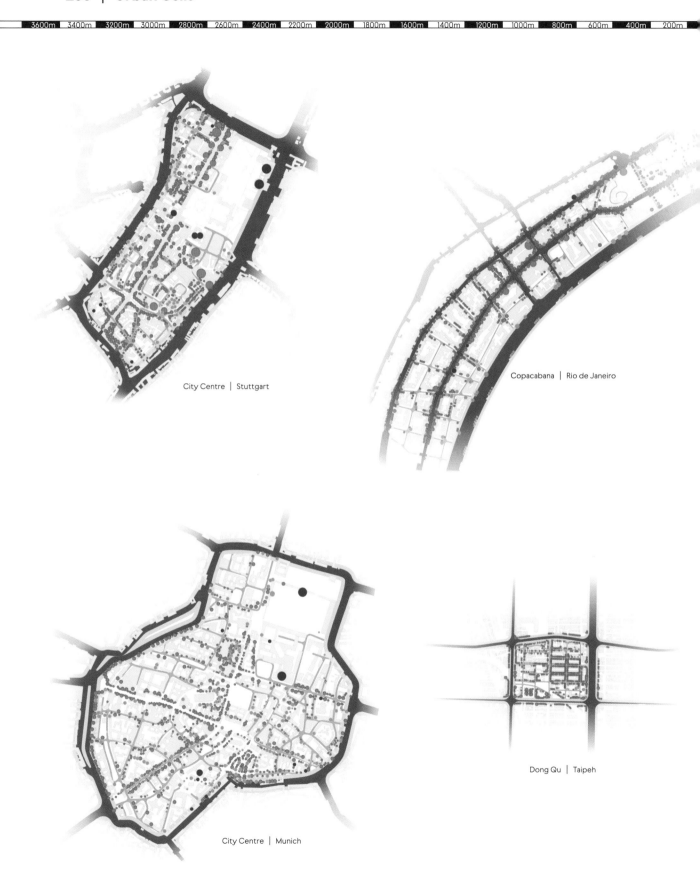

3600m 3400m 3200m 3000m 2800m 2600m 2400m 2200m 2000m 1800m 1600m 1400m 1200m 1000m 800m 600m 400m 200m

City Centre | Stuttgart

Copacabana | Rio de Janeiro

City Centre | Munich

Dong Qu | Taipeh

200m 400m 600m 800m 1000m 1200m 1400m 1600m 1800m 2000m 2200m 2400m 2600m 2800m 3000m 3200m 3400m 3600m

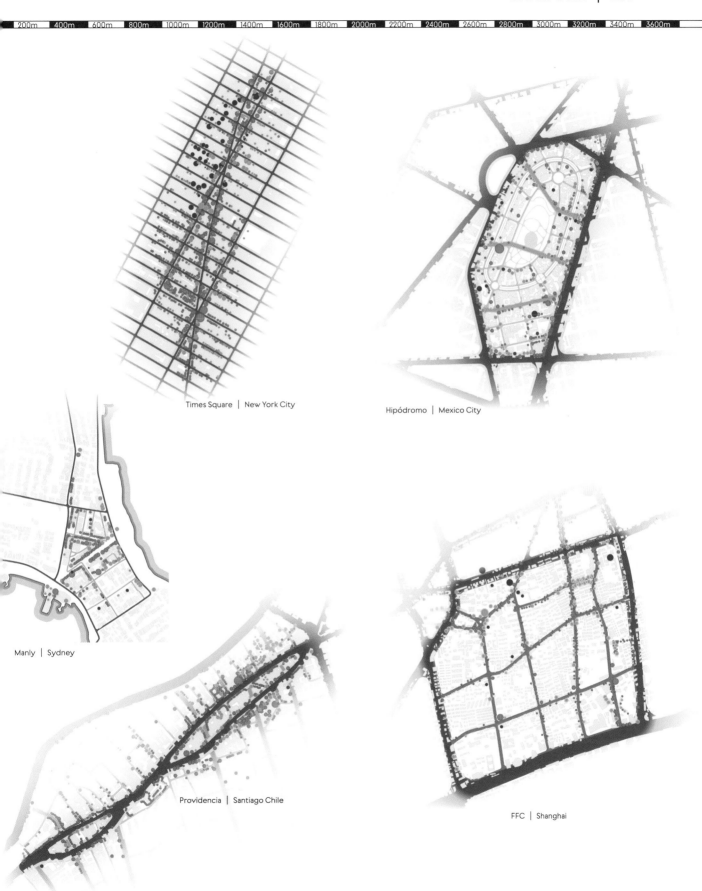

Times Square | New York City

Hipódromo | Mexico City

Manly | Sydney

Providencia | Santiago Chile

FFC | Shanghai

Urban Cell

Urban Nutrition Arteries

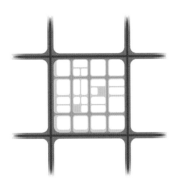

  public transport
öffentlicher Nahverkehr

  fast traffic
schneller Verkehr

 slow traffic
langsamer Verkehr

 pedestrian
Fußgänger

There are countless ways to design a main artery. The examples here seek to describe principles to increase the functionality.

Main arteries are the intersection of cars and humans. The prime focus is not to disturb the traffic flow, as well as to offer qualities for humans. The traffic flow is optimised by the separation of speeds. This separation can be achieved by greenery, height differences or low walls. Pedestrian bridges and tunnels minimise interference of traffic lights. The the car speed of 50 km/h should be disturbed as little as possible. Parallel parking on fast roads should therefore be avoided. A separate lane can offer parking.

Main arteries are ideal for bicycle tracks. The cycle track should be clearly separated from the car track to improve the safety of cyclists. Parked cars should protect the cyclists, not the other way round. A simple height difference enhances this security. Footpaths should be fairly wide. Public transport on the main thoroughfare increases the pedestrian flow. Arcades can bundle this flow and create ideal conditions for a commercial network. Wide footpaths can also support gastronomy, if they create an intimacy. Trees and vegetation, as well as elevated platforms facilitate this intimacy.

The clear separation of speeds creates qualities for cars and humans. It is the foundation for all traffic participants, as it responds to the different needs. Additional functions such as commerce and gastronomy increase the quality of life in the vicinity of the main artery.

Es gibt unzählige Möglichkeiten, Hauptverkehrsadern zu gestalten. Die hier vorgestellten Beispiele beschreiben lediglich Prinzipien, um die Funktionalität zu erhöhen.

Hauptverkehrsadern sind der Schnittpunkt zwischen Auto und Mensch. Die oberste Priorität einer Hauptverkehrsader ist es, den Verkehrsfluss nicht zu stören sowie Qualitäten für den Menschen zu bieten. Der Verkehrsfluss wird durch eine Trennung der verschiedenen Geschwindigkeiten optimiert. Diese Trennung kann durch Grünstreifen, Höhenversprünge oder Mäuerchen erreicht werden. Fußgängerbrücken und -tunnel minimieren die Störung durch Ampeln. Die Geschwindigkeit der Autos von 50 km/h sollte so wenig wie möglich behindert werden. Parkplätze an schnellen Straßen bewirken genau diese Störung. Parkmöglichkeiten sollten daher nur auf separaten und langsamen Spuren angeboten werden.

Hauptverkehrsadern eignen sich hervorragend für Fahrradwege. Der Radweg sollte klar von der Autospur getrennt werden, um die Sicherheit der Radfahrer zu garantieren. So sollten parkende Autos prinzipiell die Radfahrer schützen und nicht andersherum. Ein einfacher Höhenversatz ist ausreichend, um diese Sicherheit zu garantieren. Fußwege sollten eine angemessene Breite haben und vor dem Autoverkehr geschützt sein. Verläuft der öffentliche Personennahverkehr auf der Hauptverkehrsader, erhöht sich auch der Fußgängerstrom. Arkaden können diesen Strom bündeln und ideale Voraussetzungen für ein kommerzielles Netzwerk schaffen. Breite Fußwege können aber auch Gastronomie ausbilden, wenn sie eine Intimität erzeugen. Bäume und Begrünung sowie erhöhte Podeste begünstigen eben diese Intimität.

Die klare Trennung der Geschwindigkeiten schafft Qualitäten für Auto und Mensch. Sie ist die Grundlage, um allen Verkehrsteilnehmern gerecht zu werden, da sie auf die unterschiedlichen Bedürfnisse eingeht. Zusätzliche Funktionen wie Kommerz und Gastronomie steigern zudem die Lebensqualität in der näheren Umgebung der Hauptverkehrsader.

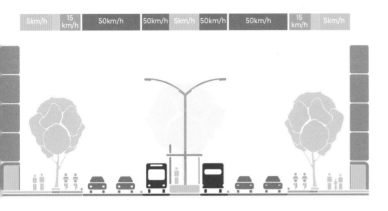

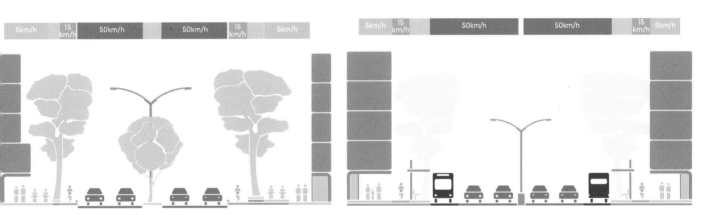

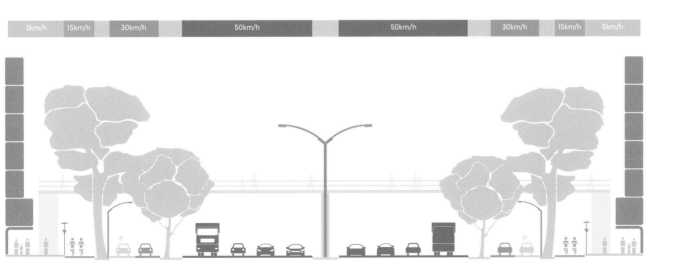

There is a variety of options for capillary streets. The examples shown illustrate only a few principles. Residential streets are part of the human city. To increase the quality for people, it is necessary to avoid fast traffic. This is achieved by traffic calming measures, such as continuous flooring, narrow and winding lanes, etc. The streets become easy to cross and usable. The parking areas further slow down the speed and are ideally located near the housing.

However, pedestrians and cyclists need enough space. But not too much, since large roads can appear empty and unfriendly. Different speeds can be combined to raise the awareness of traffic participants. The street lighting is ideally located on the sidewalks, since people are the only traffic participants without lights. The lanterns provide additional safety at night.

To increase the quality further, a high amount of trees and plants is advantageous. Trees provide shade, fresh air and serve as a visual screen. The calming effect on humans is another benefit. Grasslands filter and drain the rainwater. Larger green areas within the street can function as neighbourhood parks. They should be activated with playgrounds, fitness equipment or similar measures. Gardens, green stripes or a mezzanine floor protect the homes from prying eyes.

A relaxed pace, places to stay and nature are the basis for high-quality living. Residential streets should only have slow and human speeds. If the use for humans is maximised, they develop their full potential as places of neighbourly encounter.

Auch für Kapillarstraßen gibt es eine Vielzahl von Möglichkeiten. Die hier vorgestellten Beispiele verdeutlichen lediglich ein paar Prinzipien. Kapillarstraßen sind Teil der menschlichen Stadt. Um die Qualität für den Menschen zu erhöhen, sollte schneller Autoverkehr unbedingt vermieden werden. Dies wird durch verkehrsberuhigende Maßnahmen wie durchgängige Bodenbeläge, schmale und kurvige Fahrspuren oder geringen Platz für Autos erreicht. Durch den langsamen Verkehr ist die Straße für den Menschen einfach zu überqueren und auch nutzbar. Der ruhende Verkehr, also Parkplätze, verlangsamt den Verkehr weiter und befindet sich hier nahe der Wohnungen.

Fuß- und Radwege brauchen hingegen ausreichend Platz. Sie sollten aber auch nicht zu groß dimensioniert werden, da die Straße sonst leer und unfreundlich wirkt. Verschiedene Geschwindigkeiten können hier kombiniert werden, wodurch sich die Achtsamkeit der Verkehrsteilnehmer erhöht. Die Straßenbeleuchtung befindet sich idealerweise an den Gehwegen. Da Menschen als einzige Verkehrsteilnehmer kein Licht besitzen, bieten die Laternen zusätzliche Sicherheit bei Nacht. Um die Qualität der Wohnstraße weiter zu steigern, ist ein hoher Grünanteil von Vorteil. Bäume spenden Schatten, frische Luft und dienen als Sichtschutz. Ihre beruhigende Wirkung auf den Menschen ist ein weiterer Nutzen. Grasflächen filtern und entwässern das Regenwasser. Größere Grünflächen innerhalb der Straße können als Nachbarschatfspark fungieren. Sie sollten über Spielplätze, Fitnessgeräte oder Ähnliches aktiviert werden. Neben Bäumen können auch Gärten, Grünstreifen oder ein Hochparterre die Wohnungen vor neugierigen Blicken schützen.

Ein entspanntes Tempo, Orte zum Verweilen und Natur bilden die Grundlagen für ein qualitativ hochwertiges Wohnen. Wohnstraßen sollten deshalb nur langsame und menschliche Geschwindigkeiten haben. Wird die Nutzung für den Menschen maximiert, entfalten sie ihr Potenzial als Orte der nachbarschaftlichen Begegnung.

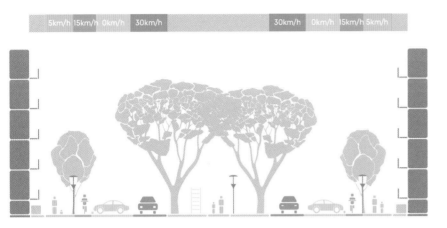

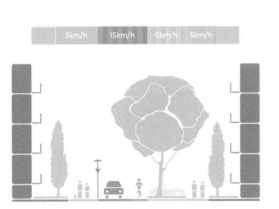

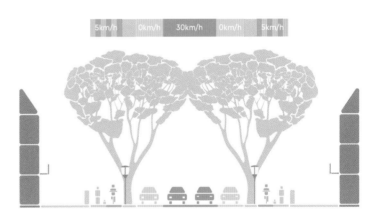

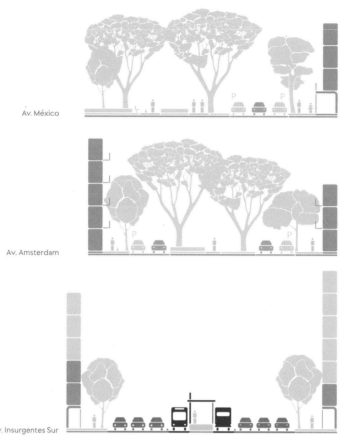

Av. México

Av. Amsterdam

Av. Insurgentes Sur

The residential cell has a strong road hierarchy. It reaches from the fast and loud main thoroughfares outside, via the slow traffic residential streets, to the almost car-free park in the centre.

Due to the narrow width of only 400 meter, the public transport on the main thoroughfare in the east is within easy reach by foot. The boundary road of the cell clearly separates the speeds in order to keep the traffic flow constant.

The streets inside the cell have slow traffic. The *Av. Amsterdam* consists of two one-way streets with parallel parking. The traffic at rest slows down the moving traffic as well. A high frequency of pedestrians and an easy to cross street section calm the streets further. In combination with the trees, these roads become ideal residential streets.

The park in the centre has only few and slow traffic, with a high amount of pedestrians.

Die Wohnzelle hat eine ausgeprägte Straßenhierarchie. Sie reicht von den schnellen und lauten Hauptverkehrsadern außen über die verkehrsberuhigten Wohnstraßen zum fast autofreien Park im Zentrum.

Durch die schmale Breite von nur 400 Metern ist der öffentliche Nahverkehr auf der Hauptverkehrsader im Osten schnell zu Fuß erreichbar. Die zellbegrenzende Straße hat klar separierte Geschwindigkeiten, um den Verkehrsfluss zu begünstigen.

Die Straßen im Zellinneren sind verkehrsberuhigt. Die *Av. Amsterdam* besteht aus zwei Einbahnstraßen mit Parkmöglichkeiten. Der ruhende Verkehr bremst den langsamen Verkehr weiter aus. Ein hoher Fußgängeranteil und ein einfach zu überquerender Straßenschnitt beruhigen die Straßen weiter. In Kombination mit den vielen Bäumen werden diese Straßen zu idealen Wohnstraßen.

Der Park im Zentrum hat nur wenigen und langsamen Verkehr, aber einen sehr hohen Fußgängeranteil.

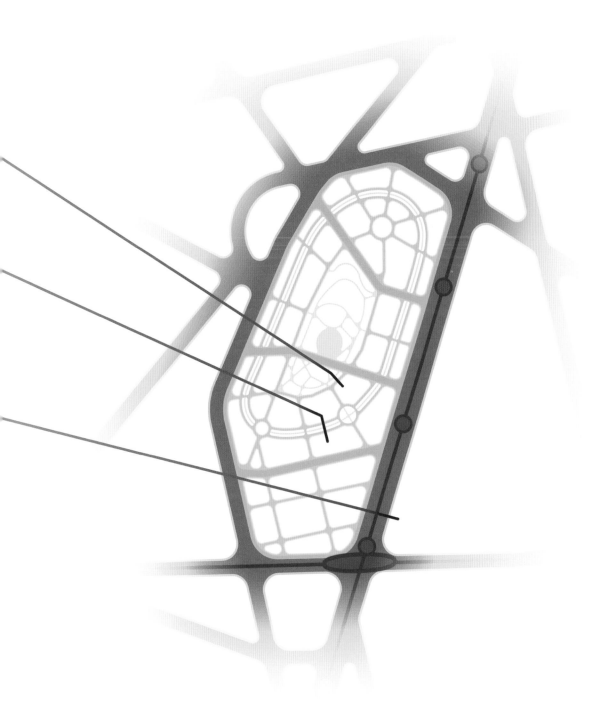

metro / bus   main street   secondary street   pedestrian

Avenida Amsterdam © Benedikt Fahlbusch

© Benedikt Fahlbusch **Avenida Insurgentes Sur**

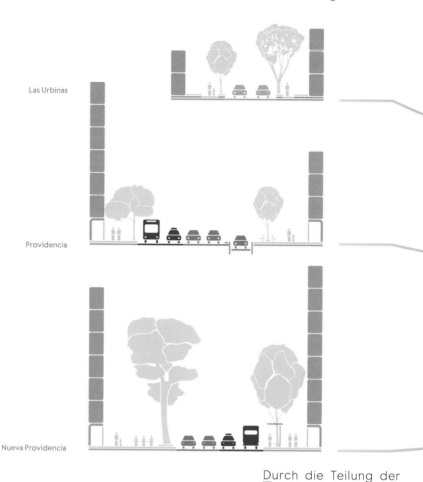

Las Urbinas

Providencia

Nueva Providencia

A linear cell is formed by dividing the main artery into two one-way streets. Both cell boundary streets use two of the four lanes for taxis and buses. The space for the cars is reduced to less than half of the road width. Their cross section is almost mirrored and the streets provide plenty of space for pedestrians. The narrow width makes it easy to cross the street. Due to that, the roads are very pedestrian-friendly and achieve an urban and mixed character. The structure of the linear cells have resulted in a sub-centre outside the Urban Nucleus.

In the north there are residential cells. Their slow traffic roads are oriented towards the river. The street section is considerably smaller and the area for traffic much lower. They only have local traffic. Small front gardens create a distance to the low houses and the space for car traffic is reduced to almost one-third of the width of the road.

Durch die Teilung der Hauptverkehrsader in zwei Einbahnstraßen entsteht eine lineare Zelle. Beide zellbegrenzenden Straßen reservieren die Hälfte, also zwei der vier Spuren, für Taxis und Busse. Der Platz für die Autos konnte auf weniger als die Hälfte der Straßenbreite reduziert werden. Die Straßen sind vom Schnitt fast spiegelbildlich aufgebaut und bieten viel Platz für Fußgänger. Der schmale Straßenschnitt erleichtert es, die Straße zu überqueren. Dadurch werden die Straßen auch für Fußgänger nutzbar und bekommen einen sehr urbanen und durchmischten Charakter. Die linearen Zellen haben ein Subzentrum entstehen lassen.

Im Norden grenzen Wohnzellen an. Ihre verkehrsberuhigten Straßen verlaufen in Richtung Fluss. Ihr Straßenquerschnitt ist erheblich schmaler und der Bereich für den Autoverkehr deutlich geringer. Sie führen nur lokalen Verkehr. Kleine Vorgärten schaffen eine Distanz zu den niedrigen Häusern und der Platz für den Autoverkehr wird hier auf knapp ein Drittel der Straßenbreite verringert.

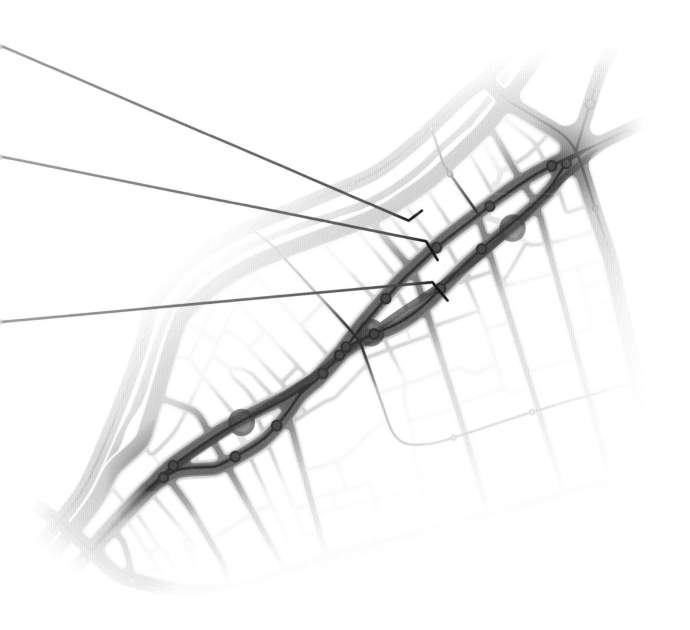

metro / bus   main street   secondary street   pedestrian

Av. Ricardo Lyon © Juan Pablo Scarafia

© Juan Pablo Scarafia **Nueva Providencia**

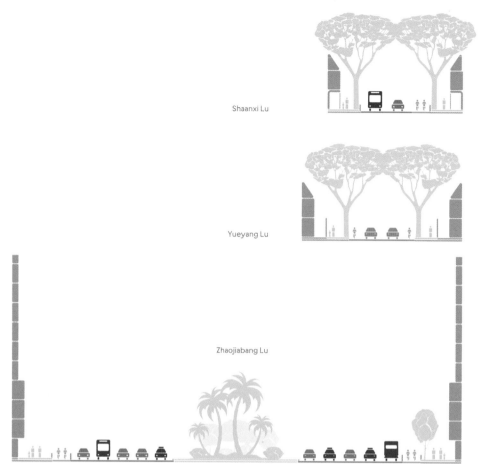

Shaanxi Lu

Yueyang Lu

Zhaojiabang Lu

The largest main artery of the Urban Cell is located in the south. The street has an enormous width of about 70 meter. The traffic is clearly separated by a green strip in the middle. There are separate bike lanes and space for pedestrians on both edges. The clear separation of the traffic participants significantly facilitates moving through the city. Even cycling on the ten-lane freeway is possible.

The boundary roads with a narrow width are designed for a continuous flow of traffic as well and perform their function perfectly. They carry the main traffic and creat a clear boundary between pedestrian and car traffic. The width is approximately the same as the slower traffic streets in the interior of the cell. This creates an equivalent street grid. Pure footpaths are almost exclusively found in the private realm. They provide access to the private compounds within the road block.

Die größte Hauptverkehrsader der urbanen Zelle liegt im Süden. Sie ist mit circa 70 Metern sehr breit. In ihrer Mitte zoniert sie den Verkehr durch einen Grünstreifen. An beiden Rändern befinden sich separate Fahrradspuren und Platz für Fußgänger. Die klare Trennung der einzelnen Verkehrsteilnehmer erleichtert das Bewegen durch die Stadt erheblich. So ist selbst das Radfahren auf der zehnspurigen Stadtautobahn gut möglich.

Auch die zellbegrenzenden Straßen mit schmaler Breite sind auf einen kontinuierlichen Verkehrsfluss ausgelegt und erfüllen ihre Funktion ideal. Auf ihnen wird der Durchgangsverkehr geleitet und sie grenzen den Fuß- und Autoverkehr klar voneinander ab. Sie besitzen in etwa die gleiche Breite wie die verkehrsberuhigten Straßen. Dadurch entsteht ein relativ gleichwertiges Straßenraster. Reine Fußwege befinden sich fast ausschließlich im privaten Raum. Innerhalb der Straßenblocks erschließen sie die eingezäunten Wohngemeinschaften.

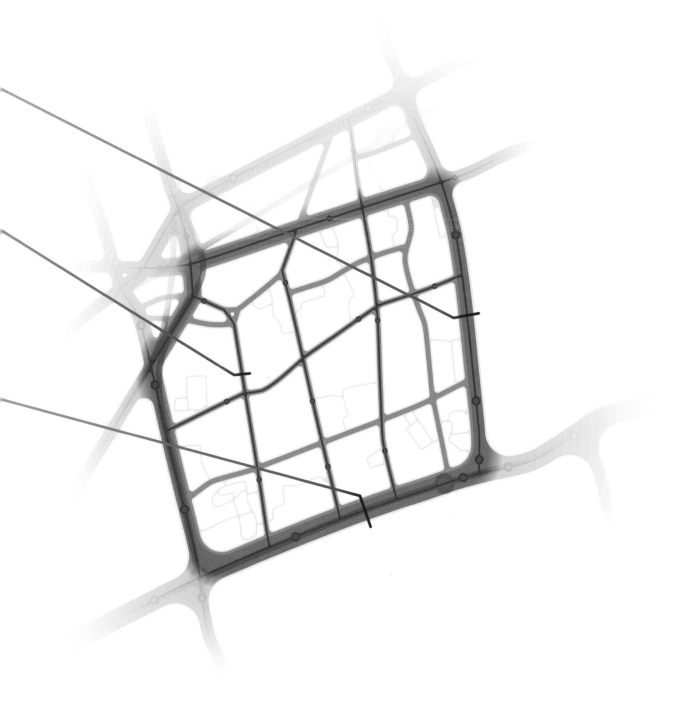

metro / bus   main street   secondary street   pedestrian

Yueyang Lu   © Daniela Gonzales Badillo

© Daniela Gonzales Badillo **Zhaojiabang Lu**

Urban Cell

Neighbourhood Parks

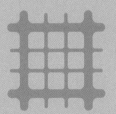

no park - not used
kein Park – nicht genutzt

park cell - barely used
Parkzelle – kaum genutzt

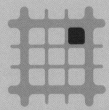

at the corner - moderately used
an der Ecke – mäßig genutzt

at the edge - used
an der Kante – genutzt

in the centre - highly used
in der Mitte – stark genutzt

1000m   900m   800m   700m   600m   500m   400m   300m   200m   100m

The calm residential cell has a high amount of green and is a fantastic example of high density inner city housing. The central park acts like a green nucleus. The cell has a small to medium size and the central park plays an important role. It is well shielded from the main thoroughfares. Thus it is highly used by the residents. It creates a pleasantly cool microclimate and the air is slightly cleaner and more refreshing. One block further out, runs an elliptical, green ring road. The *Av. Amsterdam* stands out because of its central green strip. The continuous walkway is frequently used by joggers. Fitness equipment animates the residents to exercise. Its green and calm character enhances the quality of the adjacent houses.

A pure park cell borders the living cell in the northwest. The *Parque España* is surrounded by main thoroughfares. The main roads make it difficult for people to reach the park and the traffic noise within is disturbing. The large streets relegate the status of the park to that of decorative greenery.

Die beruhigte Wohnzelle hat einen hohen Grünanteil und ist ein fantastisches Beispiel für hochverdichtetes innerstädtisches Wohnen. In ihrem Mittelpunkt befindet sich ein Park, sozusagen der grüne Zellkern. Sie hat eine kleine bis mittlere Größe und der zentral gelegene Park spielt eine wichtige Rolle. Er liegt gut abgeschirmt von den Hauptverkehrsadern und ist fast autofrei. Dadurch wird er sehr gut von den Menschen angenommen. Er schafft ein angenehm kühles Mikroklima und meist etwas frischere Luft. Einen Block weiter außen verläuft eine elliptische Ringstraße. Die *Av. Amsterdam* sticht durch ihren zentralen Grünstreifen hervor. Der durchgängige Fußweg wird viel von Joggern benutzt, die hier ihre Runden drehen. Aber auch Fitnessgeräte animieren die Bewohner zur sportlicher Betätigung. Der grüne und ruhige Charakter der *Av. Amsterdam* harmoniert perfekt mit den Wohnhäusern.

Im Nordwesten grenzt eine reine Parkzelle an die Wohnzelle. Sie ist von Hauptverkehrsadern umschlossen. In ihr befindet sich der *Parque España*. Durch die großen Verkehrsstraßen ist der Park für Menschen schwer erreichbar und auch innerhalb des Parks stört der Verkehrslärm. Die großen Verkehrsadern degenerieren ihn zur dekorativen Grünfläche.

Av. Amsterdam

© Benedikt Fahlbusch   © Benedikt Fahlbusch

Parque México

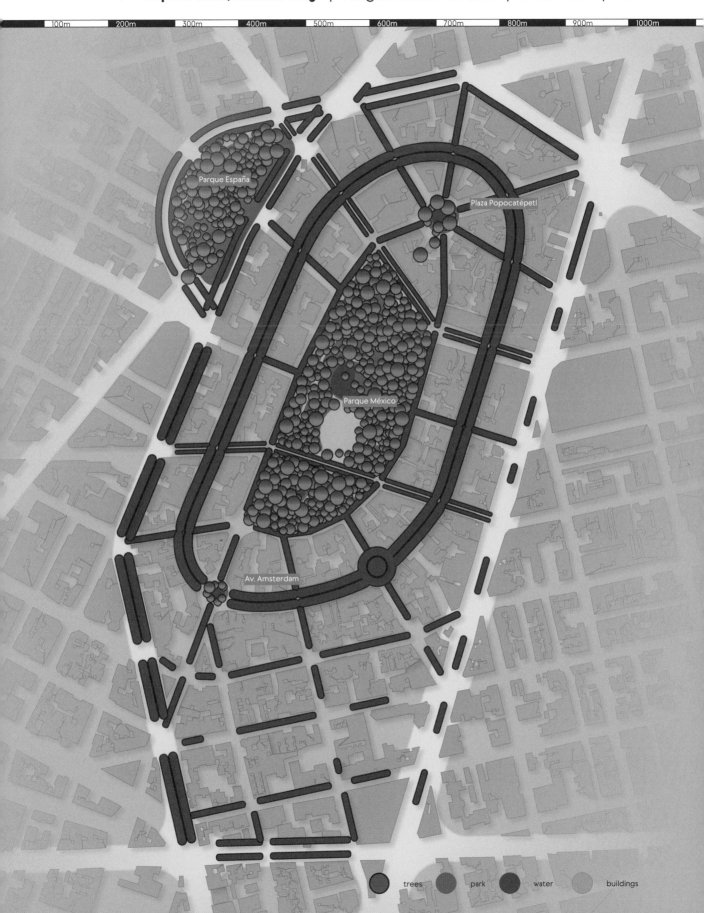

trees   park   water   buildings

1000m 900m 800m 700m 600m 500m 400m 300m 200m 100m

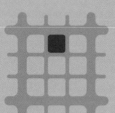

Stuttgart's city centre has a very high amount of parks. A park, the *Schloßplatz*, at the heart of the city is an exceptional example. Its location on the main shopping street makes it a very active park. It is located in the centre of the cell and is well protected from the main traffic arteries. Due to that, it is the busiest park in the Urban Cell.

A narrow connection leads to another park in the downtown area, the quieter *Oberer Schloßgarten*. It is a pleasant place to stay due to its shielded location. The small lake and the historic opera give the park its own unique charm. Nevertheless, it receives quite heavy traffic, since the park connects to a bigger green network.

The combination of pedestrian zones and parks puts Stuttgart at the top in terms of parks in the downtown area. Due to the different locations, there is a range of active and quiet public parks.

Die Stuttgarter Innenstadt hat für eine zentrale Zelle einen sehr hohen Grünanteil. Speziell ist sicherlich der Schlossplatz, eigentlich ein Park, der das Herz der Stadt bildet. Durch seine direkte Lage an der Haupteinkaufsstraße ist er ein sehr aktiver Park. Er befindet sich in der Zellmitte und ist gut vor den Hauptverkehrsadern geschützt. Durch diese Qualitäten wird er zum belebtesten Park der urbanen Zelle.

Über eine schmale Verbindung gelangt man zu einem weiteren Park in der Innenstadt, dem etwas ruhigeren Oberen Schlossgarten. Durch seine abgeschirmte Lage ist er ein angenehmer Ort zum Verweilen. Der kleine See und die historische Oper verleihen dem Park seinen ganz eigenen Charme. Trotzdem gibt es viel Bewegung, da der Park den Auftakt zu einem großflächigen Parknetzwerk bildet. Allein der Park am Charlottenplatz wird wegen der großen Verkehrsader nur mäßig genutzt.

Die Kombination aus Fußgängerzonen und Parks bringt Stuttgart bei der Begrünung in der Innenstadt ganz nach vorn. Durch die unterschiedliche Lage gibt es ein Angebot von aktiveren und ruhigeren Parkflächen.

Oberer Schloßgarten   **Schloßplatz**

100m 200m 300m 400m 500m 600m 700m 800m 900m 1000m

Oberer Schlossgarten

Schlossplatz

Charlottenplatz

Theodor-Heuss-Straße

Königstraße

trees park water buildings

1000m   900m   800m   700m   600m   500m   400m   300m   200m   100m

As in many places in Shanghai, there are no neighbourhood parks within the investigated cell. Urban life is always connected with movement, like a constantly running machine. Neighbourhood parks serve as places of rest and relaxation, but are entirely missing in this cell. Some compounds recognised this deficiency and provided private green areas. The privatisation of parks makes them a privilege for the more well-off.

However, the trees in the roads work as a linear green network and are exemplary. In the hot summer months, the plane trees create a pleasant shade and reduce the heat entry.

The rows of trees within the blocks are located mostly south of the houses. They not only create a pleasant atmosphere, but shade the houses and reduce the heat entry as well. According to Chinese Feng Shui, houses should be built facing south. In order to sell or rent an apartment, all the inhabited rooms have to be directed to the south.

Wie an vielen Stellen in Shanghai gibt es auch innerhalb der untersuchten Zelle keine Nachbarschaftparks. Das städtische Leben ist dadurch ständig mit Bewegung verbunden, wie eine konstant laufende Maschine. Nachbarschaftsparks dienen als Orte der Ruhe und Entspannung, fehlen in dieser Zelle jedoch gänzlich. Einige Wohnanlagen haben diesen Mangel erkannt und stellen Grünflächen zur Verfügung. Die Privatisierung der Parks hat aber zur Folge, dass sie zum Privileg der besserverdienenden Oberschicht werden.

Die Begrünung des Straßenraums funktioniert wie eine Art lineares Parknetzwerk und ist beispielhaft. In den heißen Sommermonaten spenden die Platanen angenehmen Schatten und mindern den Hitzeeintrag.

Die Baumreihen innerhalb der Blocks befinden sich meist südlich der Häuser. Sie schaffen nicht nur eine angenehme Wohnatmosphäre, sondern spenden in den Sommermonaten durch ihre Lage Schatten und vermindern den Hitzeeintrag. Aufgrund des Feng Shuis werden in China nur Häuser mit Südausrichtung gebaut. Um die Wohnungen verkaufen oder vermieten zu können, müssen alle bewohnten Zimmer nach Süden gerichtet sein.

Xingye Lu

© Conni Renner

Shaanxi Lu

100m 200m 300m 400m 500m 600m 700m 800m 900m 1000m

Fuxing Lu

Wulumuqi Nan Lu

Zhaojiabang Lu

trees park water buildings

3000m 2750m 2500m 2250m 2000m 1750m 1500m 1250m 1000m 750m 500m 250m

The residential cells in Southeast Edmonton have a comparatively high density for a North American city. The administrative neighbourhoods are based on the Urban Cell structure. A neighbourhood corresponds to an Urban Cell. Larger main roads combine two to four cells into groups, while smaller main roads define the cells. A green strip creates a distance to the southern highway ring.

Each residential cell has a central park. Many parks are shifted towards the interior of the cell group. There is a very high density of schools, which are always located in the parks. They serve the neighbourhood / Urban Cell and use the parks for sport activities.

Die Wohnzellen im Südosten Edmontons haben für eine nordamerikanische Stadt eine vergleichsweise hohe Dichte. Die urbane Zellstruktur findet sich auch in der administrativen Nachbarschaftsbildung wieder. Eine Nachbarschaft entspricht einer urbanen Zelle. Größere Hauptstraßen fassen zwei bis vier Zellen zu Gruppen zusammen, während kleinere Hauptstraßen die Zellen definieren. Ein grüner Streifen schafft einen Abstand zum südlich gelegenen Autobahnring.

Jede Wohnzelle besitzt einen zentral gelegenen Park. Viele Parks haben eine Verschiebung zum Inneren der Zellgruppe. Auffällig ist die hohe Dichte an Schulen, die sich ausnahmslos an den Parkflächen befinden. Sie dienen der Nachbarschaft / urbanen Zelle und nutzen die Parks für Sportflächen.

trees　　park　　water　　buildings　　schools

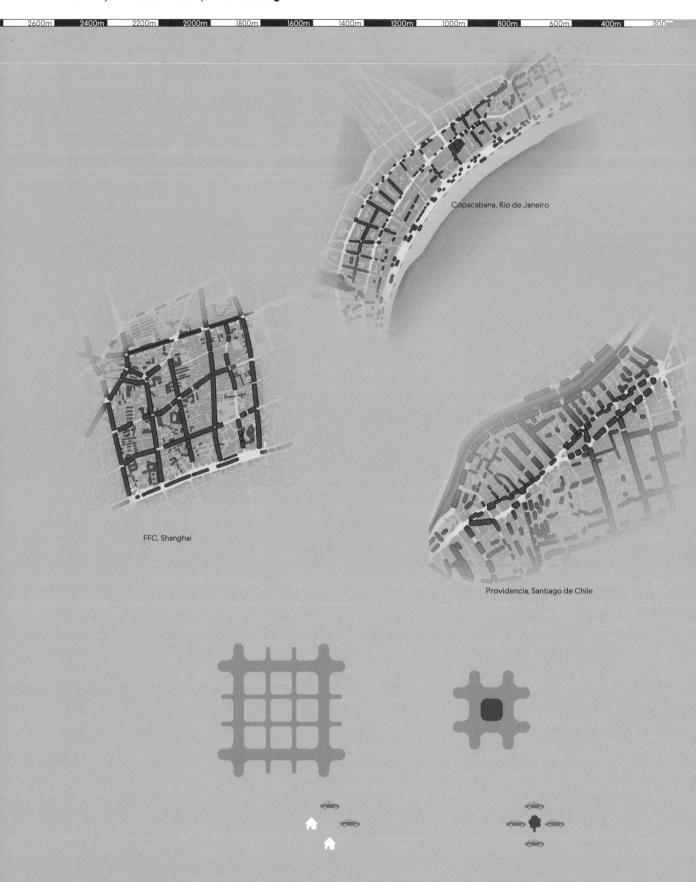

2600m 2400m 2200m 2000m 1800m 1600m 1400m 1200m 1000m 800m 600m 400m 200

Copacabana, Rio de Janeiro

FFC, Shanghai

Providencia, Santiago de Chile

200m | 400m | 600m | 800m | 1000m | 1200m | 1400m | 1600m | 1800m | 2000m | 2200m | 2400m | 2600m

City Centre, Munich

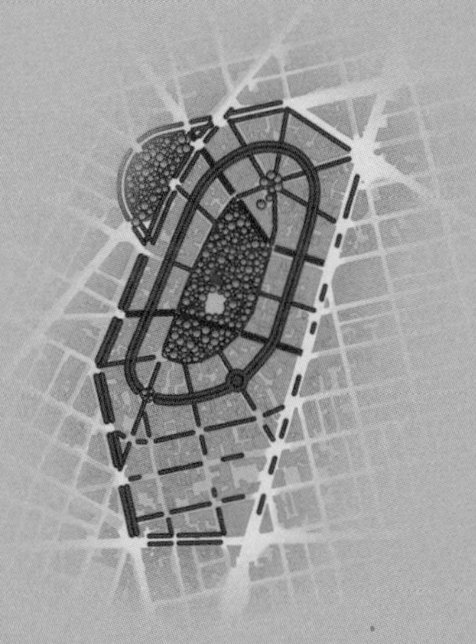

Hipodromo, Mexico City

City Centre, Stuttgart

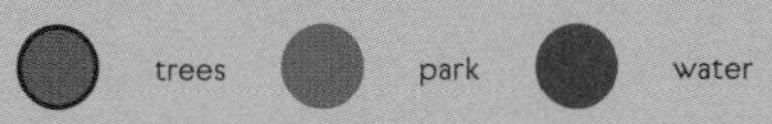

trees | park | water

Urban Cell

Commercial Network

along pedestrian areas
entlang Fußgängerzonen

along main arteries with PT
entlang Hauptstraßen mit ÖPNV

The commercial network in *Copaca-bana* does not run along the world-famous beach, but on a road block further inward. Here lies the divided main artery road, which generates two linear cells parallel to the beach. Quite centrally, this cell structure is superposed by another linear cell at a 90° angle. The superposition of the cells generates a block cell. This creates a sub-centre with a very dense commercial network. With 160 stores per kilometer it even exceeds European shopping streets. The divided main road containing the public transport, is easy to cross and has sufficiently wide sidewalk. This creates substantial foot traffic, which supports the large number of shops. The high density of the district, consisting of a perimeter block with up to ten storeys, enhances this effect further. The commercial network densifies towards the central block cell. With the *Galeria Menescal* it further reduces its mesh size.

In *Copacabana* verläuft das kommerzielle Netzwerk nicht entlang des weltbekannten Strandes, sondern einen Straßenblock weiter innen. Hier befindet sich die geteilte Hauptverkehrsader, die zwei lineare Zellen parallel zum Strand erzeugt. Relativ mittig wird diese Zellstruktur von einer anderen linearen Zelle im 90°-Winkel überlagert. Die Überlagerung der Zellen generiert eine Blockzelle. Das somit ausgeformte Subzentrum hat ein sehr dichtes kommerzielles Netzwerk. Mit 160 Läden pro Kilometer übertrifft es sogar europäische Einkaufsstraßen. Die geteilte Hauptstraße führt den öffentlichen Nahverkehr, ist einfach zu überqueren und hat ausreichende Gehwegbreiten. Dadurch wird sehr viel Fußverkehr generiert, der die hohe Anzahl an Läden ermöglicht. Die hohe Dichte des Viertels, bestehend aus einer Blockrandbebauung mit bis zu zehn Geschossen, unterstützt diesen Effekt weiter. Zur zentral gelegenen Blockzelle hin verdichtet sich das kommerzielle Netzwerk. Mit der *Galeria Menescal* verringert es seine Maschenweite weiter.

100m 200m 300m 400m 500m 600m 700m 800m 900m 1000m 1100m 1200m

Rua Barata Ribeiro

Av. Nossa Sra de Copacabana

Block Cell

Galeria Menescal

shops

<u>A</u>s a typical European city centre, the central cell has a complex commercial network. The many shops and pedestrian zones function in a similar way to a modern shopping mall. People move along a main axis, with a very large number of shops. Gastronomy is located in more sheltered areas. A modern shopping mall maximises the main axis of movement to increase the value of the stores. The historic centre gains more quality through the smaller branches of the commercial network. The result is a greater variety of shops, which a specialised shopping mall cannot compete with. Nevertheless, the major axis remains clearly visible. The main shopping street, the *Königstraße* cuts lengthwise through the cell. It has the highest frequency of pedestrians and a high density of 150 shops per kilometer. In contrast, the park in the northeast has no commerce at all.

<u>A</u>ls typisch europäische Innenstadt hat die zentrale Zelle ein verzweigtes kommerzielles Netzwerk. Die vielen Läden und Fußgängerzonen ähneln in ihrer Funktionsweise einem modernen Einkaufszentrum. Die Menschen werden auf eine Hauptbewegungsachse, geleitet, an der sich eine sehr hohe Anzahl an Läden befindet. Punktuell ist Gastronomie in stärker geschützten Bereichen entstanden. Ein modernes Einkaufszentrum maximiert jedoch die Hauptbewegungsachse um den Wert der Läden zu steigern. Die historisch gewachsene Innenstadt gewinnt gerade durch die kleineren Nebenarme an Qualität. Es entsteht eine größere Vielfalt an Läden, mit der ein spezialisiertes Einkaufszentrum nicht konkurrieren kann. Trotzdem bleibt die Hauptachse klar ablesbar. Als Haupteinkaufsstraße zieht sich die *Königstraße* einmal längs durch die Zelle. Sie hat die höchste Fußgängerfrequenz und eine hohe Ladendichte von 150 Läden pro Kilometer. Im Gegensatz dazu besitzt der Park im Nordosten gar keinen Kommerz.

100m 200m 300m 400m 500m 600m 700m 800m 900m 1000m 1100m 1200m

Königstraße

shops

Taipei has one of the highest densities of shops in the world. The reason for this is the small dimensions of the shopping areas, which produces a high diversity. The examined cell *Dong Qu* is similar to a central cell and has a small size of 13.4 hectar. A typical feature of Taipei are the arcades along the main traffic arteries. They protect pedestrians from traffic and support a high number of shops. This structure can be found in the less lively residential cells as well.

The commercial cell *Dong Qu* has its highest store density in the east. The narrow streets resemble pedestrian zones, but allow a little car traffic. The small shops have a width of a few meters, resulting in an extremely high density of up to 430 shops per kilometer. In contrast to European shopping streets, these streets have more gastronomy and a greater variety of shops. The commerce and the gastronomy are spread over several streets and enliven the entire urban cell.

Taipeh hat eine der höchsten Ladendichten der Welt. Grund dafür sind die kleinen Dimensionen der Lokalitäten, die eine hohe Vielfalt erzeugen. Die untersuchte Zelle *Dong Qu* ist vergleichbar mit einer zentralen Zelle und hat eine kleine Größe von 13,4 Hektar. Eine für Taipeh typische Struktur sind die Arkaden entlang der Hauptverkehrsadern. Sie schützen die Fußgänger vor dem Verkehr und fördern eine hohe Anzahl an Geschäften. Diese Struktur ist auch in den weniger belebten Wohnzellen anzutreffen.

Die stark kommerziell geprägte Zelle *Dong Qu* hat ihre höchste Ladendichte im Osten. Die schmalen Straßen ähneln Fußgängerzonen, da sie wenig Autoverkehr zulassen. Die kleinen Läden besitzen eine Breite von wenigen Metern, wodurch eine extrem hohe Dichte von bis zu 430 Läden pro Kilometer entsteht. Im Gegensatz zu europäischen Einkaufsstraßen besitzen diese Straßen einen hohen Gastronomieanteil und eine größere Ladenvielfalt. Der Kommerz und die Gastronomie werden auf mehrere Straßen verteilt und beleben die gesamte urbane Zelle.

100m 200m 300m 400m 500m 600m 700m 800m 900m 1000m 1100m 1200m

shops

Epping is located in the outskirts of London. Besides being the final stop of the London Underground Central Line, it is mainly known as a market town. Despite the small size of the town and its rural surroundings, the main road reaches a remarkable shop density of 147 shops per kilometer over a length of more than 700 meter. This makes the town a strong sub-centre.

The metro station in the southeast of the city is not visible in the commercial network at all. The shops focus exclusively on the central area of the main road, which has a continuous road edge. The structure of the road favours the commercial network. Due to the moderate car traffic, pedestrians can cross it without traffic lights. The wide sidewalks and the approximately 20 different bus lines also increase the pedestrian frequency.

Epping liegt in den Randbezirken von London. Neben der Endhaltestelle der Londoner Metro ist es vor allem als Marktstadt bekannt. Trotz der geringen Größe des Städtchens und der ländlichen Umgebung kommt die Hauptstraße auf eine beachtliche Ladendichte von 147 Läden pro Kilometer auf einer Gesamtlänge von über 700 Metern. Das macht das Städtchen zu einem starken Subzentrum.

Die Metrostation im Südosten der Stadt ist im kommerziellen Netzwerk überhaupt nicht zu erkennen. Die Läden konzentrieren sich ausschließlich auf den zentralen Bereich der Hauptstraße, der eine durchgängige Straßenkante besitzt. Die Struktur der Straße begünstigt das kommerzielle Netzwerk. Durch den mäßigen Autoverkehr ist sie auch ohne Ampeln für Fußgänger überquerbar. Die breiten Gehwege und die circa 20 verschiedenen Buslinien erhöhen zudem die Fußgängerfrequenz.

100m 200m 300m 400m 500m 600m 700m 800m 900m 1000m 1100m 1200m

shops

The densest commercial network has grown on the eastern arterial road, which also contains the Metrobus. A special feature of Mexico are the informal street stalls, that are found on the sidewalks. They are an excellent indicator for the best location of commerce. The pedestrian flow of the residential cell concentrates towards public transport. The highest concentration is in the southeast corner, at the metro station. Here is also the highest density of the commercial network, mainly informal street stalls. The informal commerce follows no legal requirements, but arises only where it finds the best conditions. Overall, the main artery with public transport comes to a density of 115 shops per kilometer.

Inside the cell, the large supermarket is located on an exceptional site. It is not close to public transport. Since many residents use both, public transport as well as the grocery store, a high pedestrian frequency is created in the central park.

Am dichtesten sind die Läden auf der östlich gelegenen Hauptverkehrsader gewachsen, die auch den Metrobus führt. Eine Besonderheit Mexikos sind die informellen Straßenstände, die auf den Gehwegen entstehen. Sie sind ein ausgezeichneter Indikator für die beste Lage des Kommerzes. Der Fußgängerstrom der Wohnzelle konzentriert sich in Richtung öffentlicher Nahverkehr. Am dichtesten ist er in der südöstlichen Ecke, an der Metrostation. Hier befindet sich auch die höchste Dichte des kommerziellen Netzwerkes, vor allem informelle Straßenstände. Der informelle Kommerz folgt keinerlei gesetzlichen Vorgaben, sondern entsteht ausschließlich dort, wo er die besten Bedingungen vorfindet. Insgesamt kommt die Hauptverkehrsader mit öffentlichem Personennahverkehr auf eine Dichte von 115 Läden pro Kilometer.

Im Inneren der Zelle liegt der große Supermarkt an einer außergewöhnlichen Stelle. Er befindet sich nicht in der Nähe des öffentlichen Nahverkehrs. Da viele Bewohner sowohl den öffentlichen Personennahverkehr als auch den Supermarkt nutzen, entsteht eine hohe Fußgängerfrequenz im zentralen Park.

100m 200m 300m 400m 500m 600m 700m 800m 900m 1000m 1100m 1200m

supermarket

Metro Insurgentes

shops

Urban Cell

Gastronomy

outdoor seating areas
außenliegende Sitzgelegenheiten

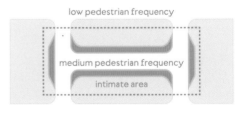

low pedestrian frequency

medium pedestrian frequency

intimate area

high pedestrian frequency

intimate areas with medium pedestrian frequency
intimer Bereich mit mittlerer Fußgängerfrequenz

The central cell has several gastronomic hotspots. *Hans im Glück* and the area south of the *Markthalle* create small pedestrian plazas. They are very intimate, have a medium pedestrian frequency and many gastronomic offerings. Due to the high amenity value, these areas developed many cafes and bars.

The *Calwer Straße* and *Gloria* are secondary pedestrian areas. They have large, outside seating areas and a certain intimacy. These conditions favoured the emerging of restaurants.

The remaining gastronomy is within the urban cell. Pedestrian frequency and intimacy play a certain role as well. A small exception is the *Theodor-Heuss-Straße*. Gastronomy has formed because of its amenity value. The other large streets are free of gastronomy.

Die zentrale Zelle hat gleich mehrere gastronomische Verdichtungen. *Hans im Glück* und der Bereich südlich der *Markthalle* bilden kleine fußläufige Plätze. Sie sind sehr intim, besitzen eine mittlere Fußgängerfrequenz und viel Gastronomie. Durch die hohe Aufenthaltsqualität hat sich die Gastronomie in Richtung Cafés und Bars entwickelt.

Die *Calwer Straße* und das *Gloria* sind sekundäre Fußgängerzonen. Auch sie besitzen große, außenliegende Sitzgelegenheiten und eine gewisse Intimität. An ihnen haben sich verstärkt Restaurants gebildet.

Die restliche Gastronomie liegt ebenfalls innerhalb der Zelle. Fußgängerfrequenz und Intimität spielen auch hier eine Rolle. Eine kleine Ausnahme bildet die *Theodor-Heuss-Straße*. Wegen ihrer Aufenthaltsqualität hat sich Gastronomie gebildet. Ansonsten sind die großen Autostraßen frei von Gastronomie.

Hans im Glück

100m 200m 300m 400m 500m 600m 700m 800m 900m 1000m 1100m 1200m 1300m 1400m 1500m 1600m 1700m 1800m

Gloria

Theodor-Heuss-Straße

Markthalle

Calwer Straße

Hans im Glück

restaurants, bars, cafes

Shanghai consists of a very uniform street grid that is similar to a block cell structure. The only short road that offers a certain intimacy is the *Yongkang Lu*. The street has become a gastronomic hotspot. Restaurants, as well as bars and cafes, lie close together. The sidewalks are used for outside seating. On weekends the street is so packed with people, it is forcibly transformed into a pedestrian zone. Problems arise in the combination of apartments located above the restaurants, where late night noise levels always lead to conflicts.

The triangular plaza to the west has an increased intimacy as well. However, it has no outside seating and only a slight densification in gastronomy.

Shanghai besteht aus einem sehr gleichmäßigen Straßenraster, das eher an eine Blockzellenstruktur erinnert. Die einzige kurze Straße, die eine gewisse Intimität biete, ist die *Yongkang Lu*. Hier hat sich eine hohe gastronomische Verdichtung gebildet. Sowohl Restaurants als auch Bars und Cafés liegen dicht beieinander. Die Gehwege werden für außenliegende Sitzflächen genutzt. An Wochenenden ist die Straße so voll mit Menschen, dass sie sich gezwungenermaßen zur Fußgängerzone wandelt. Problematisch ist die Kombination mit den Wohnungen über der Gastronomie. Der nächtliche Lärmpegel führt immer wieder zu Konflikten.

Der dreieckige Platz westlich davon hat ebenfalls eine erhöhte Intimität. Er bietet jedoch keine außenliegenden Sitzgelegenheiten und hat daher nur eine leichte gastronomische Verdichtung.

Yongkang Lu

© Daniela Gonzales Badillo

100m 200m 300m 400m 500m 600m 700m 800m 900m 1000m 1100m 1200m 1300m 1400m 1500m 1600m 1700m 1800m

Yongkang Lu

restaurants, bars, cafes

The gastronomy concentrates in intimate pedestrian areas, a little bit aside from the main traffic arteries. The *Passeo General Holley* consists of a T-shaped pedestrian area with no direct connection to the main artery. Here, the largest concentration of restaurants, bars and cafes has developed. The narrow pedestrian zone provides intimate niches with outside seating.

Paseo Orrego Luco is based on similar principles. The access to the courtyard is over a small road. On the edge of the intimate space several restaurants and bars have emerged. They use the plaza for outside seating. Since it has no connection on the other side, the pedestrian frequency is very low.

The *Plaza Lyon* is mainly used for lunch. It is a little off the main thoroughfare, offers intimacy and outside seating as well.

Etwas abseits der geteilten Hauptverkehrsader liegen intime Fußgängerbereiche, in denen sich die Gastronomie konzentriert. Der *Passeo General Holley* besteht aus einer T-förmigen Fußgängerzone ohne direkte Verbindung zur Hauptverkehrsader. Hier findet man die größte Konzentration von Restaurants, Bars und Cafés entstanden. Die schmale Fußgängerzone bietet intime Nischen mit außenliegenden Sitzgelegenheiten.

Nach einem ähnlichen Prinzip funktioniert der *Passeo Orrego Luco*. Über eine kleine Stichstraße wird der Innenhof erschlossen. Am Rande des intimen Platzes sind mehrere Restaurants und Bars entstanden. Sie nutzen den Platz für Sitzgelegenheiten. Da der Platz eine Sackgasse ist, besitzt er eine sehr niedrige Fußgängerfrequenz.

Der *Plaza Lyon* wird verstärkt mittags genutzt. Auch er liegt etwas abseits der Hauptverkehrsader, bietet Intimität und außenliegende Sitzmöglichkeiten.

Passeo General Holley

© Juan Pablo Scarafia

Gral. Holley

Plaza Lyon

Orrego Luco

restaurants, bars, cafes

Urban Cell

Commercial Network &

Gastronomy

In the Old Town of Munich, commerce is found along the main motion axes of pedestrians. The *Neuhauser-straße* is the main shopping street and has the highest density of shops. A second axis of movement runs from the southwest to the north. The western edge of the central cell contains the public transport and has adequate walkways. These conditions have supported the emergence of a commercial network.

Gastronomic hotspots are found on the intimate public spaces *Frauen-platz* and *Platzl*. Even the main motion axes have gastronomy, but in the somewhat less frequented areas.

Two special features are the *Viktualienmarkt* and the *Fünf Höfe*. The historical market and the modern shopping centre form highly concentrated collections of commerce and gastronomy.

In der Münchener Altstadt verteilt sich der Kommerz auf die Hauptbewegungsachsen der Fußgänger. Die höchste Ladendichte hat die Haupteinkaufsstraße, die *Neuhauserstraße*. Eine zweite Bewegungsachse verläuft von Südwesten nach Norden. Der westliche Rand der zentralen Zelle führt den öffentlichen Nahverkehr und hat ausreichende Gehwege. Hier ist ebenfalls ein dichtes kommerzielles Netzwerk entstanden.

Gastronomische Hotspots bilden die intimen öffentlichen Räume *Frauenplatz* und *Platzl*. Auch auf den Hauptbewegungsachsen liegt Gastronomie, allerdings in den etwas weniger frequentierten Bereichen.

Zwei Besonderheiten sind der *Viktualienmarkt* und die *Fünf Höfe*. Der historische Markt und das moderne Einkaufszentrum bilden hochverdichtete Ansammlungen von Kommerz und Gastronomie.

Frauenplatz

Neuhauser Straße

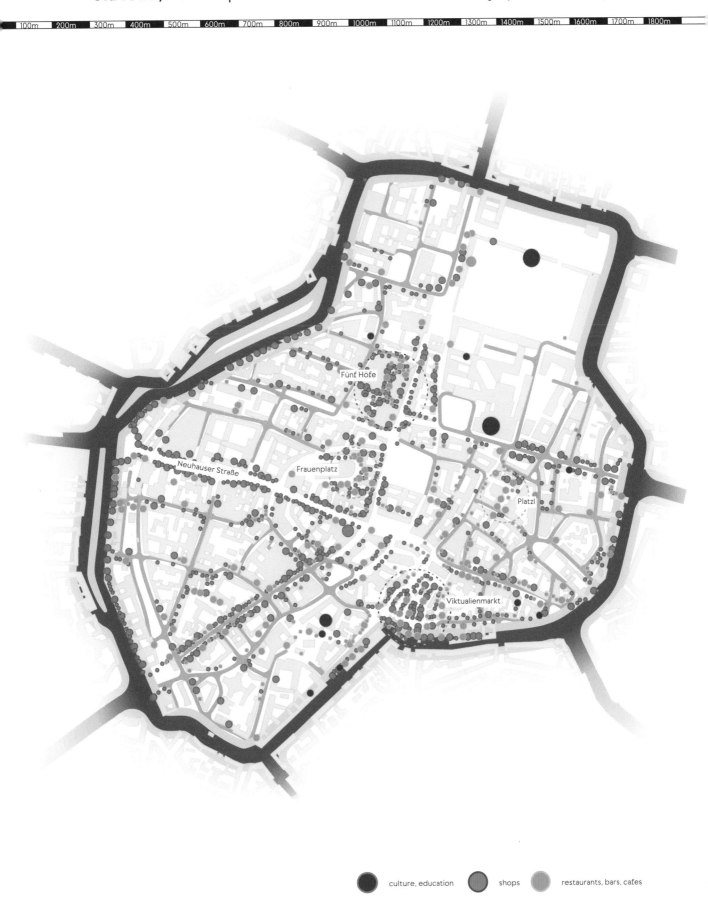

100m 200m 300m 400m 500m 600m 700m 800m 900m 1000m 1100m 1200m 1300m 1400m 1500m 1600m 1700m 1800m

Fünf Höfe

Neuhauser Straße

Frauenplatz

Platzl

Viktualienmarkt

culture, education · shops · restaurants, bars, cafes

Manly is a northern suburb of Sydney. It is located between the bay and the open sea and forms a strong commercial and gastronomic sub-centre. *The Corso* is the main motion axis of pedestrians and runs between the pier of the ferry in the south-west and the beach. It is where the main shopping street has developed as a pedestrian zone. It has the highest density of shops. Two further axes of movement from the west and southeast form the side branches of the commercial network.

The gastronomy is spread over the somewhat quieter beach promenade and more intimate places around the centre with a medium pedestrian frequency. They are almost exclusively in observing locations.

Manly ist ein nördlicher Vorort von Sydney. Er liegt zwischen der Bucht und dem offenen Meer und formt ein starkes kommerzielles und gastronomisches Subzentrum. *The Corso* ist die Hauptbewegungsachse der Fußgänger und verläuft zwischen der Anlegestelle der Fähre im Südwesten und dem Strand. Hier hat sich die Haupteinkaufsstraße in Form einer Fußgängerzone gebildet. Sie hat die höchste Dichte an Läden im Vorort. Zwei weitere Bewegungsachsen vom Westen und Südosten formen Nebenarme des kommerziellen Netzwerkes.

Die Gastronomie verteilt sich auf die etwas ruhigere Strandpromenade und intimere Plätze um das Zentrum mit mittlerer Fußgängerfrequenz. Sie befinden sich fast ausschließlich in beobachtenden Positionen.

The Corso　　　　　© Helen Renner　© Helen Renner　　　　　**Market Lane**

100m	200m	300m	400m	500m	600m	700m	800m	900m	1000m	1100m	1200m	1300m	1400m	1500m	1600m	1700m	1800m

The Corso

culture, education   shops   restaurants, bars, cafes

The city lives.

It's man who
brings it alive.

Imprint

The Deutsche Nationalbibliothek lists this publication in the Deutsche Nationalbibliografie; detailed bibliographic data are available on the Internet at http://dnb.dnb.de

ISBN 978-3-7212-0968-6
© 2018 Niggli, imprint of Braun Publishing AG, Salenstein
www.niggli.ch

1st edition 2018

All of the information in this volume has been compiled to the best of the editor's/author's knowledge. The publisher assumes no responsibility for its accuracy or completeness as well as copyright discrepancies and refers to the specified sources.

Die Deutsche Nationalbibliothek verzeichnet diese Publikation in der Deutschen Nationalbibliografie; detaillierte bibliografische Daten sind im Internet über http://dnb.dnb.de abrufbar.

ISBN 978-3-7212-0968-6
© 2018 Niggli, ein Imprint der Braun Publishing AG, Salenstein
www.niggli.ch

Dieses Werk ist urheberrechtlich geschützt. Jede Verwendung außerhalb der engen Grenzen des Urheberrechtsgesetzes, der keine Berechtigung durch den Verlag erteilt wurde, ist unbefugt und strafbar. Dies gilt insbesondere für Vervielfältigungen, Übersetzungen, Mikroverfilmung und das Abspeichern oder die Verarbeitung in elektronischen Systemen.

1. Auflage 2018

Alle Informationen in diesem Band wurden mit dem besten Gewissen des Autors zusammengestellt. Der Verlag übernimmt keine Verantwortung für die Richtigkeit und Vollständigkeit sowie Urheberrechte und verweist auf die angegebenen Quellen.

Special thanks goes to my wife Fanny, who has not just shared the experience, but supported me in every possible way. Without her the book wouldn't exist.

Great thanks goes as well to Daniel Perraudin of Bureau Perraudin, who helped with the layout and graphic design of the book, Max Kögler for all the inspiration and graphic advices, Max Gane for helping with the English text and Jana Fritz (TEXTECHT) for proofreading.

A special mention goes to all the great people and conversations during my years abroad. They have shaped the content of this book significantly.

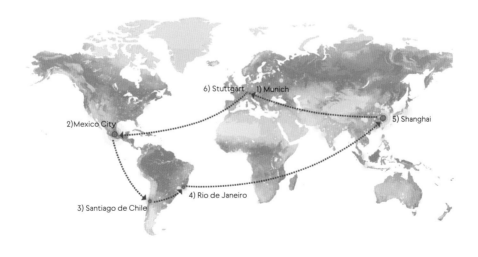